A New Prescription for Addiction

Subutex, Prometa, Vivitrol, and Campral—
The Revolutionary New Treatments for Alcohol,
Cocaine, Methamphetamine, and Prescription
Drug Addiction

Richard I. Gracer, MD

With additional material contributed by
Steven M. Peterson, LCSW, CADC III

A New Prescription for Addiction

Library of Congress Cataloging-in-Publication Data

Gracer, Richard I.
 A new prescription for addiction : subutex, prometa, vivitrol, and campral—
the revolutionary new treatments for alcohol, cocaine, methamphetamine, and
prescription drug addiction / Richard I. Gracer, with additional material
contributed by Steven M. Peterson. — 1st ed.
     p. cm.
 Includes index.
 ISBN-13: 978-1-60070-029-3 (hardcover)
 ISBN-10: 1-60070-029-2 (hardcover)
 ISBN-13: 978-1-60070-030-9 (softcover)
 ISBN-10: 1-60070-030-6 (softcover)
 1. Drugs of abuse. 2. Substance abuse—Treatment. 3. Substance abuse—
Patients—Services for. 4. Chemotherapy. I. Peterson, Steven M. II. Title.
 RC564.G7338 2007
 362.29—dc22
                              2007009349

Cover image by David Ridley, from Images.com

The opinions expressed herein are solely attributable to Richard I. Gracer,
MD, and do not reflect the opinions of any author, individual, or company
listed herein. This book was produced without financial support from any of the
individuals or companies whose products are discussed in this book. Richard I.
Gracer, MD, is a licensee for the Prometa procedure and has lectured on behalf of
Cephalon, Inc. and Reckitt Benckiser Pharmaceuticals Inc. Fully reprinted articles were secured by permission from appropriate authors or magazines, and any
quotes are attributed fully by author, name of publication, and date of issue.

The content in this book is offered for informational and educational purposes only, and is not intended to be a substitute for medical advice, diagnosis
or treatment. The reading of this book does not create a doctor/patient relationship of any kind between reader and Richard Gracer, MD, or his affiliates.
Instead, the Content is intended to support, not replace, the relationship that
exists between readers and their physicians.

All patient names have been changed to protect their identities and their
personal stories have been altered somewhat for clarity or brevity.

For further copies of *A New Prescription for Addiction,* information regarding Gracer Behavioral Health Services, or to contact Dr. Gracer, please visit:
www.gracermedicalgroup.com. To contact the author, please e-mail: info@
gracermedicalgroup.com and write "Question about Dr. Gracer's Book" in the
subject line.

Contents

Acknowledgments

When I first thought about writing this book it seemed such a huge task that I almost let it go. It was only after discussing the project with family, colleagues, and friends that I was able to get some perception on what it would really take to do the job correctly. I held my breath and took the leap. Once I got started, there was no turning back. No one can produce this type of book on his or her own, certainly not I. I relied on the support and work of many others, whom I would like to thank.

First, and most important, my wonderful wife Alice (and stepdaughter Nicki) had to do without my company many days and evenings due to my research and writing schedule. Alice was always loving and supportive, even when I had to neglect other parts of our life. Alice's help was invaluable in rewriting many passages in order to make it easier for the layperson to understand. She also worked tirelessly to make sure that the diagrams were correct. Her love and support makes all that I have to do not only possible, but easy. Thanks, Alice.

Steve Peterson, LCSW, CADC III, the program director for Gracer Medical Group, wrote much of the psychosocial material. His help was invaluable throughout the project and his input and many years of experience in treating addicted patients continues to give me vital perspective. His work was the inspiration for the Readiness to Change Quadrant evaluation and the result is our work together. He is an important reason that our program and clinic are so successful.

John Havens helped me with primary research, interviews, and writing. He put spirit in many of the patient stories that make this book come alive. Laine Cunningham helped make sure that the book flowed correctly and spent many hours helping get things right. Dawson Church, the publisher of this book and my "guru," guided me through the process and really made this book possible. His wonderful, positive energy makes it a pleasure to be with him.

Ann Tepperman, MSW, helped with the psychosocial portions of the book and is an important part of our team. She is currently working on several research projects to validate our smoking program and improve the Readiness to Change Quadrant Evaluation.

Leni Felton, CCN, produced the diet suggestions and gave me additional insight for the nutrition chapters. Her work in the clinic gives us a unique edge that makes an important difference for many patients.

Alon Marcus, DOM, is an old and trusted friend and a published author in his own right. We have worked together for almost 20 years. He was the source of information for the acupuncture and Chinese medicine portions of the book. Our patients get important input and treatment from Alon.

Jeri Stegman, the director of clinical programs at New Connections, our program partner, has given me her knowledge and encouragement.

Barry Sears, PhD, gave me guidance and ideas for the nutrition chapters. His work is one of the important foundations upon which this book rests.

I value the work of Joan Mathews-Larson, PhD, and enjoyed my conversations with her while doing my research.

Kathleen Gragano, RN, of Yale Addiction Research, and Tim Lepak, the founders of NAABT.org, gave me vital information and perspective on the science and practical use of buprenorphine. Their work is extremely valuable.

Special thanks to Rusty Payne of the DEA for linking me to Special Agent Mark Caverly, who heads the DEA section that enforces laws for Internet pharmacies, and who helped me understand the internet pharmacy problem and what we can do about it.

The work of Malcolm Gladwell, the author of *The Tipping Point* and *Blink* gave me the impetus to start thinking "outside the box," with what I hope are positive results.

Sanjay Sabjani of the Hythiam Corporation gave me an interesting perspective on the physiologic basis of addiction, which I used in the book.

Jennifer Bolen, JD, former Assistant United States Attorney with the U.S. Department of Justice and founder of J. Bolen Group (thelegalsideofpain.com) taught me how the law views prescription drugs and the best way to help physicians and patients deal with this complex area.

My brother, James Gracer, MD, is a gifted internist/psychiatrist. He has taught me much of what I know about psychiatric diagnosis and psychopharmacology.

My sister's husband, Lester Adler, MD, has been more than a friend. He is a constant positive influence and a font of knowledge on nutritional and internal medicine. We have spent many hours discussing esoteric, important medical subjects. These conversations are a valuable part of my ongoing medical education.

My son, Erik M. Gracer, MD, worked in my practice as my partner for four years before leaving to open his own urgent care center two years ago. During the time he was with me, I was able to narrow and concentrate my practice on chronic pain and addiction. This specialization has enabled me to develop my programs and write this book. He has also remained a close friend and advisor, whose input I value and heed.

In the text I relate how many incredible persons have influenced and taught me what I know and how to think. I truly "stand on their shoulders." Of all of them, the most important is always my father, Martin. Although he died in 1983 he is with me every day. While my dad taught me how to "think," my mother, Estelle, taught me how to "feel." From early childhood I saw her empathy and care for others. She is the amazing paragon toward which I strive.

I would also like to thank my friends and colleagues who spent time on this project. They include Deanna Anderson, J. P. McDermott, Isabella Michon, Randy Peyser, Michael Lobl, Don Miller, Carl Lyle, Maury Schwartz, my sister Lea Gracer, my daughter Merrill Grimmer, and Lance Longo, MD, for the help he gave Steve Peterson for the counseling chapters.

A special thank you goes to Joseph Volpicelli, MD, PhD, who taught Steve Peterson much of what he knows about empathy, motivational interviewing, and combining medication with psychosocial treatment, allowing him to develop many of our successful counseling techniques. He also did much of the original research on naltrexone.

The office and professional staff at Gracer Behavioral Health Services makes this all possible. Thanks to Sheri Epperson, Mani Chokmowh, Rhodia Wilson, Tanya Etu, Jackie Julty, and Gerrie Ugaddan.

Finally thank you to all of the patients who have taught me so many things over more than 30 years of medical practice. A physician who does not constantly learn from those he cares for will always be treating his first patient.

Richard I. Gracer, MD
San Ramon, California

February 2007

How to Use This Book

By reading *A New Prescription for Addiction,* you will:

Learn more about the nature of addiction so you can recognize signs of trouble in loved ones or friends.

Learn about the latest, cutting edge medical breakthroughs and treatments to tame the cravings that cause relapse.

Take the questionnaire to determine if addiction is present in you or in a friend or family member.

Help a loved one you suspect is either dependent on or addicted to alcohol, cocaine, methamphetamine, opiates, marijuana, or even nicotine.

Find help because you suspect you may be addicted.

Find out if you're ready to change and how to deal with the answer if you are addicted.

Discover how to get help *right now.*

Part One:
The State of Addiction

Chapter One
The Addiction

A re you or a loved one addicted? This book was written to help those people who are struggling with addiction to alcohol, cocaine, methamphetamine, opiates, nicotine, and marijuana. Since people who know addicted individuals are also impacted, this book can help family and friends understand and support people as they work to free themselves from drugs and alcohol.

The Gracer Behavioral Health team has worked with many people to break the bonds of addiction. Our approach is humane and holistic. If there are underlying medical, pain or psychiatric issues, we understand that these must be treated along with the addiction for the best chance of success. Most importantly, we recognize that addiction is a disease that requires medical treatment, just like diabetes or heart problems.

It all starts when the addicted person realizes that there is a problem and that they can get help that works. We've developed a questionnaire to help you and your loved ones realize whether addiction is an issue and how it might be affecting your life. We strongly urge you to answer these questions for yourself or a loved one. This tool, along with others we've developed such as the Readiness Quadrant (RQ), help determine the addicted person's perception of prior substance abuse treatment and the course of current treatments, as well as their willingness to try new treatments.

Extra copies of this questionnaire can be downloaded from Gracer Medical's website.

Note: A drink is defined as a 12-ounce beer, a glass of wine, or a shot of liquor. A 40-ounce beer is equal to three drinks.

To be Answered by MEN UNDER 65 ONLY:		Circle one:	
1.	Do you typically drink more than two drinks per day?	Yes	No
2.	On average, do you drink more than 14 drinks per week?	Yes	No
3.	Do you ever drink more than five drinks at any one time?	Yes	No
To be Answered by ALL WOMEN and MEN OVER 65:			
1.	Do you typically drink more than one drink per day?	Yes	No
2.	On average, do you drink more than seven drinks per week?	Yes	No
3.	Do you ever drink more than four drinks at any one time?	Yes	No
To be answered by EVERYONE:			
4.	Do you use any drugs other than tobacco or those prescribed by a physician?	Yes	No
5.	Do you take more medication than you need or is prescribed?	Yes	No
6.	Do you get pain medication from more than one physician?	Yes	No

7.	Have you ever felt you should cut down on your drinking or drug use?	Yes	No
8.	Have people ever annoyed you by criticizing your drinking or drug use?	Yes	No
9.	Have you ever felt bad or guilty about your drinking or drug use?	Yes	No
10.	Have you ever had a drink or used a drug first thing in the morning (eye-opener) to steady your nerves or to get rid of a hangover?	Yes	No
11.	Has your drinking or drug use caused family problems?	Yes	No
12.	When drinking or using drugs have you ever had a memory loss or blackout?	Yes	No
13.	Would you be interested in speaking with a counselor about your or a loved one's alcohol or drug use?	Yes	No

1-1: Questionnaire

Scoring Section One: Questions for Men or Women

For Men:

1. Drinking more than two drinks per day signals potentially damaging drinking habits.

2. Drinking more than 14 drinks per week is correlated with significant health problems such as cancer, accidents, liver disease, and so on.

3. Consuming five or more drinks per occasion is considered a binge-drinking episode.

One or more "Yes" answer is a concern, especially if excessive drinking behavior is related with problems (driving intoxicated, arguments with others, mood swings, and so on).

For Women:

1. Drinking more than one drink per day signals potentially damaging drinking habits.

2. Drinking more than seven drinks per week is correlated with significant health problems such as cancer, accidents, liver disease, and so on

3. Binge drinking for women is four or more drinks per occasion.

One or more "Yes" in this section signals a need for further inquiry. This is especially true if drinking causes life problems (driving intoxicated, arguments with others, mood swings, and so on).

Scoring Section Two

If you answered "yes" to three or more questions, you (or your loved one) may have a problem with addiction. I strongly urge you to read the rest of this book to become as informed as possible about the disease of addiction. Use the resources included here and in the appendices and remember: *you can stop.*

The Time for Change

It is time for change in both the treatment of and society's attitude toward substance abuse. America is at a juncture, ready to break the stigma associated with the disease of dependence and addiction. For far too many years the public has associated addiction with junkies splayed on street corners or prostitutes turning tricks so they can buy their next hit.

The typical middle-class person addicted to prescription pain medication (or alcohol, or stimulants like cocaine and methamphetamine) looks just like you or me. They "fly under the radar." When we meet them, we have no idea there's a problem. Even their families and physicians are often unaware. While they may have first taken the drug to get high, they soon need the drug to keep from suffering physically and mentally.

Ignorance keeps millions of people quiet about their growing dependence on or addiction to prescription medications. Countless others are suffering from the effects of alcohol, cocaine, nicotine, marijuana, and the epidemic of methamphetamine. Due to an out-dated puritanical mindset, countless individuals hide their problems until they're saddled with full-blown addiction.

A central hope of this book and the Gracer Program is that the public will see that addiction is a medical disease, the same as diabetes or cancer. After the shock, pain, and scarring associated with trauma or surgery, the body mends itself. Physical changes to the brain also occur, and are augmented by opiate medications. When the brain is damaged, natural neurotransmitters and hormones may no longer be effective in giving comfort, creating the physical basis of addiction. Alcohol, nicotine, and the stimulants cocaine and methamphetamine create similar changes.

As you'll discover, the first step for most patients is not *admitting* they have a problem (as the familiar adage of Alcoholics Anonymous states) but *realizing* they have a problem. Equally important, they must realize that there are effective ways to change. These are based in science rather than faith; and while they include social programs and therapy, they begin by treating the very real physical damage that makes cravings so powerful.

Most addicted people are desperate to break their habit—they just don't know how. The methods we've developed at Gracer Behavioral Health Services will help families and physicians find and give support to these desperate people and the ones they love.

Remember:

- The situation is *medical,* not moral.

- Family and friends can find immediate and readily available solutions to help bring loved ones from the dark world of addiction to a life free of pain and terrifying secrets.

- Patients can be treated in a holistic, comprehensive fashion so they can return to their lives as whole and healed as possible.

- There's hope. There's *A New Prescription for Addiction.*

Chapter Two
The Cravings

"How many Norcos?" I asked, thinking that due to my harried schedule I may have misheard the young woman sitting in my office.

"Fifty a day," she responded sheepishly.

"Five-zero, not 15? A day?"

"Yes. Is that a lot? I didn't think it was that big of a deal because a friend of mine ordered the pills over the Internet. I'm assuming if they can sell it over the Internet, it's safe, right?"

She was the second young, middle-class woman that week who had asked the same question.

* * *

I wrote this book to save lives.

Norco is a drug that contains ten milligrams of hydrocodone, the most abused prescription drug in the USA. Norco's dosage is double that of the common painkiller Vicodin, which contains only 5 milligrams. Both pills contain acetaminophen, the active ingredient in Tylenol and a major cause of liver failure from intentional and accidental overdose. Even fifty *acetaminophen* pills a day would be fatal to anyone without tolerance. The only reason those two women were still alive was that they were relatively young and their livers had adapted to the gradually more toxic doses.

Many patients aren't so lucky. Most middle- or upper-class patients who struggle with addiction don't present their problem to their doctors or families until it's too late. Due to the stigma created by the moral attitudes toward addiction, people would rather die than have anyone think they're hooked.

John

It's 7 AM and the alarm goes off. I can barely move. My back hurts and as soon as my mind starts to click over, the anxiety starts. My stomach hurts. God, I need my Vicodin! I pop a couple of pills with coffee. By the time I shower I feel much better.

It's now 9 AM and I'm at work. My back is starting to hurt again and the gnawing uneasiness is taking over. I take a couple more Norco and things get better. I have an important meeting with a client, so to be sure things go well I take a couple more pills.

By the time I get home I must have taken over 30 tabs. This cycle started after I had a mild back injury and my family doc gave me a few Vicodin. Not only did they take away the pain, they gave me a wonderful sense of well-being I hadn't felt before. When the prescription ran out, I called and got some more.

I never thought I would get hooked. I should have known better, as I had had a real problem with methamphetamine ten years before. I finally shook it, but not until I had gotten kicked out of the Navy and had a felony conviction for writing a phony check.

Over the next few months I worked up to 20 Vicodin a day then escalated to Norco, which has a double dose of hydrocodone. By that time I wasn't sure if I still had back pain, but if I missed a dose I felt like a truck had run over me. I tried to stop but could never make it through the time it would take to get it out of my system. I also felt really depressed when I tried to quit. I couldn't think clearly or even work.

I finally got into a residential rehab program and was given buprenorphine. It immediately took away the cravings and other symptoms. I felt better than I had in a very long time. Then they told me I could only be on the meds for a few days to detox. As soon as I went off the meds, I was ill and the cravings were massive. I signed myself out of the clinic, got online, and got going on my drugs as soon as I possibly could.

* * *

John is a typical patient with opiate addiction. After a careful evaluation I started him on buprenorphine (Subutex/Suboxone), a medication that takes away the cravings of opiate addiction. He also started seeing Steve Peterson, program director for Gracer Behavioral Health Services. He was able to taper and then stop his medication over a few months. John also had severe anxiety, but with proper medical treatment this is also now under control.

Many people like John are desperate to stop using, but can't go cold turkey or even survive a short detoxification program and then maintain abstinence without getting ill. Even if they do, they may have other untreated problems. They need a personalized program that treats the cravings that cause relapse.

Today John has a great job. He is in the process of clearing his record and is free from back pain and cravings.

Cravings 101

The National Alliance of Advocates for Buprenorphine Treatment (NAABT) website features an excellent article, "What it is Like to be Addicted," which conveys the hopelessness experienced by any individual under the influence of drugs. Reading the entire article will give you insight and compassion toward their experience. Here are some of the highlights:

> Many people are treated with prescription painkillers for legitimate pain only to discover they have exchanged a pain problem for an addiction.

> Soon they notice the level of euphoria is not as great as it was the first few times and they start to feel less than normal without the drug... Now the opioid only causes feelings of *normality* not *euphoria*.

> As time goes on they need more and more to feel normal and to prevent withdrawal. Eventually a depression starts to take over even while taking the drugs... They are just medicating themselves to lower the depression. To stop would mean being overwhelmed with depression and feelings of despair not to mention the extreme physical effects of withdrawal.

> This is why it is so hard to quit. They are trying to do the hardest thing they have ever done in their lives, while feeling worse then they ever had. **Only 2 percent report remaining drug free after quitting "cold turkey."** The rest need some kind of treatment. The root problem (the reason for drug use in the first place) must be addressed if they are to remain abstinent.

> Some will do almost anything to prevent withdrawal. The symptoms of withdrawal are described by thousands of patients as "The flu times 100." The symptoms include prolonged nausea, vomiting, diarrhea, chills, sweats, painful goose bumps, uncontrolled leg movement, dilated pupils, anxiety, irritability, depression, insomnia for several days on end, anger, stomach

pain, cramps, muscle and joint pain, tremors, nasal congestion, tearing eyes, and feeling like they are going to die. Some patients have reported that they keep toughing it out but after two weeks or more they just can't fight the depression any longer...[1]

Although this article deals with addiction to opiates, the information applies to **alcohol, cocaine, methamphetamine, opiates, marijuana, nicotine,** and any other substance. Self-denial is not a viable decision once a substance alters the basic brain chemistry; patients need to recognize that their problem requires consistent, ongoing care. If you're wondering whether you or a loved one falls into this group of people, use our questionnaire.

While behavior is part of addiction, once brain receptors are damaged, higher levels of the addictive substance are physically needed to feel normal or even to avoid nausea, anxiety, stomach cramps, sweating, and other withdrawal symptoms. Cravings fuel addiction and are the primary cause of relapse.

These cravings occur with addiction to alcohol, cocaine, methamphetamine, opiates, nicotine, and even marijuana. After addiction has chronically (and sometimes permanently) damaged receptors, the hardest part is dealing with the long-lasting, post-acute withdrawal syndrome (PAW).

If you don't find a way to deal with the cravings, you face a bleak future of constant struggle and mental duress. The odds are stacked so that you'll probably return to addictive behavior in a matter of weeks or even days. You've exposed your body repeatedly to foreign elements that drastically altered your brain chemistry. Your brain adapted. In a sense, cravings are the brain complaining that it's taken the time to reset itself according to your behavior and now it doesn't want to change back!

Along with the physical side, it's important to understand social triggers. If you're addicted to alcohol and you go to a bar, your cravings will be stronger than while sitting in the library.

Let's say that before you become addicted, you relax by watching TV with your family. After a tough day's work you can count on *Everybody Loves Raymond* reruns and your son's laughter to take it down a notch. Once you're addicted that process won't work anymore. The social trigger that used to create natural relaxation chemicals was TV and playing with your son. Now it's alcohol.

Not only has your life turned upside down, but your notion of relaxation has done the same. Cravings are difficult to manage because you're reorienting yourself to the world before addiction took hold. So now the chemical, physiological, and social ramifications of addiction are working against you. These triple assailants can be invincible unless you know how to battle them with a comprehensive, holistic method of treatment.

Post-Acute Withdrawal Syndrome (PAW)

I want to touch on some of the specifics of post-acute withdrawal to further demonstrate how cravings affect a patient. Below is an excerpt from an excellent book called *Staying Sober: A Guide for Relapse Prevention* by Terence T. Gorski, a pioneer in the development of Relapse Prevention Therapy.

> Post-acute withdrawal is a group of symptoms that occur as a result of abstinence from addictive chemicals. In the alcoholic/ addict these symptoms appear seven to fourteen days into abstinence, after stabilization from the acute withdrawal.

> Recovery causes a great deal of stress. Many chemically dependent people never learn to manage stress without alcohol and drug use. The stress aggravates the brain dysfunction and makes the symptoms worse.

> The symptoms of PAW typically grow to peak intensity over three to six months after abstinence begins. The damage is usually reversible, meaning the major symptoms go away in time if proper treatment is received. But the adjustment does not

occur rapidly. Recovery from the nervous system damage usually requires from six to 24 months with the assistance of a healthy recovery program. People recovering from long term opiate and stimulant use often have PAW symptoms for no apparent reason for up to 10 years after they have stopped using. Individuals who intend to have consistent long-term recovery must learn to recognize these symptoms and learn how to manage them.

Symptoms of Post-acute Withdrawal

The most identifiable characteristic is the inability to solve usually simple problems. There are six major types of PAW symptoms that contribute to this. They are the inability to think clearly, memory problems, emotional overreactions and numbness, sleep disturbances, physical coordination problems, and general problems in managing stress. The inability to solve usually simple problems because of any or all of these symptoms leads to diminished self-esteem. A person often feels incompetent, embarrassed, and "not okay" about themselves. Diminished self-esteem and the fear of failure interfere with productive and challenging living.

Use of alcohol or other drugs can temporarily reverse the symptoms of the damage. If alcoholics drink, or drug addicts use, they will think clearly for a little while, be able to have normal feelings and emotions for a little while, feel healthy for a little while.

For this reason it is necessary to do everything possible to reduce the symptoms of PAW. It is necessary to understand PAW and to recognize that you are not incompetent and you are not going crazy. Because post-acute withdrawal symptoms are stress sensitive, you need to learn about PAW and methods of control when stress levels are low in order to be able to prevent the symptoms or to manage them when they occur.

The chronic nature of PAW needs a chronic treatment plan. Your body can't act like a computer and simply reboot after continuous drug or alcohol use. You can't quickly and automatically return to normalcy through abstinence or even with medication. The journey has to start somewhere. You need to be informed to fight the disease of addiction. Knowing the symptoms of PAW will help you recognize when they appear and convince you that your process of healing is normal.

A New Prescription

This book is divided into two major sections: the current state of addiction and addiction treatment in America, and the Gracer Behavioral Health Services Addiction Craving Management and Recovery Program. This book is a proactive manual on how to see your (or loved one's) circumstances as they really are. Then you can move forward to a positive future through specific advice and useful resources to escape relapse and addiction.

Relapse is normally attributed to a moral failing rather than understood as a response to a wrenching chemical/physical change within the body. Treating the physical components of cravings is a large portion of Gracer Medical's program.

In addition to medical treatment for cravings and addiction, our program also diagnoses and treats the underlying problems that may have caused addiction in the first place. Chronic pain, depression or anxiety, even serious undiagnosed mood problems such as bipolar disorder can lead people to "medicate" their problems with alcohol, nicotine, marijuana, opiates, or street drugs. We at Gracer Medical believe the patient deserves, and must have, relief from these underlying conditions for the best possible chance at long-term success.

Finally, long-term success also depends on how much social support a person can gather. If a patient is open to group therapy, Gracer Medical provides it. We also encourage participation in other programs such as twelve-step and other public support groups. Many middle-class patients, however, feel more comfortable discussing their issues in a private setting. These patients are accommodated in an environment that provides the best that counseling can offer in a private, supportive setting. Whenever possible, family members and friends are brought in to provide additional support and understanding.

This book will show you how a body responds to addictive foreign substances; yet doctors and patients need to address the underlying causes of addiction rather than the substances themselves. While I'll discuss treatments for specific addictive substances such as opiates, alcohol, nicotine, cocaine, methamphetamine, and even marijuana, I will also provide general solutions for overall mental and physical health.

Finally, note that although I use the term "flaws" to refer to certain aspects of addiction treatment in America, my intent is to indicate the lack of a comprehensive program rather than an error or disservice done to patients. I firmly believe that twelve-step and other programs can be of great service in the right circumstances.

However, most current programs are insufficient *in and of themselves.* The *huge failure rate* we see with these programs proves that they don't provide complete and lasting recovery from the many medical, psychological, and social ramifications of addiction. Unless all three areas are addressed, the program will remain flawed because patients will remain at enormous risk of relapse.

---

1 www.naabt.org

Chapter Three
Dr. Gracer and the Gracer Medical Program Team

The Gracer Medical program has gathered a team of doctors, clinically certified nutritionists, Level III substance abuse counselors, and affiliates to help their patients battle addiction. Our evaluation and diagnostic methods strive to treat the whole person rather than just the disease of addiction.

Just like our patients are individuals with individual needs, our professional staff members are individuals with specific areas of expertise. We want you to feel comfortable not only with our treatment methods but also with the people you'll meet as you break free of addiction. In this chapter you'll meet our staff and learn how they can help you on your difficult journey.

Meet Dr. Gracer

In over 30 years of medical practice, I have been fortunate to encounter great men and women whose work has influenced my thinking as I developed novel and effective treatments. It all really started with my father, Martin.

He was an engineer-turned-businessman with an inquiring mind. In the mid-1960s he sold his successful business, went back to school to get a master's degree in computer science, then got a job as a computer technician at a local hospital. He was an optimist who believed in a bright and interesting technological future.

When I first started medical school, I almost decided to get a PhD in biochemistry along with my medical degree. I ended up as a family doctor because I enjoyed interacting with people and the satisfaction of seeing positive changes in my patients over time.

In 1978 I was involved in an automobile accident. A bone in my neck was fractured and I was unable to work for about six months. During that time I learned firsthand that the medical profession knew very little about treating soft tissue orthopedic problems. I finally went to a physical therapist who had studied in Europe and was familiar with James Cyriax, MD, a famous British orthopedic physician often called the Father of Orthopaedic Medicine.

In about two weeks I was able to return to work. The spinal manipulation used by this gifted physical therapist was not only missing from my medical education, but it was frowned upon as ineffective and unscientific. My neck told me that outlook was wrong. I decided to make the treatment of musculoskeletal problems and chronic pain my life's work.

When Dr. Cyriax gave a one-week course at St. Mary's Hospital in San Francisco, I couldn't believe how much I learned. I soon made several trips to Britain to study under Dr. Cyriax. I was lucky enough to spend time with him in his private practice in London. I joined the Institute of Orthopaedic Medicine and the Society of Orthopaedic Medicine, both British medical societies.

During this time, I first used prolotherapy for treatment of low back problems. Not until several years later did I discover that, according to Western medicine, "prolotherapy doesn't work."

Fortunately I had already treated close to one hundred patients successfully, so I knew better.

About fifteen years ago I realized there was a group of patients who could not be helped with any of the medical techniques I had learned and developed. I realized something I should have known all along—that all orthopedic problems reside in a human body. Even today, orthopedic problems are treated as solitary specific defects that need to be corrected mechanically with surgery or drugs. The fact that problems within the overall body system can lead to orthopedic problems was, and still is, generally ignored.

The gifted physicians I met in nutritional and holistic medicine usually had very little knowledge of orthopedic medicine and body mechanics. Obviously, knowledge of *all* areas is necessary for the best results. I was lucky to be a medical school classmate of Jonathon Collin, MD, the publisher of the *Townsend Letter for Patients and Doctors*. My brother-in-law, Dr. Lester Adler, is an experienced, practicing preventative and nutritional physician in Sedona, Arizona. Their guidance gave me an excellent start.

Again, the general medical community considered many of the treatments to be ineffective. This included, for example, the use of glucosamine sulfate for degenerative arthritis, a treatment that today is common. I constantly found myself out ahead of the medical pack...just like my father.

My practice evolved to include chronic pain. Because anxiety, depression, and even bipolar disorder are present in many chronic pain patients, I also became expert in the treatment of mood problems, with the guidance and help of my brother, James Gracer, MD, a noted internist and psychiatrist.

Drug addiction can come hand in hand with the use of opiates for chronic pain, and it soon became obvious that I would need to treat these patients as well. In fact, the most challenging dilemma is how to treat patients with valid and serious pain who also are addicted. The program I developed brings together all the important elements. Other gifted practitioners have come together under the Gracer Program to provide the content and services necessary for this comprehensive approach.

Other Pioneers in the Treatment of Addiction

Another influential medical thinker I've been lucky enough to know is Barry Sears, PhD. Dr. Sears is the author of the successful *Zone* series. I first met him in the mid-1990s, just after he had written his bestseller *Entering the Zone*. His concepts of "silent inflammation," the effects of too much insulin, and the need for taking high doses of pharmaceutical-grade fish oil have revolutionized the way physicians look at degenerative problems. In the years since, Dr. Sears has expanded his concepts to many treatment-resistant medical conditions such as aging, heart disease, and degenerative arthritis.

In 1992 I first read the work of Joan Mathews Larson, PhD. In her paradigm-shifting book, *Seven Weeks to Sobriety,* she outlined her successful program that helps alcoholics in her Health Recovery Center in Minneapolis, Minnesota. In her 1999 book, *Depression-Free, Naturally,* she extended her methods to treat depression. She discussed the need for specific nutrients and describes the different mechanisms for alcoholism and depression, along with strategies for their treatment. I have refined and expanded many of these principles for nutritional treatments used at The Gracer Medical Group and Gracer Behavioral Health Services.

During the writing of this book, I discovered the Prometa protocol. While double-blind, placebo-controlled studies from UCLA, Cedar Sinai in Los Angeles, and the University of South Carolina are currently under way as this book goes to press, Prometa is so promising that it couldn't be left out of this book. We're hopeful that these studies will show what the initial studies indicate: that this is a safe, efficacious way to treat alcohol, cocaine, and methamphetamine addiction. This treatment has already transformed the lives of many of my patients, and I want to thank the physicians, researchers, and staff of Hythiam, Inc. for their input.

Finally, I recently read the work of Malcolm Gladwell. In his best-selling books *The Tipping Point* and *Blink,* he describes the way social revolutions come about. *A New Prescription for Addiction* is intended to start just such a revolution. The current process to treat drug addiction is broken. Addiction is a disease that affects neurotransmitters and receptors in the brain. Abstinence alone does not work.

Using what I have learned from Dr. Sears, Dr. Larson, and other gifted teachers and physicians, along with my own knowledge of neurochemistry and nutritional medicine, I have developed a treatment for pain and addiction that utilizes the body's own healing system as a powerful agent for change.

The Search

After meeting with the two young women who were taking enough Norcos to kill, I researched programs that dealt with the social and psychological aspects of addiction, along with the medical. To help members of this "hidden minority," I would have to use a more holistic treatment. I also discovered the extent that the issue of cravings affects patients struggling with alcohol, methamphetamine, cocaine, opiates, marijuana, and even nicotine. These cravings are so overpowering that even with therapy and treatment for underlying psychiatric conditions, most patients quickly relapse.

The research came up short. The programs focused solely on either medical treatment (methadone), psychological treatment (therapy), or social treatment (twelve-steps). Although all of these help some patients, none addressed the entirety of a patient. They treated portions of an individual with separate cures, much like you take your car to a mechanic, a body shop, and car wash. But people are interconnected and must be treated that way.

Around this time I discovered a marvelous medication called Subutex, which the FDA had just made available for private physician use. Its active ingredient is buprenorphine. This medication helps treat and can even reset brain receptors damaged by chronic exposure to opiates. It is the first medication of its kind to provide a major turning point for patients suffering from opiate addiction.

Until recently, methadone was the major treatment of choice for people addicted to heroin or other opiates. Unfortunately, methadone is itself an opiate as addictive as heroin. It is also typically distributed in public clinics where many middle- and upper-class patients feel uncomfortable and, therefore, won't seek treatment.

Buprenorphine provides an effective way for patients to break their dependence on opiates while treating them in a private office on a one-to-one basis. The research also led me to the Prometa protocol, a potentially revolutionary way (pending the double-blind study results in 2007) to recondition the neuroreceptors involved with alcohol, cocaine, or methamphetamine addiction.

The Program

To understand why patients so often relapse, the mechanics of craving must be known as a physical and psychological presence. We all understand the notion of cravings because we've all been intensely hungry or thirsty, or been struck by an urge for caffeine or sugar. Cravings related to withdrawal, however, can be longer lasting as well as far more intense and debilitating.

Gracer Medical specializes in treating the cravings that fuel addiction and bring on relapse. Evidence-based treatments are individualized for each patient. The client-centered approach is both empathic, to support the person, and action-based, to support the person's change.

Most programs stress stopping the drug (including alcohol and opiates) through rapid detoxification followed by a short course of therapy, then discharge patients to a twelve-step program. However, many middle- and upper-class patients are uncomfortable in a public group so they drop out almost immediately. The detox–therapy–twelve-step process has a success rate of about 15 percent, worse in the case of methamphetamine. Yet the usual response to relapse is to put the patient through the same type of program again and again.

Addiction is a brain disease that chronically—and sometimes permanently—damages neuroreceptors. That's why the hardest part is the long-lasting, and occasionally permanent, post-acute withdrawal. Symptoms include fatigue, joint and muscle aches, depression, and cravings. With medications like buprenorphine (Subutex/Suboxone) for opiates, a monthly injection of naltrexone (Vivitrol) for alcoholism, camprosate (Campral) for alcohol cravings, and Prometa for cocaine, methamphetamine, and alcohol, the Addiction Craving Management and Recovery Program can treat post-acute withdrawal like the medical illness it is.

Just like with other chronic problems such as hypertension or diabetes, treatment of post-acute withdrawal must be long term and comprehensive. Any underlying pain or medical problems must also be treated for best results. Recovery must also include the diagnosis and treatment of any psychiatric disorders commonly associated with patients struggling with addiction.

The Staff

Steven M. Peterson, LCSW, CADC III

Mr. Peterson believes that compassion for his clients is core to the treatment of addiction. This approach involves harnessing his clients' motivation for change while they learn new recovery skills. He emphasizes family involvement in most therapeutic interventions to support change in both the individual and the family.

When appropriate, Mr. Peterson integrates his supportive therapy methods with medications prescribed by medical doctors to help manage both drug cravings and mental health symptoms.

Mr. Peterson has worked at both inpatient and outpatient substance abuse treatment agencies and has been in private practice since 1990. For ten years, he served as an ad hoc professor at the University of Wisconsin at Milwaukee. There he taught undergraduate and graduate students in the application of social work methods with substance abusers and their families. He is a frequent presenter at Social Work and Substance Abuse Counselor conferences on evidence-based intervention methods. He also served as a trainer for the Minority Counselor Training Project.

In 1999 Mr. Peterson started his research career with the Center for Addiction and Behavioral Research. He was trained in Combined Behavioral Intervention and served as the Lead Research Therapist for Project Combine at the Milwaukee site. He has also been a research therapist for the Arrive Project, the Nalmefene Study, the Medisorb Study, and the Aripiprazole Study.

Steven Peterson is a licensed clinical social worker (LCSW) and a certified alcohol and other drug abuse counselor (CADC III). He is a 1986 graduate of the University of Wisconsin at Madison where he received his master's degree in social work. He is certified in several evidence-based therapy methods including Combined Behavioral Intervention, BRENDA therapy, and EMA therapy.

Ann Tepperman, MSW

Ann Tepperman has been using her gift of healing and her education in clinical social work within the field of substance abuse counseling for many years. She first became interested in the field while working with at-risk youth. During that time she also participated in years of training in therapeutic bodywork.

She went on to receive a Masters in Social Work from California State University East Bay focusing on children, youth and family and substance abuse. She currently works at Gracer Behavioral Health, where she strives to incorporate complementary healing modalities with clinical social work.

Alon Marcus, DOM

Alon Marcus received his licensed acupuncturist degree from the American College of Traditional Chinese Medicine in San Francisco, California in 1984. Two years later, he received a Doctor of Oriental Medicine (DOM) degree from SAMRA University of Oriental Medicine in Los Angeles, California. He also trained in Japan and China, completing his internship at the Traditional Chinese Medicine Municipal Hospital in Guangzhou.

Dr. Marcus studied orthopedic and osteopathic medicines with several well-known physicians. He has published numerous articles in both Eastern and Western medical journals. His books include *Foundations for Integrative Musculoskeletal Disorders: East-West Approach* (North Atlantic Books, 2005); *Musculoskeletal Disorders: Healing Methods from Chinese Medicine, Orthopedic Medicine and Osteopathy* (North Atlantic Books, 1998); and *Acute Abdominal Syndromes: Their Diagnosis and Treatment According to Combined Chinese-Western Medicine* (Blue Poppy Press, 1991).

In 1995 Dr. Marcus became a diplomate of the American Academy of Pain Management. He has lectured internationally and taught courses in medical and Chinese medical orthopedics for several years. In 1997 he was named Educator of the Year by the American Association of Oriental Medicine. Dr. Marcus is currently in private practice in San Ramon and Oakland, California.

Leni Felton, Certified Nutritionist

Leni Felton is a clinical nutritionist certified by the Clinical Nutrition Certification Board. She specializes in nutritional therapies and healthy living practices for people with chronic health issues. She has been in private practice since 1995 and is a professional member of the International & American Association of Clinical Nutritionists.

Every nutritional program Leni develops reflects her underlying philosophy: cleanse, build, and balance. Leni developed spa-friendly nutrition and cleansing programs for an award-winning day spa. She was an early practitioner of Metabolic Typing, for which she co-developed and taught a curriculum for doctors and adjunct practitioners. Leni joined the Gracer Medical Group in August 2006.

Two pivotal experiences contributed to her decision to pursue therapeutic nutrition as a full-time career. One was helping to research alternatives with a team who successfully supported a friend's recovery from a lymphoma diagnosis. The other was the death of her father at age 52 following four years of debilitating and, at the time, little-understood panic attacks. One experience was deeply satisfying, allowing her to see that much can be done through nutritional and natural therapies. The other developed compassion for those suffering from conditions thought to be untreatable due to misunderstood or unknown etiologies.

Chapter Four
The Stigma

Joan

It started because I couldn't sleep. I never had an alcohol problem, although my father and brother have been in rehab more than once and my brother now lives on the streets. I went to parties and had a couple glasses of wine just like everyone else. When I started having problems sleeping it felt just fine to take a drink before bed. One glass of wine led to two...then I found that vodka was even better. Before I realized I had a problem, I needed to drink constantly to keep from getting ill.

I was ashamed and my husband and children were overwhelmed. I kept it a secret from our friends and the rest of the family, but I had to make excuses when I couldn't make it to family get-togethers or even go shopping. I hated the way I felt—shaky, nauseated and always tired. When I tried to stop, I would shake and vomit. I never made it more than a few hours.

This continued for over two years. I finally went to my doctor and told the truth about my "little secret." My physician referred me to a well-known program where I was placed on drugs to help me get off of alcohol. I went to groups, ate well, exercised, and learned all about alcoholism and drug addiction. I didn't identify with most of these folks but they were my family for twenty-eight days. After the program I was told to remain dry and was referred to a twelve-step program in my neighborhood. There was no medical follow-up. I was not given any medication for depression.

I couldn't wait to go home. The next day my husband went to work and as soon as he left, I felt alone and anxious. I finally gave in to the awful craving for "just one drink." By the time he got home I was drunk again. I was ashamed, but I was not able to get past the physical need to drink.

I was powerless to break the cycle and even more depressed each time I thought of the wasted time and money spent at the rehab facility. If they couldn't help me, who could?

* * *

Joan's husband heard about our clinic in a news story and then on the Internet. He called and made an appointment. When I met Joan she was shaky and afraid. After a thorough medical evaluation we decided she was an excellent candidate for the Prometa protocol, which we now believe helps reset the brain receptors damaged by alcohol.

I put her in the hospital overnight to make sure she was safely detoxed and started her Prometa treatment the next day. By the second day she was much better. After the third day she felt better than she had in years. She started a nutritional regimen that I outlined for her, supervised by our certified clinical nutritionist. She also saw Steve Peterson, head of the Gracer Behavioral Program, for counseling. Joan's treatment was complex as her depression was the result of bipolar disorder. It was only after taking a mood stabilizing medication that she really started feeling well. Over the next months she maintained her sobriety and her feeling of well-being continued to improve. She was exercising, eating right, and even sleeping without extra medication.

* * *

After the Prometa treatment, things really changed. I was sleeping and the terrible anxiety that had plagued me for so long was gone. I have learned how to deal with the stressful issues in my life. I know I can never drink again, but I now have a normal life. Thank God!

* * *

The Stereotype

Julie

I remember seeing a blinding white light.

I was walking upstairs, turned the corner on the landing, and heard a soft clicking. The fifty-pound antique mirror had come loose. The glass was angled so I could see my own terror as the wooden frame crashed into my skull. The glass shattered around my head and shoulders, turning my face into a thousand shards before I was knocked unconscious.

That's when the light came. The light heralding a life of constant pain and the skewed perceptions of doctors, friends, and family members who thought my desire for relief was a moral weakness or lack of self-control. I never wanted to become addicted to Vicodin. People who haven't suffered chronic pain think you've somehow brought the pain on yourself or that you

take medication to get high. But if you've ever lived with chron-
ic pain you'd understand vividly that's not what you want.

   You just want the pain to stop.

* * *

Stereotypes surrounding addiction create cultural pressures for people trying to quit. Although their intentions are good, friends and family can often prevent people from improving by pushing them into inadequate programs.

Julie's journey began because she walked upstairs at the wrong time. She's a mother and grandmother, a great friend to many, and a woman filled with warm humor and compassion.

But she's labeled a druggie because she takes medication on a regular basis. If you knew, you'd probably avoid being alone with her or whisper about her if you saw her in the supermarket. Perhaps you'd consider calling child welfare if you saw her pushing her grand-son on the swing unsupervised.

* * *

After the incident with the mirror, pain never left me. I also had another accident in which I was thrown through the windshield of my car. I was astounded when one of my doctors called me a "drug seeker." What else did I have to suffer to prove that I was in genuine need?

I couldn't wait for the doctors to figure it out. Eventually I was up to twelve pills a day, each containing 10 milligrams of hydrocodone and 325 milligrams of acetaminophen [note: she was taking Norco]. I was terrified at the idea of being an addict but didn't know how to escape. I felt so bad if I missed a dose that I saw no way to stop.

* * *

At this time Julie came to my office and started buprenorphine (Subutex). The medication finally brought her some relief. It stopped her cravings and also treated her pain. (Buprenorphine is FDA approved for opiate addiction but is also used as a pain medication.)

Julie was actually a pseudo-addict; she was not an actual addict. She suffered genuine pain but wasn't getting adequate pain treatment because her behavior marked her as an addict. I decided to use buprenorphine in her case because the dosages of Norco that were sufficient to treat her pain caused her to suffer from withdrawal symptoms—which in turn caused her to increase the dosage higher and higher. Pseudo-addiction is an extremely common problem that understandably causes confusion. After all, most people will assume that if someone needs pain medication beyond what their doctor has prescribed, they must be looking for something other than pain relief. They must be hooked on the drug's high.

Maybe. Maybe not. Full-blown addiction involves chronic, aberrant behavior (online shopping for pharmaceuticals, spending large sums of cash for illegal drugs, heightened emotional states, continued use of drugs despite dire consequences) that continues after adequate pain treatment has begun. In Julie's case, once she began treatment with buprenorphine, she experienced great relief and didn't need to pursue other venues for medication. As a non-addict, taking medication made Julie more functional because her pain was lessened.

The Assumptions

So what? You may feel sorry that a rusty nail and car accident impacted her life so terribly, but you begrudge her use of medication no matter what her official label.

It's okay. Go ahead and think that for a moment. The first step to eradicating prejudice is to recognize a lack of understanding. If you aren't fully informed, you shouldn't be blamed for not knowing. You should, however, be encouraged to find out.

According to a 2003 government study called *The National Survey on Drug Use and Health:*

- 4.7 million teenagers and adults misused opioid painkillers.

- Almost 2.5 million people used opioid painkillers for non-medical reasons for the first time—an increase of 335 percent from 1990.

- 31.2 million teenagers and adults (over 13 percent of the population) said they had misused prescription painkillers at least once.

- Approximately 1.5 million people used heroin.

Name ten friends or family members. Odds are that at least one of them has misused or is misusing prescription painkillers or has another drug or alcohol problem. Ten to 15 percent of the population has a genetic predilection to develop addiction under the right circumstances. This is addiction in all its forms: to prescription medication, alcohol, cocaine, amphetamines, marijuana, even nicotine or gambling.

Most people aren't aware that their genetic makeup makes them a candidate for addiction. It's kind of like discovering you're allergic to peanuts and then discovering your grandfather had the same condition. Only peanuts don't alter your brain chemistry and create a chemical, physiological craving that can't be cured by abstinence or willpower alone.

The National Drug Intelligence Center reports that the availability of pharmaceuticals has increased sharply since the late 1990s. The increase is due to the increase in legitimate commercial production of many drugs, which are then diverted to the illegal market through forged prescriptions, doctor shopping, theft, and the Internet.

Prejudices about the kind of people who use drugs makes recognizing the problem even worse. Kathleen Thompson-Gargano, a nurse practitioner involved at Yale University's Buprenorphine Studies program and co-founder of The National Alliance of Advocates for Buprenorphine Treatment (NAABT) says:

> Dangerous and common misconceptions are helping the spread of opioid abuse and addiction into neighborhoods we used to believe were safe. Many parents and teens believe that if it is a prescription medication, it must be safe!

There is no place where "those types" *don't* live. More importantly, you can't go on pretending that nobody you know suffers from addiction issues. The numbers don't lie, even if people struggling to keep their problems a secret do.

Are you beginning to see why it's so important that you analyze your preconceived notions about addiction and update them with facts? Prescription medication addiction is an epidemic that encroaches on your life whether you realize it or not.

My point in writing this book is not to terrify or lecture. I'm also not going to pull any punches. My life's work has been as a healer and I am tired of the social stigmas and political correctness that keeps millions of suffering individuals from receiving the treatment they need to "come out of the medicine cabinet" and lead productive and fulfilling lives.

However, let me set a couple of ground rules before moving on. Although you'll see quotes from pharmaceutical companies and patients about the relief gained from treatments like buprenorphine (Subutex/Suboxone), Prometa, monthly injectable Naltrexone (Vivitrol), or camprosate (Campral), my colleagues and I do not advocate the blanket use of any medication or treatment to serve the dependent/addicted population. That would be the same as the current one-size-fits-all approach that uses detox, therapy, and twelve-step programs. *Patients are unique individuals whose background, medical history, and specific situation should determine the course of care.*

Definitions and The Disease

In grasping the concept of how medications affect the brain and body, you need to know what *opioids* are. Reckitt Benckiser Pharmaceuticals, Inc., the manufacturer of buprenorphine (Suboxone/Subutex), states that opioids derive directly from opium (drugs like morphine and codeine) or are manufactured (oxycodone, hydrocodone, and fentanyl). Patients with severe pain find these medicines extremely effective and most do not become dependent. Their literature clearly states that addiction is a long-term brain disease that will worsen the longer it is left untreated.

Dr. Nora D. Volkow, director of the National Institute on Drug Abuse (NIDA), also says that drug addiction is a brain disease. Imaging studies, in which the brain is scanned and compared to the brains of non-addicts, shows specific abnormalities in affected individuals.

Knowing that dependence and addiction issues are as multifaceted as the broken shards of Julie's mirror is important to providing the comprehensive, compassionate care patients need.

Doctor Denial

Numerous individuals in the medical profession harbor as much ignorance about addiction issues and pain management as the general population. Many times, people who have found the strength to go to their doctors are treated with a lack of sympathy and knowledge that is both stupefying and shameful. As Kathleen Thompson-Gargano, RN, says:

> Often we hear that doctors are not interested in having "those patients" in their waiting rooms… The fact is, "those patients" are, more often than not, indistinguishable from the rest of us.

I have asked almost all of the 400-plus patients in our studies if they have a primary care doctor. They almost always do. When I ask them if their doctors know about their addiction they categorically say no. The reason they give is that, "I don't want my doctor to think of me as one of those people."

Doctors need to ask certain basic questions to screen patients before prescribing opiates. Many times those physicians who inadvertently create the problem then stigmatize the patient who becomes hooked. Worse, doctors might prescribe escalating doses to treat the pain and drag the patient deeper into addiction.

An example came to light while this book was being written. A patient had been seeing a professional, capable pain doctor to control the suffering from hepatitis C. Every month her doctor prescribed 120 tablets of 40 mg Oxycontin and 120 tablets of 30 mg rapid release Oxycodone. Since the doctor wasn't being asked every month to provide increasing amounts or doses, he assumed she was taking the medications as directed.

But she was a heroin addict. After picking up her prescription every month, she took *all 240 pills in four days*. The rest of the month she used heroin. In fact, the hepatitis C the doctor was treating had been contracted through her heroin use.

If the doctor had performed a preliminary drug screening, he would have known she was using heroin. But when a nice, middle-class person is sitting in the exam room, concern over existing addiction is the last thought to enter most people's minds.

Prescribing opiates without any kind of basic screening leads to trouble. A list of questions to ask before prescribing any opiate medication is included in the chapter entitled Pain Issues. If the doctor didn't ask these questions before treating a friend or family member with opiates, *just ask* them yourself. And if you recognize yourself in the questions, get help properly managing your pain and possible addiction issues before it's too late.

Chapter Five
Helping "The Hidden"

Barbara

Sunday, 5:00 PM at Church

"Barbara?"

Where is my purse? I have at least another hour here prepping tables for the potluck supper.

"Barbara?"

Where is my god-damned purse!

"Barbara, are you okay?"

It's Janice, giving me the look she's been giving me the past few weeks—part sympathy, part suspicion.

"I'm fine, Janice, thanks. Just a bit of a migraine. How many tables do we have left to set?"

"About five," *she says, lifting my purse onto the table. As it lands there's a distinct sound of pills shaking in a bottle and Janice's eyebrows shoot up. I grab the purse and head out of the kitchen.*

"*Thank God you found this, Jan. I could sure use one of those aspirins right now.*"

I jog up the stairs to the second story. Nobody from the dinner will be up here in this bathroom, but I lock the door anyway. Soon I'll be back to normal. For an hour, maybe more, I'll be the mom, wife, and churchgoer I was meant to be.

I fish through my purse so quickly that I don't notice when the nail clippers slice my left ring finger. I feel the pain and notice the slim line of blood, but don't bother wiping it off until after I take my Vicodin.

After

Just seeing the white oval calms me down, even though blood has soaked two of the pills. Etched into the face of the chalky shape it reads 10 mg. Maybe I should cut one in half. But it's the Christmas potluck. I'm here for another three hours.

I pop two pills and swallow them without water. I notice the bitter taste of blood.

Monday, 10:30 at Dr. Shapiro's office

"*I'm sorry, Mrs. Robbins. You say your regular doctor is in Europe and that's why you can't get your prescription refilled?*"

He's got the look. The Janice look.

"*Helsinki, actually,*" I say. "*I suppose that's Scandinavia rather than Europe, isn't it? Or are they the same thing?*" I laugh too loudly and put my hand on his shoulder, wondering about the last time any woman came this close to him. His muscles tense and then relax and I know he's enjoying my touch.

"*Whatever it is, it's cold. But is he not responding to e-mail? And didn't he leave a number for a colleague who knew your medical history?*"

"*They're in Finland together, if you'd believe it.*" I let my hand trail down his arm. He blinks rapidly and clears his throat as I step closer. He's not listening to what I say. It's about playing the game until he breaks out that little white pad.

"*Yes, well,*" he says, blushing. He clears his throat again and I almost smack his puffy white face.

Write it.

"*Um…*" He's looking at the floor now, shifting his weight. I have to interrupt his thoughts.

"*Yes, doctor?*" I say it in a way so I know he'll look at me. I lock eyes with him and smile in a very specific fashion—warm, mysterious, mischievous.

Write it now.

"*Okay, Mrs. Robbins, this is for fifty more Vicodin but I'd really appreciate your getting back in touch with me when you're done with these and when your doctor gets back.*"

"*Certainly, doctor.*" I try to keep myself from ripping the paper from his pudgy hands.

Whatever you say.

Wednesday, 9:30 at the Allen's House

"*Mom? Are you okay?*"

I open my eyes to see my two kids, my husband, and the entire Allen family staring at me in surprise.

"*What? Yes, I'm fine,*" I answer, loud enough to make my four-year-old's eyes well up with tears.

"Just asking. You look really tired."

Susan's staring at me now with The Look. "You haven't eaten anything, Barbara. Can I get you something else? Was the chicken too dry?"

"The chicken's delicious, really. I just feel another migraine coming on. Do you have any aspirin?"

"Yes, it's in the bathroom." She starts to stand.

"Wait! I'll go—I've also got a bit of a stomach cramp."

The Look has gone from subtle concern to full-blown shock. It takes about two seconds for me to get over my embarrassment as I pound upstairs and nearly rip the door off the medicine cabinet.

Susan was on Percocet after her C-Section. I rifle through dental floss, toothbrushes, deodorant. As I slam the door closed I catch a glimpse of my face and turn away.

She must keep the pills in the bedroom.

I open the door quietly. Their three-week-old son, Jack, is asleep in a crib next to their bed. Of course it's on Susan's side, which means I'll have to be extra quiet. I make it to her bedside table and pull it open without a sound. But as I move the books and papers she's got in the drawer I get more anxious—there's no bottle here. I'm dying to turn on the light but can't because of Jack. Then I see the small white shape sitting on top of the table and grab the top to open the bottle and pour out some pills.

But it's the baby monitor and my thumb hits the volume knob. A loud squelch emanates from the box and Jack immediately wakes up, shrieking. I try to turn it off but throw it aside when I see three white shapes sitting in a day-by-day pill holder. I snap open the Wednesday portion and am just tipping my head back when the door opens and the light snaps on.

*My husband stands next to Susan. Both have looks of horror
on their faces. Susan grabs Jack and backs against the wall as if
I had shoved a steak knife through his chest. My husband shakes
his head, bewildered and sad. "Barbara," he says, "what the hell
is wrong with you?"*

* * *

Barbara's not a heroin junkie, living in a flophouse and making money through prostitution. She's not buying drugs off street
corners in the middle of the night. She's an average, middle-class,
church-going mom who found herself addicted to Vicodin…and her
situation is getting worse.

Why do middle-class or white-collar folks get hooked on prescription medication? One answer, of course, is the same reason
everyone does—they start to combat pain or to achieve a high. Some
feel that the drug in Vicodin (hydrocodone) lifts their depression
and gives them energy. They use it to make life "a little easier." They
continue using it to maintain their pain relief/euphoria or to combat
the horrifying and painful effects of withdrawal as the dose they need
escalates and the time between doses decreases. Without realizing it
until it's too late, they are hooked!

Perhaps they need the medication to combat real pain but cannot get the proper prescription, entering into pseudo-addiction while
appearing to be full-blown addicts. If they can't get the pain relief
they need and have access to drugs, they may become true addicts
as well.

Why Middle-class/White-collar
Patients ("The Hidden") Don't Seek Treatment

- *Private in Public.* Due to their status or public standing,
  these patients resist group meetings and public settings and

will drop out of treatment quickly if forced into this model. Private treatment has proven much more successful.

- *Demographic Denial.* These patients typically have the money and resources to fuel their addictive behavior much longer than other addicts. They learn early on how to trick their doctors and friends to get medications, or lie to health insurance providers about prescription doses.

- *Virtual Vicodin.* Internet pharmacies provide easy and plentiful medications without the need for a prescription. The Hidden can get their fix from the safety of their homes.

- *Condemning Culture.* The stigma surrounding addiction accelerates the terror and loneliness felt by patients struggling to overcome dangerous behavior. They fear the destruction of their picture-perfect lives.

- *"Sticky" Statistics.* The renowned author Malcolm Gladwell provides clues as to why certain behaviors or trends captivate a large body of people. Addiction loves company.

Common Characteristics

- As much as 15 percent of the population is either physically or genetically predisposed to becoming addicted after taking medication for a legitimate medical purpose. These same people are also susceptible to alcohol, marijuana, cocaine and methamphetamine, nicotine addiction, and even other self-destructive behaviors, such as gambling.

- People suffering from the disease of addiction often don't have adequate coping mechanisms or the support of family and friends.

- Many people unknowingly become dependent on and addicted to their prescription medication.

- Many people suffering from addiction were abused (often sexually) as children.

- Many people suffering from addiction have a psychological disorder (such as depression or bipolar disorder) that makes treatment much more complicated.

- Many people suffering from addiction have chronic underlying pain or medical problems that may have triggered substance abuse.

- People suffering from addiction often (usually) have family members who have substance use or serious psychiatric problems.

These factors, and addiction in general, affect every segment of the population regardless of economic or cultural conditions.

Definition of Dependence

It's important to note the differences between abuse and dependence. The American Psychiatric Association has developed strict criteria for diagnosis of abuse and dependence. *The Diagnostic and Statistical Manual-IV (DSM-IV)* provides the following definitions.

Abuse is:

A pattern of use leading to significant impairment or distress, such as failure to fulfill major role obligations at work, school, home; recurrent use during dangerous situations such as driving a car; recurrent related legal, social, or interpersonal problems within a twelve-month period.

Dependence is defined as:

A pattern of use leading to significant impairment or distress marked by three (or more) of the following: tolerance, withdrawal, or taking the substance in larger amounts or over a longer period than intended; a desire or efforts to cut back;

large amounts of time spent obtaining, using, or recovering from the substance; giving up social, work, or recreational activities because of use; continued use regardless of its worsening of a physical or psychological problem occurring at any time in the same twelve-month period.

Tolerance is defined as the need for more of the drug, or loss of effect with the same amount.

Withdrawal is a rebound syndrome that occurs when heavy, repetitive doses are decreased.

Private in Public

I am a middle-class professional woman with a family and very traditional and conservative thoughts. I am embarrassed that I got caught up in this problem and was very embarrassed to discuss it with anyone. It is a shameful experience, not one I intend to repeat. There has to be a feeling of safety for people so they can discuss the problem with their doctor.

These are the actual words of a patient who became addicted to prescription drugs by ordering massive amounts over the Internet. The fact that she was able to deal with her problem alone and in my office is the primary reason she overcame her excess. People like her do not feel comfortable in a clinic or twelve-step setting, at least not before coming to grips with their situation in the privacy and protection of a doctor's office with people they trust.

Before buprenorphine arrived, the main treatment for opioid addiction was methadone maintenance treatment (MMT) in public clinics. Patients visit the clinic daily to receive their medications. This public setting, along with a lack of personal attention and anonymity, is one of the primary reasons that The Hidden avoid treatment until it's too late.

Now many middle-class persons are seeking private treatment in their physician's office much the same way that they are treated for diabetes of high blood pressure. I have heard it said that, *"Buprenorphine has brought the treatment of addiction into the mainstream, allowing the 'mainstream'(The Hidden) to get treatment."*

Kathleen Thompson-Gargano (from NAABT) provides further insights:

> In any other hospital or clinical setting, HIPPA [Health Information Patient Privacy Act] laws make patient privacy a priority. In methadone clinics the setup does not protect privacy at all. Patients stand in lines waiting to be medicated by a nurse in a glass booth. Patients have to give observed urines and attend group therapy sessions. Other disease states and treatment modalities do not require patients be humiliated and give up their privacy. This is itself a reflection of the stigma associated with addiction.

Other common reasons are inconvenience and, for the employed, even cost. If the patient has a job, they are charged significantly more than those who are unemployed. This discourages working and impedes peripheral recovery efforts such as getting out of debt. Achieving a normal lifestyle becomes very difficult. The patient feels the effort is futile, making relapse inevitable.

The concept of control is paramount in modern society, especially for middle-class and white-collar folks determined to keep a positive standing in their communities. Up until recently they had only public courses of action available. Most doctors didn't understand the subtleties involved in treating opioid addiction or were legally mandated to recommend patients to clinics.

But the tide has turned. Laws have changed so doctors can prescribe medications like buprenorphine (Subutex) and give patients the private care they need and desire. Prometa promises dramatic relief of cravings for alcohol, cocaine, and methamphetamine. Depot Naltrexone (Vivitrol) is a monthly injection that helps control alcoholism. Note that I'm not advising that only blue-collar or poverty stricken individuals continue to attend clinics, or that anyone likes public scrutiny of a devastating personal problem. The point is that now an entire demographic have options they can consider.

Demographic Denial

There are times when having money or resources can be a bad thing—especially if they allow someone to buy drugs and/or alcohol without raising red flags for family or friends. Many of The Hidden enjoy positive financial circumstances and can sink deep into addiction before funds run short.

Those who carry health insurance typically spend only the co-payment for their medication of choice. Jeri Stegman is the Associate Director of Programs and Services at Concord, California-based New Connections, one of the country's 20 top intensive outpatient treatment programs. She says, "Most of these people have health insurance, a factor normally associated with the middle-class. Opiate addicts certainly buy prescription drugs on the street, but for the most part, [The Hidden] get drugs from hospitals and physicians and are paying with insurance."

Our society respects wealth and suspects those without it. When health insurance pays for medications, why would friends and family assume anything was wrong? Unfortunately, people suffering from addiction learn how to work the system and can "doctor shop" or frequent the ER for a fix. Health insurance can often prolong the period in which they're able to buy excessive drugs, as they only need a co-payment.

If you do notice a loved one buying or seeking excessive medication, just ask people around them if they've noticed similar behavior. If appropriate, plan a time when you and a close group of friends can confront this person to tell them, "You can stop," and that there are new ways to help them. Provide them with the information in this book and find a local resource to address their specific circumstances.

Doctors deal with hundreds of patients a week and are put into highly stressful situations all the time. Although they're responsible for their actions, sometimes they assume their patients are also acting responsibly. They don't suspect that patients are doctor shopping. According to Jennifer Bolen, JD, former Assistant United States Attorney with the US Department of Justice and founder of J. Bolen Group/The Legal Side of Pain, it's an all too common practice.

> I struggle with pain issues and am white-collar so I can speak with authority on this subject. I'm also a professional female that can go into any doctor's office and convince a physician to prescribe a medication without even giving me a drug screening. I could go to a doctor, then a psychiatrist, then an OB/GYN and get enough drugs to start my own little pharmacy.

The training and experience that has allowed these patients to be successful in their careers has also allowed them to deceive others as effectively as they have themselves. Many alcoholics only drink at night to hide their problem. It isn't until they start missing work or have to drink all day long to keep withdrawal at bay that their lives unravel.

With stimulants, anger and irritability, and then work absence may be the only signs. Most stable adults do not change their personalities without a major cause. Drug addiction is a common reason.

Virtual Vicodin

Just type "Vicodin" into any search engine and you will find hundreds of sites to purchase medications online. Then you have a phone "appointment" with a doctor and they send you to a pharmacy (typically in Florida) that fills the prescription—they FedEx your order to your door. The process can make things a lot easier for someone who can't afford a doctor's appointment every month. But it's very easy to abuse the system.

These are the words of a patient who came to me after becoming addicted to medications received via the Internet. Later you'll hear from Mark Caverly, chief of the Pharmaceutical Internet Intercept Coordination section of the Drug Enforcement Administration (DEA), about just how prevalent these Internet pharmacies have become. In my opinion, the system is abusing the patient rather than the other way around.

Improvements in communications technologies mean that people can be connected to the Internet more quickly than ever before. Whether they're surfing on PDAs or on their phone, access to illicit substances has never been easier. This setup distorts the doctor/patient relationship. Diagnosis and treatment should never be based solely on information obtained over the phone or the Internet. When patients interact with these Internet doctors they know from the start that the treatment that will be prescribed will automatically be the medication that they desire. This is in contrast to a normal doctor visit in which diagnosis and treatment are based on a careful examination. Treatment may or may not be a specific medication, depending on the best interests of the patient, *not* on the commercial interest of a drug dealer. This problem is so prevalent that laws have been instituted to make giving a prescription without a face-to-face meeting illegal.

Many people repeatedly receive telemarketing calls from foreign pharmacies (usually in Canada) selling opiates. Imagine being hounded every day by these calls while you're struggling with addiction and cravings. Perhaps the worst part is that people think that because medications are being offered on websites that look official, they must be safe. That assumption can be deadly.

Condemning Culture

It's one thing to say you'd like to help a friend who is addicted to drugs. It's another thing to understand the repercussions—social and otherwise—involved in the disease of addiction. Here are some thoughts from Cynthia, a patient who struggled with addiction after being prescribed morphine for the agonizing pain of a baseball-sized tumor in her ankle.

Initially my doctor prescribed a long-acting form of morphine called Kadian. Because the name was uncommon I wasn't treated like an opium-den freak. The social taboos associated with "The M Word" [morphine] vanished. It seems to me the more affluent [you are], the more important image is. My drug therapy is strictly private. Only my very best friend, who is a nurse, knows because she understands I suffer from an actual disease.

I believe whole-heartedly that American society equates beauty and financial success with strong character and goodness. Therefore, a family pulling in seven figures probably won't be scrutinized the way their housekeeper would be. A mom in our school recently made a drunken stink at a casual event. But oh-so-many do love to attend her parties and gather in that historical home of hers. Yet a single mom with a slight drinking problem is sure to be ostracized.

Cynthia's perspective provides a welcome candor in our politically correct society. Why do some individuals escape public scrutiny while others are judged and condemned? Why do we ignore the overt addictive behavior of some yet point our fingers at others?

Cultural stigmas surrounding addiction need to stop on both ends of the economic spectrum. People in less fortunate circumstances need to be provided with the resources to help them address their addictions. And The Hidden need to be compassionately confronted by people who will just ask.

"Sticky" Statistics

In his popular book, *The Tipping Point: How Little Things Can Make A Big Difference,* Malcolm Gladwell introduces "the stickiness factor." For instance, teens almost always begin smoking because they perceive cigarettes and those who smoke as being cool. Even after being presented with overwhelming evidence of the health risks, teenagers continue to take up smoking at alarming rates. The 20 to 30 percent who have the genetic predisposition get hooked for life, while most of the others grow out of the habit. The way to cut down on smoking is to make it "uncool" so teens never start. Smoking is amazingly "sticky."

Prescription drugs, like cigarettes, have an allure that helps them spread. Intentionally or not, people dependent on or addicted to drugs may convince people around them that they're thriving. Ironically, some people herald their medication as the reason they can function, without realizing that they may be slipping into addiction or may already be addicted.

Certainly anyone who lived through the drug-embracing culture of the 1960s, 1970s, and even the 1980s would understand that although *addiction* to drugs may have been perceived as dangerous or socially unacceptable, *experimentation with and the recreational use of drugs was commonplace.* When Julie began taking Vicodin, one of her friends said, "Ooo! Can I have one?"

This same mentality applies when someone gets amphetamines from a co-worker, goes drinking after work, smokes marijuana on the weekend, or even bums a cigarette from a friend. It's far too easy—and acceptable—to get the substances that can lead to a downward-spiraling addiction.

Think how influential people can become when they're not only convinced that something is helping them but their body is craving the substance they're touting. That level of intensity could convince potential drug users to try a medication. Or perhaps the prevalence of a drug gives rise to a curiosity that leads to experimentation.

For his article, "Tipping Point Marketing: A Primer" (*Brand Strategy Magazine,* April 2004), Paul Marsden had students at the London School of Economics administer street-corner questionnaires to 100 individuals. During the first 50 questionnaires, the student was drinking a can of Coke. For the final 50 questionnaires, Pepsi was consumed. No other mention of brands was made.

At the end of each interview, the student offered a free can of Coke or Pepsi to participants. When the student drank Coke, more people chose Coke (72 percent). When he drank Pepsi, 54 percent chose Pepsi. The results were significant.

A second experiment was run using students who were less attractive and/or less popular. This individual had no significant influence on respondents. In fact, people were *less* likely to choose Coke when exposed to the interviewer drinking Coke and *less* likely to choose Pepsi when exposed to the interviewer drinking Pepsi.

Every day we deal with numerous emotional and cultural influences that we aren't aware exist. Although a person may avoid drinking because of a history of alcoholism in his family, he won't bat an eye when his doctor prescribes Vicodin after surgery. When we're aware of how culture affects our opinion of what we put into our body, we're taking a measure of common sense along with our medication.

Gladwell has another theory that's applicable to middle-class addiction. In *Blink,* he describes "the ability of our unconscious to find patterns in situations and people based on very narrow 'slices' of experience." This ability, which he calls "thin-slicing," is often referred to as intuition. When identifying a middle-class, white-collar person who suffers from drug addiction, we encounter a "thin-slicing error." Our predisposition to believe that a certain type of person *couldn't* be an addict is as damaging a stereotype as believing that only lower-class impoverished neighborhoods have drug problems.

The fact that middle-class people are embarrassed to share their problems is a primary cause of the thin-slicing error. When people become expert at masking their feelings or hiding their problems, it becomes impossible for their friends or loved ones to help.

Likewise, the Internet is powerfully persuasive because online pharmacies are businesses—they convince you to purchase their medications because otherwise they'll go under. The above-board pharmacies will provide you with information on working with your doctor and the legal procedures you'll have to follow to procure medications over the Internet. The illegal ones will simply ask you for your credit card. In either case, the ubiquitous availability of medications online implies acceptance that could be construed as permission to purchase and use at will.

Once someone starts taking drugs, the stickiness factor turns physiological—when opioids enter the bloodstream, they attach themselves to receptors in the brain. As the drug leaves the body, trouble begins. People feel a strong desire to experience the well being and freedom from pain again. They begin to suffer intense cravings. Soon they need to use just to keep from feeling awful.

Short-acting opiates such as hydrocodone can be especially dangerous because they flood the receptors and are gone quickly, thereby increasing the intensity of cravings and potential for addiction. Vicodin, which is hydrocodone in combination with acetaminophen, is a commonly abused version.

A 2001 study by the DEA on its Diversion Control Program for pharmaceuticals gives a sense of how particularly "sticky" the hydrocodone problem has become. In 1998, over 56 million new prescriptions were written for hydrocodone products. By 2000, there were over 89 million. Average consumption nationwide has increased by 300 percent since 1990.

A primary reason why this particular drug is so sticky is that it has relatively few side effects and is more likely to cause euphoria. Even more dangerous is the fact that addiction comes gradually through Vicodin, causing people to get "stuck," or addicted, without knowing. People start using Vicodin to "round out the corners of their lives" or to relieve stress. Soon they are hooked.

How We're Different

We've discovered compelling proof that the ability to seek addiction treatment in a private office setting is one of the most important factors in treating middle-class addiction. It is my profound hope that the more the mainstream seeks treatment, the less power the stigma will have on the entire population. Then people suffering in private can come out of hiding and find the care they so desperately need.

It's time to stop the stigma associated with addiction and deal with these issues in as scientific, yet humane and holistic, a manner as possible. This book is designed to help you get a better picture of your relationship to addiction so you can discuss your concerns with your doctor as an informed and educated individual. Whether you suffer from these issues yourself or are concerned for a loved one, this book will help you solve your problem.

The Gracer Behavioral Health Services
Five-step Program

This program diagnoses and treats the underlying cause of substance abuse.

1. Proper diagnosis and treatment of the real causes of pain

   - A complete medical evaluation, including possible hormonal problems such as thyroid and sex hormones in men and women

   - A thorough nutritional evaluation by a certified clinical nutritionist to assess food allergies, toxic exposure, and silent inflammation, often a major source of pain

2. Psychosocial treatments

   - Substance Abuse Check Up and other brief therapy approaches

   - Solution-focused therapy

   - Combined behavioral intervention

   - Family therapy

   - Intensive outpatient program (IOP) in conjunction with New Connections, a non-profit organization

3. Medical treatment for cravings

   - Buprenorphine, an FDA-approved outpatient treatment for addiction to opiates such as Vicodin, Norco, Oxycontin, methadone, and morphine/heroine

   - Prometa, a treatment plan for alcohol, cocaine, and methamphetamine dependence

   - Vivitrol, a monthly injection for alcohol dependence—recently approved by the FDA (also used off-label for opiate addiction)

- Other medications for cravings management
- Acupuncture and Chinese herbal medicine evaluation

4. Treatment for underlying psychiatric problems including:

- Major depression and anxiety disorders
- Bipolar disorder

5. Support groups led by experienced professionals

5-1: The Gracer Behavioral Health Services Five-step Program

You Can Stop

As soon as you're comfortable I urge you to use this book and the resources described here to seek out The Hidden in your own life. I realize that it may be awkward. But if you don't risk confronting this issue, the people you love may wind up sick or dead.

Take this book to your local physician, minister, rabbi, therapist, political leader, and friends. Create a network of informed, compassionate people who are willing to *just ask* if they recognize the signs listed here. *Just ask* is a call to action and a program of behavior you can follow to help people in need. Tell these people, "You can stop," and let them know about the paradigm-shifting treatments now offered in private office settings.

The fact is that most addicted people are desperate to stop. They just don't know how. They are afraid they will fail. Some have already tried and failed, sometimes many times. With the current treatment methods, most *do* fail. Now they can get treatment and walk the road to recovery without shame or public scrutiny.

A final note: getting treatment in private doesn't necessarily mean that a patient is unwilling to admit they have a problem. More likely they're terrified and need a private consultation with a trusted health practitioner rather than a one-size-fits-all clinic or program. At the end of the day, if patients are seeking treatment that can prevent relapse or future addiction, does it matter where they get treated and the precise format?

Certainly a support network of individuals who have struggled through similar circumstances can provide accountability. But that's a decision patients can make *after* they have started treatment for the chemical, physiological damage done to their bodies. Wanting it any other way means we're letting a stigma or a stereotype mandate behavior. And that's a slippery slope indeed.

Do you believe you or your loved one has a disease? Are you deeply aware that the stigma associated with addiction needs to be lifted? Are you in John's shoes, struggling with a growing addiction to opiates? Or are you like Joan, relying on alcohol to relieve problems that seem to double and triple when you're not drinking?

Perhaps you're like Julie and suffer from genuine pain but can't get anyone to believe that you're in agony. You might be addicted to marijuana or nicotine, not realizing that cigarettes exacerbate other addictions and have negative impacts on your brain physiology as well as your overall health.

Whatever your situation, keep reading. Doctor's orders. This is your *New Prescription for Addiction*.

Chapter Six
The Flaws
(and the Goal)

Rick

"You're a drug addict, Rick. Just say it."

I stared at the nerdy therapist, wishing he'd leave me alone. Ten other people in our circle gazed at me with patronizing smiles. The middle-aged woman wearing a bad wig patted my knee and whispered, "You can do it."

I cleared my throat. "Well, I'm here because I have a problem, I guess."

"You're an addict," nerd boy interrupted. "If you don't say it, you can't own it."

Nods from the group.

"We're here to help you, Rick. I've told the group about your addiction to Norco and they all understand. They heard how you even hit your wife when she kept your pills from you. We all know how you feel."

A teenaged boy with a lip ring spoke up. "Yeah, but eighty Norcos a day, dude. That's a lot. I'm surprised your liver didn't explode or whatever."

Wig woman said, "And we haven't even mentioned the fact that he's an alcoholic. Rick, tell the group you're an alcoholic."

An elderly man across the circle nodded. "That's the only way to recognize your higher power, Rick. It worked for me. I was on the juice even before I did the Oxycontin."

"You mean Hillbilly Heroin," said the boy. The elderly man turned purple and put his head to his chest in shame.

"So what's it going to be?" Nerd boy asked. "What are you going to do right now to change your situation?"

I knew what I wanted to do—get out of the clinic as fast as humanly possible. But I had told my wife I'd give rehab a shot. All I could do was squirm in my chair and try to think of the right thing to say.

"Um," I began, vividly picturing a handful of Norcos as I tried to speak. "I have a problem. I'm addicted to Norco and I'm also an alcoholic."

Nerd boy smiled like I'd just written him a check for five grand. Nods all around. I kept up the lip service. "So I'm really glad to be here with all of you today so I can start on my journey of healing and get my life back in shape."

Wig woman started to mist up. I went for the jugular—I sniffed like I was about to cry. "I need to get clean so I can be the best husband I can be; my wife is my best friend and she doesn't deserve to be treated the way I've been treating her. I'm doing this for Jill." I paused for effect and hid my face in my hands. "I love you, baby. I'm sorry. I'm so sorry."

Everyone got choked up. Even lip-ring had to turn his head away so he wouldn't lose his cool. I got some patronizing hugs from a bunch of people and went back to my room, where I could almost see my skin crawling on my arms and legs from the power of the drug cravings that had overtaken my body and mind. The stress of having to perform for these idiots had tripled my desire to use. I'd probably end up worse off for coming to this place.

* * *

This story dramatically reflects the experience of one patient in particular, but is typical of many. Most twelve-step programs employ a confrontational model of treatment. The idea is that patients can only change a problem once they recognize and admit (usually publicly in a group setting) that they have a problem. First, I want to state again that any program that helps a patient quit addiction in a healthy manner is fine. Millions of people have been helped with twelve-step programs and I recommend them to my patients as part of their overall treatment.

However, I say *part* because, for most patients, twelve-step programs by themselves aren't the solution. The programs only focus on the social aspect of the problem and not the physical or psychiatric areas. Would it make sense to have a Diabetics Anonymous where diabetics had to admit they have a problem in order to heal their disease? Since addiction is a physiological disease as much as a social one, it needs to be treated on all fronts.

The confrontational model itself doesn't work for many people due to embarrassment and public scrutiny. There are many twelve-step programs that foster a supportive, educational community. I couldn't recommend anything better for a patient undergoing long-term treatment for chronic addiction. However, timing is key. Shoving someone into confrontation during intense cravings or the beginning stages of post-acute withdrawal is a recipe for disaster. The wife of one patient described it this way:

> My husband went to a thirty-day rehab facility where they only gave him buprenorphine for a few days. He only lasted about two weeks before he made me come get him. Their whole deal was the twelve-step program and finding their higher power. His only higher power is himself. Dr. Gracer's program is working because Dr. Gracer isn't just a revolving door. There is no set date for my husband to be done and they work on his issues one-on-one. My husband and I do not feel comfortable sharing our stories at meetings. I want to keep this whole thing discreet. Only my husband and my mother know.

It is interesting to add that the rehab program he left prescribed buprenorphine (Subutex) to detox him, but only for a few days. He was feeling well until the buprenorphine was stopped as part of the program's abstinence policy. This left him depressed, with intense cravings. On the way home he scored some Norco. Since the program didn't focus on treating his cravings, it failed.

Support for Holistic Treatment

What Gracer Medical does is not revolutionary, and we're not the only organization advocating this approach. The National Institute on Drug Abuse's (NIDA) *Principles of Effective Drug Addiction Treatment* states that a successful addiction treatment program should include:

- Treatments tailored to the individual
- Treatment that is readily available
- Treatment that attends to multiple needs, not just drug use
- Ongoing assessment of patient needs, which may change
- Treatment for an adequate period of time

- Individual and/or group counseling and other behavioral therapies
- Medications—an important element for many patients
- Integrated treatment for coexisting mental disorders
- Recognition that medical detoxification is only the first stage
- Recognition that treatment does not need to be voluntary
- Continuous monitoring for drug use during treatment
- Assessment for HIV/AIDS, hepatitis B and C, tuberculosis, and other infectious diseases
- Recognition that recovery from drug addiction can be a long-term process

Even though these principles were introduced back in 1999, few addiction programs follow NIDA's suggestions. Both the medical community and the population at large still view addiction as an insular problem and focus on sociological issues without regard to brain chemistry, cravings, or psychiatric disorders.

In addition, Stanton Peele has been writing about addiction since 1969. His seminal book, called *Love and Addiction,* caused quite a stir in the medical community and established him as a leading authority on approaches that didn't focus on opiates or drugs. Here are some thoughts from his compelling article, "What Treatment for Addiction Can Do and What It Can't; What Treatment for Addiction Should Do and What It Shouldn't," from the *Journal of Substance Abuse Treatment.*

> Addiction occurs along a continuum, and even those at the extremes of addictiveness show the capacity to act in other than an addicted way under the right circumstances... Changing the means of administering a substance or the setting of administration can alter the addictive experience sufficiently to render it ineffective...

A similar approach is represented by aversive conditioning to drug and alcohol effects or by simply convincing the person to abstain... A more direct approach to shifting this balance is to improve the person's personal and situational resources.

Therapy for addiction only rarely and very inexactly accomplishes these things, in part because addiction treatment is preoccupied with the nature of the substance involvement rather than with the person's relationship to self, others, and the world.

A compelling article, entitled, "Psychosocial Treatments for Substance Use Disorders: Guiding Principles for Promoting Behavioral Change," was published in *Primary Psychiatry* in February of 2006. The authors, Kenneth M. Carpenter, PhD, and Adam C. Brooks, PhD, also contend that a person's relationship to themselves and the world plays a vital role in determining behavior toward addiction and abstinence. Their studies also demonstrate that non-confrontational methods are most effective in promoting lasting change.

Carpenter and Brooks introduce the idea of Coping Skills Training (CST), which assumes that "substance users can learn new behavioral, cognitive, and interpersonal skills to prevent relapse." These approaches are non-confrontational and encourage an empathetic relationship between doctor and patient. Rather than using shame to force change, they help patients set up specific treatment programs.

The methods include teaching a patient about triggers and identifying specific circumstances, people, or substances that increase risk for a patient. CST also provides coping behaviors for cravings. Lastly, although effective in group setting, CST is ideal for office settings. It can be delivered once or twice per week, or as much as every other week. This approach caters to The Hidden.

The term "competing reinforcers" means that patients are provided with a positive result to reinforce their positive behavior. These can take place privately with a doctor, or in a community. An example would be vouchers given for drug-free urine samples. The first sample might get 50 cents and the tenth $5.00 at a popular café or mall. While these may seem to be very small amounts, research shows that it works. Negative (addictive) behavior is traded for activities that promote feelings of self-worth and/or community approval.

Another principle of Carpenter and Brooks, the importance of the doctor-patient interaction, is of special interest. At Gracer Medical, our innovative Readiness Quadrant (RQ) evaluation is a unique test we've developed to measure a patient's willingness to embrace non-addictive behavior. The RQ is one of the first ways we open a dialog with people who come to us for help. Not only does it help us determine what treatments might be best suited to individuals, but it also helps patients realize things they might not have known about their own journey.

Here's the thing about addiction—it's hard to change your behavior. It sounds simplistic, but I want to make sure you understand what people struggle with when trying to wean themselves from dependence or addiction. As an example, think back to the thrill you felt at learning to drive. Since you were so young when you started, you might have pushed the limits a little. You might have taken corners too fast, peeled away from stop signs, or swerved through traffic.

Let's say that you never settled down and became a safe driver. Instead, you found the high-stakes risks of defying accidents and death a rush. Every time you go out on the freeway now, you see how high you can push the speedometer needle. If traffic is heavy, you swoop down on the other car's bumper until they get the hint and move out of your lane. Whenever you can't feed your need for speed, you feel irritated and are on edge for the rest of the day.

In fact, your addiction to speed causes you to alter your behavior to such a degree that your daily schedule is now dictated by how often you can drive fast. You leave work early to beat the traffic and fly on empty highways. The jackrabbit starts are wearing out the transmission, so you have to spend more money on car maintenance. Rather than stay home on your days off, you prefer to drive into the mountains to pit yourself against hairpin curves.

Maybe your family is tired of your weekend absences, your irrational behavior when you can't speed, and the heavy expenses for gas and newer, faster cars. You may think your enjoyment of speed isn't that big a deal. But your family and colleagues see how much of a financial strain is on your family and how much danger your kids are in when they ride with you. Even your wife refuses to get in a car with you because even when she's driving, you demand she drive faster.

Then you get help and a doctor tells you that you're in trouble. She presents you with the medical facts and outlines a program of treatment. But you still don't want to change. Why? Because your life revolves around speed!

Changing addiction doesn't just mean you stop taking drugs or alcohol. It means you reverse your worldview, your daily activities, even your friends. Because it changes everything, it's a huge deal. It's no wonder people don't want to embrace change. That's why our RQ evaluation is vital. Not only does it measure a patient's willingness to change, it also shows the patient when and why they're not ready or willing to do so.

The interaction with a doctor or clinician can determine a patient's motivation to change or lack thereof. This is separate from a patient's independent *desire* to change. Thus the style and methods employed to treat a patient during the delicate initial stages are critical. Empathetic and supportive methods are far superior to a confrontational mindset.

The "Addiction Industry"

So if the fundamentals that are needed to effect change are well known and available, what's the problem? Sadly, as Carpenter and Brooks point out, these elements are rarely found in current treatment programs. The good news is that more individuals and organizations are recognizing that social models for treatment of substance abuse in and of themselves are not as effective as we have thought. The bad news is that many people in the "addiction industry" are just as reluctant to change as the patients are. Sometimes clinicians are determined to stick with a familiar program they've utilized for years.

I do not doubt that many or most of these programs are run by people who truly want to help patients recover. It is my hope, however, that they will realize that their efforts will bring more fruit if they incorporate a more holistic treatment rather than focusing on just one branch of care.

Flaws in the Mainstream Treatment Model
1. The most commonly seen model for the treatment of substance abuse (rapid detox, short treatment, abstinence, and discharge to a social program) just doesn't work.
2. Deficiencies within twelve-step programs.
3. Treatment based not on evidence but on tradition or physician preference.
4. Substance abuse seen as separate from mental health, and/or substance abuse staff has little training in treating mental health issues.
5. Confrontation (shame or moral judgment) approach lacks empathetic counseling/treatment.
6. Treating the manifestations of pain and/or addiction rather than their symptoms/causes.

7. Medicine/pharmacology prescribed without regard to psychological/sociological issues.
8. No evaluation or treatment of nutritional problems.
9. No alternative medical approaches.
10. Doctors and medical community don't deal with legitimate pain issues.
11. No diagnosis or treatment of underlying hormonal imbalances.
12. No evaluation of neurotransmitter status.
13. No craving management.
14. Most programs only deal with substance abuse, rather than the whole person.
15. Programs don't always recognize social preferences for how the middle class wants to be treated.
16. One-size-fits-all mentality.

6-1: Flaws in the Mainstream Treatment Model

1. The most common model just doesn't work.

The current system of rapid detox, short treatment, abstinence from even medically useful drugs, and discharge to a social program does not work. Recurrence rates are about 85 percent or more. The single focus of most programs practically guarantees failure for most people. If the underlying reason why they became addicted isn't treated, and if their cravings aren't managed, patients simply can't be expected to do the hardest thing in their lives when the stress of confrontation is their only "support."

The Gracer Program uses an integrative approach. We understand that every person is an individual who needs a program designed specifically for them, aimed at ensuring that they will not drop out and giving them the best possible chance to succeed. This provides a caring and scientific environment free from moral assessments and emotional stigmas.

Note that we agree that abstinence from the abused drug is critical. However, medicines used to treat other diseases or ailments can and should be prescribed. Telling anyone they are no longer allowed the relief or treatment provided by medicines (whether prescribed or over the counter) creates unnecessary suffering. Even in the case of opiate addiction, opiates can be prescribed if absolutely necessary under extremely careful scrutiny. For more information, refer to the short- versus long-acting opiate section in the Opiates chapter.

Rather than focusing on simply abstaining from the substance or behavior that led a patient to become addicted, we employ the specialists and partners that can truly provide the greatest overall assessment for each patient. Once we reach a conclusion about the patient's status we can provide the strongest program for their care, as compared to simply pursuing a temporary plan of detoxification and encouragement for abstinence. Any effective plan must treat the long-term cravings that are main the cause of relapse.

In all fairness, Narcotics Anonymous does recognize that abstinence only works in the context of a strong support network. Surprisingly, they also condone prescribed medications for NA members where appropriate. Nonetheless, my overall concern is for a patient's well being. I cannot advocate abstinence alone if patients will suffer needlessly when they could be safely detoxified and receive the long-term care that will deliver them from addiction.

2. Deficiencies within twelve-step programs.

- While in our program we find that they are vital for some patients and an important support for many others, a 15 percent success rate is nothing to write home about.

- They don't satisfy the desire for privacy characteristic of The Hidden.

- The predominant model of "shame for change" is largely ineffectual and has negative psychological consequences.

- They do not stress self-reliance. They trade one addiction for another (going to meetings).

- They lack treatment for the disease as well as other co-existing problems and do not fully consider cravings or post-acute withdrawal.

Twelve-step programs are social in nature, rather than scientific. Successful treatment of addiction also focuses on medicine and pharmacology. Addiction treatment can be helped by social means, but lasting or permanent damage to the brain cannot be treated by talking or through group support. Some individuals may be able to withstand the dramatic and traumatic physiological changes of withdrawal and abstinence. If they prefer suffering, so be it. Their physician or counselor may feel taking any kind of medication is too risky at their stage of treatment.

But let's admit that this choice is largely philosophical in nature. If you crush your finger in a car door, you're going to need a doctor. No one thinks it strange for you to rush to a hospital; they only think it's strange if you don't. When you're afflicted by addiction, it's as if your brain has thousands of tiny open wounds. I don't blame anyone for being concerned about taking a new prescription after suffering from addiction. However, I am always amazed that people will choose to not try a method that could stop their pain and heal their bodies.

Proponents of twelve-step programs, as well as many clinicians and other health care professionals, have faith that this type of program is the only thing that works. Science (or even logic at times) doesn't enter the picture. But belief in something can't stand up against the medical and scientific nature of addiction. An 85 percent relapse rate is a deficiency I will not accept.

3. Treatment is not evidence-based.

Many doctors prescribe a treatment that works for them, not the patient. If their methodology results in a high percentage of recovery with low relapse, show me your evidence! Group therapy has been the foundation of substance abuse treatment for more than forty years, but only minimal research has been conducted to document its effectiveness.

Over the past decades, research has revolutionized medical and psychological treatments. This stands in contrast to substance abuse treatment, where most programs are slow to adapt. Too few counselors keep current with ongoing research; even fewer try to implement new methods.

It is important to change as new ideas develop. Most medical diseases are treated differently today than they were 50 years ago...why not substance abuse?

4. Substance abuse is seen as separate from mental health and/or substance abuse staff has little training in treating mental health issues.

The biochemistry of addiction often coincides with psychiatric illness such as depression and anxiety. This is one of many reasons that substance abuse treatment should not be segregated from mental health treatment. Many times this problem is bipolar disorder, which must be treated differently from common depression and anxiety disorders. The Gracer Program recognizes that many people with addiction are self-treating psychiatric symptoms.

All too often substance abuse counselors have little or no training in mental health diagnosis and treatment. In addition, after discharge from the acute part of most programs, there is no mental health follow up. The usual twelve-step referral addresses social rather than psychiatric, medical, or craving issues.

The converse is also true: many psychologists and even psychiatrists have little experience with substance abuse. They may treat patients for depression or other mood problems, even bipolar disorder, without addressing the "elephant in the room." Many times, physicians and mental health providers are ignorant of their patient's real problem. They might not know about substance abuse at all because, often, family doctors and therapists are never told. That's why it's important to *just ask*.

Only the integration of the two fields can achieve optimal outcomes.

5. Confrontation (shame or moral judgment).

Shame doesn't work. It ostracizes rather than embraces. It intensifies a patient's feelings of isolation and can cause lasting psychological damage. Momentary peer or doctor pressure can never replace long-term, positive reinforcement from a professional or other supporting individual.

"Traditional" programs also ignore the fact that middle-class patients often won't participate in group settings. People are reluctant enough to admit to themselves or their doctors that they have problems—why would they spill their guts to a roomful of strangers?

Change through shame also has lasting psychological ramifications. People may initially change but eventually resent such treatment and often rebel. This often reinforces their desire to participate in addictive behavior.

Empathetic models are more successful because, when patients elicit positive responses from a mentor/doctor/friend, they want to repeat that behavior. Likewise, if they do relapse or step backward, they respond much better to positive encouragement to try again than to a verbal spanking.

6. Treating the manifestations of pain and/or addiction rather than their symptoms/causes.

Treating only the symptom (i.e., addiction) does not treat the cause. Gracer Medical, through extensive testing and analysis, determines where a patient's pain comes from in order to treat it effectively over the long term.

An analogy from Ted. J. Kaptchuk's marvelous book, *The Web That Has No Weaver: Understanding Chinese Medicine,* demonstrates this point beautifully. In this scenario, a group of patients with duodenal ulcers was treated by Chinese medicine rather than by the traditional Western medicine regimen.

The Chinese methodology involves diagnosis through checking the pulse, looking at the tongue, and examining the skin. The chief concern is to restore the natural balance (the yin and the yang) of the body's energy system (called *chi*). The typical treatment is largely acupuncture, herbs, and dietary changes. These are prescribed to correct the body's system toward normal function, rather than directing treatment to the ulcer. The diagnoses themselves were Chinese and did not have specific reference to the duodenum.

At the time the book was written, Western physicians focused on the duodenum, the first part of the small intestine, rather than the whole system. Doctors thought the ulcers were caused by excess acid from the stomach. The stomach acid was created by a patient's poor dietary choices or chronic anxiety. Antacids like Mylanta were prescribed for short-term care. For long-term care, the duodenum was surgically cut and reattached so the acid wouldn't be as damaging to the duodenum. The surgical procedure was being prescribed more and more often as patients that took Mylanta had recurrences of ulcers and even internal bleeding.

It is interesting to note that, many years later, ulcers were proven to be caused by a bacterium called Helicobacter Pylori. Treatment now consists of antibiotics for a couple of weeks. The bacterium was discovered by two Australian physicians, Dr. Barry Marshall and Dr. Robbin Warren, who bucked the accepted medical dogma linking ulcers to acid. Due to Marshall and Warren's work, multitudes of patients have been spared the knife for a highly invasive procedure that didn't treat the cause.

The Western doctors were focused on the manifestation of a problem rather than the whole picture. This is typical of Western medical practice: diagnosis based on one part of the system (a broken bone, ulcer, or lesion) instead of the whole.

When doctors focus on drug addiction rather than on the patient, they're likely to miss major clues. When doctors focus on the moral aspect and recommend a twelve-step program, they're missing the patient's medical/pharmacological needs.

7. Medical/pharmacological-only approaches that do not address the psychological or sociological issues.

Just as sociological treatments should not exclude medical options, medical treatments for cravings and psychiatric conditions should not be the sole treatment. Thankfully, more and more enlightened individuals are beginning to recognize the positive effects multidisciplinary approaches have on addiction patients. Medicine, therapy, and support groups provide a trinity of care that addresses a patient's overall concerns.

8. No evaluation or treatment of nutritional problems.

Medications affect and alter brain chemistry. Food does the same. When you ingest sugar or caffeine, your energy spikes. Plus you may have a feeling of pleasure associated with your scone and coffee, so your dopamine levels increase. There is a connection between your brain and what you ingest. Some foods can be toxic. Others, such as carbohydrates, stimulate insulin production and can cause chronic illness such as diabetes and degenerative arthritis in some genetically predisposed individuals.

Diet and supplements can be manipulated for positive effects. Dr. Joan Larsen documents a direct connection between hypoglycemia and alcoholism for a specific group of alcoholics in her book *Seven Weeks to Sobriety*. Since some people become alcoholics because they are self-medicating this condition, doctors who diagnose and treat that patient's hypoglycemia obtain greater success rates than those who don't. Physicians who understand a patient's nutritional history and habits can provide the most holistic and informed care.

9. No alternative or integrative medical approaches.

Integrative medicine provides the best of both worlds. The Gracer Program includes many treatments based in alternative medicine. This includes acupuncture and Chinese medicine, herbal treatments, use of amino acids, and other functional medical testing and treatments usually overlooked by conventional medicine.

10. Doctors and the medical community don't deal with legitimate pain issues.

Physical problems ranging from migraine headaches to chronic back pain must be treated if there is to be a successful outcome. These are often the inciting reason for the addiction syndrome. If left untreated, they remain an important factor for relapse. We also recognize that patients with legitimate, under-treated pain issues may appear to be addicted without actually being addicted (pseudo addiction).

It's one thing for a doctor to recognize drug-seeking behavior and empathetically work with a patient to help them recognize their problem. But if they disregard a patient's claims out of hand due to negative experiences with other patients, they might miss information critical to correct diagnosis and treatment.

11. Not diagnosing and treating underlying hormonal imbalances.

Subtle, often overlooked hormone deficiencies such as low thyroid function and low sex hormone levels can cause fatigue, treatment-resistant depression, chronic pain, and other symptoms. It is important to evaluate and treat these problems. Often, correcting this type of problem can dramatically impact a patient's success.

12. No evaluation of neurotransmitter status.

Testing for neurotransmitter levels can be used to design specific supplementation programs of amino acids, minerals, and vitamins to increase and balance the brain's neurotransmitters. This augments a patient's response to other medications to the point that medication can often be decreased or even stopped.

13. No craving management.

I cannot fathom how any treatment program could be successful without addressing this vital issue. Cravings are the single highest reason patients relapse and live in misery during withdrawal. Cravings are powerful, physiological urges that cannot be dismissed as behavioral. They are a result of brain dysfunction and are triggered by social situations and prior behavior. They require proactive, chronic care to avoid almost certain relapse.

14. Most programs (and general public mindset) only deal with the substance abuse aspect.

People aren't cars—they aren't fixed by replacing a part. They are emotional beings living in a highly developed social community. Dealing with the drug itself is just the first step of many. More importantly, if patients aren't treated like human beings, their feelings of isolation will increase and they'll likely relapse. Only after getting to know a patient can I best treat them as an individual. Prescribing the wrong treatment means I haven't done my job.

15. Programs don't always recognize social aspects of how the middle class wants to be treated.

A large number of people are seeking care now because they can see a doctor in a private office setting. For some strange reason, how people want to be treated for addiction has often largely been taken out of the equation. In the mainstream treatment mindset, because of their apparent moral failing, drug addicts don't deserve to have a say. That mindset is both skewed and erroneous. In a paradigm where it's so vital for a patient to feel empowered, a method of care they can champion for themselves must be found.

16. One-size-fits-all mentality.

To illustrate this flaw, let me share a classic tale. Long ago, the Buddha's disciples asked which of the wandering hermits and scholars were right: those who claimed the world was infinite and eternal, those who said it was finite and would decay, those who said life continued beyond the body, and so on.

Buddha told them about a raja who gathered all the blind men in his province and showed them an elephant. One man felt the elephants head, another its foot. A third grabbed its tail and a fourth its tusk. When the raja asked what sort of animal an elephant was, he received a different answer from each man.

The one who had touched the tusk said it was like a plowshare. The one who felt the foot said it was like a pillar, and the man who grabbed the tail said it was like a brush. The men began to argue, providing the raja with much amusement. As each blind man clung to his own false impression of the elephant's true nature, so too did the wandering hermits and scholars see only one side of a matter.

This metaphor shows how the medical field deals with patients suffering from addiction. Most practitioners are blinded by their prejudices, experiences, and training. They only see what they believe.

My old friend and noted medical philosopher, Thomas Dorman, MD, once said this is the "Believing is Seeing Disease." Since many physicians already know that a given treatment does not work or that another is effective, they see any data to the contrary as bogus and explain it away. In other words, "Don't confuse me with the facts; I've already made up my mind!"

Another aspect is that experts only see what they know. A sociologist may only focus on the social impact of addiction while the physician focuses on the medical impact. They're not willing or able to take off their masks and see the whole elephant. There is an overemphasis on placing a patient's problems into tidy little boxes instead of treating people in a holistic manner.

It's time we give doctors the resources they require so they can refer addiction patients to the places that will best suit their needs. And it's time we demonstrate to patients that we understand they are not a problem to be solved but a person to be saved.

Chapter Seven
The Deceivers and the DEA

Frank*

>"I'm going to start you on Vicodin," the doctor said.

>"Why is that?" Frank asked.

>"Your headache isn't responding to the other meds. Let's try Vicodin for a bit and see if it helps at all. Sound good?"

>"Sure. Thanks, doc."

>*Two Weeks Later*

>"The pain is still pretty severe. Do I need to take more Vicodin?"

>"Let's change to double-strength Norco. I want you to get relief from your pain and also see which medication will help you best."

>"Okay. Thanks."

A Few Weeks Later

"Doc, I've got a weird situation going on. When I take the meds, the pain only goes away for an hour or two. Every time I turn around I've got a bottle up to my lips; my wife's giving me dirty looks and people at work think I have a bladder infection because I'm going to the bathroom so much. Do you have a different pill or whatever I can take to get rid of the pain?"

Prescription pad in hand, Frank's doctor stared at his patient for a long moment. Finally he said, "Frank, I think you need to take a break from the meds."

Frank was stunned. "But you just increased my dosage a few weeks ago."

"I know. But I'm worried you may be seeking drugs for the drugs' sake versus getting relief from your pain."

"You're calling me a liar?"

"Not a liar, no—just a confused and troubled patient trying to find help."

Frank's mouth hung open in disbelief. "So help me! Whether it's drugs or a program or something, what should I do?"

Frank's doctor shrugged and rubbed his eyes under his glasses. "I have some pamphlets I can give you, but unfortunately I'm not trained as an in-depth pain specialist."

Frank left his doctor's office, angry and terrified. He paused just long enough to tear the pamphlets to pieces and throw them all over the waiting room.

Two Weeks Later

Frank's spam filter missed an incoming e-mail. The subject line read "Notes on our Project at Work" so he didn't realize it was an ad until he had opened it. The words "Online Vicodin" *were followed by a link. Two clicks later, Frank had his credit card out and was entering his information for his first shipment.*

The shipment came quickly. It just said "Vicodin" on the label, no warnings or information on what company had produced it. Frank took them anyway, by the handful, along with his Norco tabs. And he started drinking—slowly for the first few weeks, then binge drinking as solitude, pain, and loneliness overtook him.

The night he left the bar and got behind the wheel with a stomach full of pills and booze, a cop arrested him on a DUI charge. His license was revoked and he was fired from work. His headaches only got worse.

*This is a dramatic story and not from a real patient.

* * *

The Deceivers

As mentioned earlier, this book was inspired by two young patients who became addicted via the Internet. Initially I was flabbergasted at how easy it was to order the medications over the Internet. Now I am spammed (as I'm sure you are) dozens of times per week—even per day—by offers to buy these drugs with the click of a mouse.

Sadly, Frank's story is commonplace. A genuine problem with pain can lead to dependence or addiction when doctors aren't adequately trained in pain management. Patients who are unaware of their dependence can become confused under the influence of powerful chemicals that undermine common sense. DUIs, loss of jobs, and estrangements from family and friends are typical in a person's downward spiral. The Internet is often the devastating blow that seals their fate.

Internet pharmacies have become prevalent and are dangerous. First, the majority of them are illegal. Period. There are official protocols to follow to legitimately receive drugs via the Internet, and the process should take more than a quick phone call.

Second, the notion of *caveat emptor* (buyer beware) has never been more applicable than with buying drugs online. Think of purchases you've made over the Internet before—books, clothes, gifts. If you get a defective product, you return it. How can you return your health if you ingest a faulty, fake, or even toxic drug? It is imperative to remember that just because someone *sounds* like a doctor doesn't mean they're acting in your best interest. And just because you receive something in the mail that *looks* like a standard pill bottle, it may not contain safe or even properly formulated medication.

The prevalence of other easy-to-find substances such as alcohol, cigarettes, marijuana, and powerful drugs means addiction can strike from a number of sources. It's vital that patients understand what they're up against and be protected.

Consumer, Heal Thyself

You're probably sick of the ads on TV where someone smiles and talks about the relief they've received from some new medication with a pretty name. People dance on the beach holding hands and butterflies form the letters of the brand name while a thirty-second litany of warnings are backed by soothing music.

I hate those commercials. They encourage viewers to have a backward relationship in which patients dictate treatments to their doctors. People come to my office and tell me they need Vicodin or Percocet without even asking me for an examination. Do you demand your auto mechanic replace a perfectly good transmission because you watched "Monster Garage" on the Discovery Channel?

Knowledge can be a good thing when used properly. Advertisements for medication can be helpful because they often bring the patient to the doctor for their problem or draw the doctor's attention to a possible treatment; but only the physician should make this decision, and only after a thorough assessment.

However, many patients feel so strongly that they'll leave their doctor if he or she won't prescribe a certain drug. This puts a physician in a very difficult situation. You want to respect your patient's wishes, but if they're asking for a medication that isn't in their best interest you have to let them know.

Doctors need to *just ask* their patients the tough questions. Remember Gladwell's idea of the thin-slicing error? It happens all the time. If a physician doesn't ask questions pertinent to the patient's care, odds are the patient won't tell them. Erectile dysfunction and other circumstances can be embarrassing. But if a doctor doesn't know all of the symptoms, he or she can't prescribe the best solution.

This is precisely why the Internet's doctor-patient "relationship" is so skewed. If a doctor can't physically examine a patient, they're trusting that the patients are telling the truth. They're also trusting that the person is in their right mind—which is often not the case with addiction. People typically resort to purchasing over the Internet when they want a certain drug rather than a proper diagnosis. And the majority of online pharmacies are primarily interested in making money, not offering the best treatment.

I understand that getting drugs online is easier, faster, and oftentimes cheaper than coming to my office and hearing a diagnosis you might not agree with. I'm worried, however, about patients ruining and even losing their lives. Internet pharmacies have greatly added to the harm of opiate addiction because patients can get huge amounts of pills without medical observation.

The FDA's response to a tragic story of a fifty-two-year-old Illinois man who died of a heart attack after buying Viagra online further underscores the potential dangers. *The Journal of Medical*

Internet Research[1] reports that the website didn't know (or ask) about the man's chest pain or history of heart disease because it only required that he complete a basic survey. "Though there is no proof linking the man's death to the drug, FDA officials say that a traditional doctor-patient relationship, along with a physical examination, may have uncovered any health problems such as heart diseases and could have ensured that proper treatments were prescribed."

More importantly, physicians should be counseling their patients only after a thorough examination. Even if patients mean to be honest, they're often wrong. The law now requires a face-to-face meeting before prescribing a controlled substance such as Norco for the first time. This makes all the pseudo-doctor visits illegal.

Most Internet pharmacies don't even require that a physician be involved at all! Take a look at these statistics from a study conducted by The National Center on Addiction and Substance Abuse at Columbia University (CASA) called, "You've Got Drugs! Prescription Drug Pushers on The Internet" (2/04).

Anyone—including children—can easily obtain highly addictive controlled substances online without a prescription from Internet drug pushers. All they need is a credit card. Of the 157 sites selling controlled prescription drugs on the Internet (January 15 through January 22, 2004):

- 90 percent (141) did not require any prescription.

- 41 percent (64) stated that no prescription was needed.

- 49 percent (77) offered an "online consultation."

- 4 percent (7) required that a prescription be faxed.

- 2 percent (3) required that a prescription be mailed.

- 4 percent (6) made no mention of prescriptions.

The number of Internet pharmacy sites has grown over the past few years. The felons who create the sites know to cancel one and create another when they may be under scrutiny from law enforcement. Going after the websites themselves is a game of smoke and mirrors. Reporting a URL to the DEA can be helpful, but odds are by the time you report the site the webmaster is long gone. The "physician" and pharmacist continue to send drugs to online patients via a new website.

Jennifer Bolen, JD, founder of the J. Bolen Group/The Legal Side of Pain, says:

> There are valid users of Internet pharmacies, where care of the patient, diagnosis, and so on is done up front and conforms to the legal requirements of the state where the Internet user resides. However, the black market and corruption elements online are really dangerous. Patients need to know that in most instances they're not dealing with qualified clinicians. You don't know who/where it's coming from, and you don't even know if it's real.

It's a different kind of drug war, one that cuts across socio-economic and racial lines.

The DEA

The US Department of Justice Drug Enforcement Administration (DEA) has made great progress in identifying and prosecuting illicit Internet pharmacies. But the danger of buying tainted or even deadly products online is still very real, especially when patients don't realize how medications will interact with their current regimen.

Beyond the extraordinary amount of information available on the DEA's website, I wanted to get an insider's perspective on the battle waged with Internet pharmacy criminals. I was fortunate to secure an interview with Special Agent Mark Caverly, who is chief of OSI, the Pharmaceutical Internet Intercept Coordination Section of Special Ops (SOD).

What's the current status of Internet Pharmacies online today?

It's difficult to gauge the extent of abuse on the Internet or for the DEA to quantify the amount of drugs being trafficked online. For instance, the other day I typed "Vicodin, no prescription required" into Google and got 11 million hits. There's no way to tell how many of these sites are linked back to each other or how long they'll stay online.

However, I can let you know about some successful operations we've recently concluded. For example, Operation "Cyber Chase" concluded in April of 2005. One organization [caught in that sting] sold 2.5 million units of controlled substances. This operation involved international Internet criminals.

On the national level, Operation "CYBERx" was also very successful. This was a domestic operation where the physicians and pharmacies involved were trafficking as much as 3.5 million dosage units of controlled substances per month.

Our experience shows that there may be one website operator involved who has twenty different websites and domain names. So if they're concerned that one of their sites is getting unwanted scrutiny, they'll take that particular site down one day and put up another one tomorrow. They're extremely fluid and change rapidly to evade the law and deceive more customers.

What's your experience with businesses telemarketing to customers about pharmaceuticals?

We're seeing some telemarketing call centers being set up internationally and nationally. People were getting phone calls when their refills were due. In other words, they were getting aggressively marketed to.

However, these 800 numbers don't last too long for the same reason the sites don't—they're too easy to set up and break down.

Our primary focus is to identify the individuals who set the sites up. These are the people who facilitate the sale of the drugs but may or may not handle the drugs themselves.

Our greatest impact is made not when we take down a website or call center but when we identify the major players behind schemes that permit this trafficking to go on. And that's where we've had the most success.

Is the general public fairly unaware of the illicit nature of many Internet pharmacies?

In short, yes. That's why we've tried to have big take-downs with lots of press coverage. We try to make as big a splash as possible to let people know that getting drugs online is not something you want to do. You don't know what you're going to get. The majority of drugs are being sold at four to *ten* times the price you could buy them with a prescription from your doctor.

Some people may not know that [ordering drugs online] is illegal. But any reasonable person has enough clues and hint that they ought to know what they're doing isn't above-board.

Any thoughts on the idea of white-collar/upper-class folks using Internet drugs more than other demographics?

A general problem here is that there's a perception that the controlled substances are safer than drugs like cocaine or heroin. They don't realize the enormous addiction potential.

I've seen lots of individuals with many years of schooling and lots to lose from their addiction. It's very sad.

Any final thoughts?

Your readers and the general public have to remember that there's a tremendous amount of money that can be made and *that's* what's motivating the sales. The people who run the sites are not trying to benefit anybody. They're exactly the same in nature as the organizations that traffic in cocaine or heroin.

Just Ask

Let me urge you to visit your doctor if you're considering going online (or anywhere else) to purchase your medications. The Internet simply makes it too easy to lure patients into unsafe purchases.

It's not just the online criminals or disreputable "doctors" who are responsible for your safety—it's you. If you're in pain or trying to help a loved one, you're not going to be objective about acquiring medications if given a cheap online alternative. When in a heightened emotional (physical/chemical) state it is no time to risk purchasing medications over the Internet. Even if you're issued actual brand-name drugs, you need medical guidance on how those substances will interact with your body.

The DEA's classifications were put into place to protect and educate consumers. They're designed to provide a buffer between patients and products that could cause them harm. In the perfect world, the main buffer is your doctor. Seek his or her counsel and explain what you've learned in this book so you can prove your due diligence. *Just ask* for advice. Research all the options to prove that your chief interest is in ridding yourself of pain rather than trying a certain medication.

If you're set on purchasing medications online, make sure to research appropriate state-licensed pharmacies to do so. You can do this by visiting the Verified Internet Pharmacy Practice site (VIPPS) of the National Association of Boards of Pharmacy (NABP).

I know you may have real symptoms that your physician is not addressing. The problem with going it alone online is that drug dosage can rapidly escalate without a trained medical perspective. I have seen patients taking huge amounts of Norco or Vicodin, as high as 80 per day. Tragically, these patients still had pain and were literally enslaved by their habit.

It's difficult, if not impossible, to remain patient when your body craves a substance. The temptation to over-order medications, along with the risks of using, is too great to face alone. Don't let Internet anonymity protect your growing dependence on or addiction to drugs. Talk to your pharmacist and doctor and keep your treatment *offline*.

---

1 *The Journal of Medical Internet Research,* Jan '01 Cyberpharmacies and the role of the US Food And Drug Administration Volume Three, Issue One (January, 2001) of *The Journal of Medical Internet Research:* Online prescriptions of pharmaceuticals: Where is the evidence for harm or for benefit? A call for papers—and for reflection, by G Eysenbach—http://www.jmir.org/2001/1/e1/).

Chapter Eight
The Addicted Brain

I looked down at the concrete slab and sighed. I'd been working all morning and my back was already throbbing, but the slab had to be moved. I figured it to be about 100 pounds. A hundred pounds for a big guy like me was no big deal.

When I felt a distinct "pop" in my back I realized I had miscalculated. The slab had to be at least 150 pounds, maybe more. Plus my back was already tired and I lifted with a jerking motion by mistake. Searing white pain shot through my back. The slab dropped to the floor with a loud crack. A couple of the guys looked over, irritated, but their expressions changed when they saw my face.

I couldn't move. It hurt to breathe, even. Getting into a car to see my doctor was agony. If you've ever pulled your back out, you know what I'm saying. And you also know the difference between hurting your back a little, where you put on a heating pad and sit in your La-Z-Boy watching the game for a few hours, and hurting your back a lot. I was incapacitated. Couldn't work.

My doctor told me to take it easy and prescribed Vicodin for pain. Eventually I returned to full duty. For the next couple of years my back got progressively worse. My doctor prescribed Vicodin and muscle relaxers, followed by Oxycontin and stronger medications. An orthopedic surgeon recommended surgery. But the success rate wasn't very high and undergoing major surgery is always a risk, especially to someone in my line of work.

Then I went to a new doctor who really took the time to talk about various options for pain management. He had a holistic view toward medicine, meaning he talked about nutrition and Eastern medical ideas, which I found very encouraging. Most importantly, he spent a good deal of time at each appointment asking about my personal life. It was obvious that my pain meds were affecting my mood and relationships, but nobody else had asked about this stuff before.

I trusted my new doctor enough to try new types of treatment. To control my suffering, we went with a pain medication called fentanyl in the form of a patch. That didn't do the trick, so my doctor prescribed oral pain meds. Then I began to feel dependent on them as well as depressed. I needed stronger doses and felt irritable, tired, and alone. My life was a mess. I didn't want to spend time with my wife, son, or any of my friends. I wouldn't even talk on the phone with anyone.

My pain was getting worse. It seemed as though nothing would make me feel better. To combat my depression, my doctor prescribed an antidepressant; but by that time I was fixated on the pain meds and didn't have an interest in the antidepressants, so I didn't take them.

We decided it was time for me to get off the opiate pain meds, as I was obviously addicted. My doctor prescribed buprenorphine and it worked really well for a couple months, but I wasn't really ready to give up the pain meds yet. It didn't take long to fall back into my addiction—visiting the ER, lying to my family, becoming depressed.

It's interesting to note here that my mom was addicted to pain meds for several years. She also started taking them due to a back injury. But I never thought I was addicted because the pills always came from a doctor. When I started taking the pain meds the feelings of addition *were almost immediate, which makes me feel that I was genetically "pre-wired" to become addicted.*

It was about this time when I lost a second job because of my addiction. I also lost many people I thought were my friends due to their lack of understanding. I was looked at as a loser who just didn't want to work and take care of his family because he couldn't pull himself together.

When I went back on the buprenorphine, I was ready to change.

It's working out very well for me now. In fact, I would even say it has saved my life and my marriage. I went from being completely dependent on pain meds to not having any desire to take them whatsoever. I still have pain but I'm learning to deal with it in other ways, and my pain has decreased since I got off the opiate pain meds. I just got a major promotion at work and life is good.

* * *

The Sticky Cycle

Jack's story is a typical example of the journey pain patients go through after they've suffered an injury. The following diagram demonstrates this cycle:

3) As addiction becomes more severe, patient loses jobs/friends due to their behavior. Patient's mood worsens as the situation progresses. Without proper treatment, patient feels hopeless and health/situation worsens.

1) Patient Suffers Initial Trauma. Visits regular doctor who doesn't have expertise in pain management. Visits orthopedist who suggests surgery. Doctor prescribes opiates.

2) Patient becomes dependent on or addicted to medication. Patient's focus becomes only on getting more medication.

8-1: Pain Cycle

You'll recall that Julie's journey after being smashed by her mirror followed almost exactly the same course. She suffered an initial trauma and was referred to an orthopedist. The orthopedist recommended surgery, a suggestion Julie was reluctant to pursue because of complications and lack of efficacy. When she went back to her doctor, she was called a "drug seeker."

Newsflash—while a person's medical team bounces them back and forth between multiple specialists and appointments, the patient is still in debilitating pain. Is it any wonder patients become addicted? And as Jack mentioned above, there are various levels of pain. Some cause discomfort; others prevent you from going to work or functioning at all. When people are suffering a heightened level of agony, they're not terribly receptive to their doctor's suggestion to "take it easy" or "grin and bear it."

This can also be the time when a person is most susceptible to addiction to other substances like alcohol, cocaine, methamphetamine, or marijuana. They may start smoking or restart if they had quit in the past.

Another danger is how opiates react with specific patients. As Jack mentioned, he feels he was genetically predisposed to be addicted because of his mother's history. This predisposition is nobody's fault but it does play an enormous part in understanding a patient's needs in terms of pain management and overall care. If a doctor is not aware of a patient's history, he or she may prescribe the very medication that will lead a patient to addiction.

As demonstrated by Jack's story, a person cannot predict how they will behave on medication. For many patients, addiction is a *chronic* disease that needs to be treated for months or even years. It is unrealistic and damaging to think that a person can instantly stop being addicted through abstinence or rapid detox. Although these treatments help certain individuals, it is safer to picture a recovering addict as someone convalescing from a major disease.

If someone completes chemotherapy and is in remission, you don't invite them to play touch football two weeks after their last hospital visit. The same is true for people who are recovering from opiate or other substance addiction—their bodies and brains have been scarred and wounded and need time to heal, no matter how the person appears on the outside. These changes can last for years and in many cases never resolve.

All of these facts contribute to what I call the sticky cycle of opiates. It is alarmingly easy for a pain patient to become addicted if they have a genetic predisposition and are not receiving adequate treatment. Treatment is inadequate if patients experience enough pain or cravings to seek relief beyond what's been prescribed by their doctor.

It's also inadequate if their pain is treated with ever-increasing doses of short-acting opiates, which have a high potential to cause dependence. Note that the Doctor Dealer section in the Pain Issues chapter further discusses this phenomenon. Gracer Medical has developed a list of questions that every physician should ask before prescribing any opiate medication; this list is found in the same chapter.

The Mechanisms of Addiction

It's important to understand how the body works when confronted by drugs and alcohol. Your body contains numerous systems that must remain in balance to keep your body in optimum health. Once you see the relation of the brain and nervous system to items that enter the body, it's impossible to condemn addiction as merely a lack of self-control.

Drug addiction is a complex process that includes many of the systems that regulate emotions and perceptions. These systems involve the brain and the nervous system, both of which are constantly changing. With severe or chronic stimulation (such as chronic pain), changes can be long lasting with repercussions on the whole body, including permanent damage to brain receptors. These changes are called neuroplasticity.

The pathology seen in drug addiction is really an exaggeration and imbalance of normal brain function. Patients suffer from a brain receptor disease rather than a moral failing. While the social aspects of this disorder are important and should not be minimized, these changes must be understood and modified as part of successful treatment of this disorder.

Much of your body's health depends upon *homeostasis,* the ability to maintain normal function under a wide spectrum of conditions. The body has to keep numerous elements in balance to avoid unhealthy results. Most biological mechanisms rely on competing actions that keep each other in check. A simple example is found in the arm. When the brain sends a signal to flex the elbow, the triceps relaxes while the biceps activates. When the arm is ordered to reach out, the triceps contracts and the biceps relaxes.

Homeostasis also is vital within the central nervous system, in which multiple processes work together to create a state of normality and health. Here, a number of complex pathways interconnect to modulate and balance each other. When basic chemicals called *neurotransmitters,* which are released by the nerve cells, act upon *receptor sites,* the chemical exchange enables us to take action and experience feelings.

Throughout the spinal cord and brain there are receptors that create the pain relief and euphoria felt with opiates or other addicting substances, such as alcohol, cocaine, methamphetamine, nicotine, and even marijuana. Each of these drugs also stimulates receptors in parts of the brain that regulate other functions. When these receptor sites are overstimulated for prolonged periods of time, the body can get out of balance and addiction can begin.

It is important to note in the example of the arm muscles that at no time is the triceps muscle completely flaccid or the biceps fully contracted. Even when the arm is still, both muscles have some activity. The concept that both systems are working at the same time and are in balance for a final result is called tone.

The Relaxation System

The simplest level of control in the nervous system is the balance between relaxation and excitation. Neurotransmitters are chemical messengers that deliver commands to neurons, or nerve cells. Serotonin, dopamine, and norepinephrine are all examples of these chemical messengers. These are called modulating neurotransmitters because they modulate, or adjust, our feelings.

GABA (gamma amino butyric acid) is a neurotransmitter that works throughout the body. It makes nerve cells less excitable and therefore less likely to fire. When they do fire, pathways in the brain are affected, resulting in a relaxed feeling. This is accompanied by the release of dopamine in the pleasure centers of the brain, which triggers contentment and enjoyment.

Each GABA receptor has several sites where different compounds can dock. Alcohol, opiates, barbiturates, the benzodiazepine class of drugs (Ativan, Valium, Librium, and Ambien), and some neurosteroids can activate GABA receptor sites. The same sites are activated indirectly by marijuana. The key effect is a decrease in anxiety and an increased feeling of well-being. There is also a relative slowing down of the central nervous system.

Just like the example of two muscles working together to move the arm, GABA has an opposite called *glutamate*. Glutamate creates excitation. While GABA decreases the number of times neurons fire, glutamate increases the amount of firing. Depending on which pathways those transmissions take through the brain, a complex variety of feelings, cravings, and pleasure that make up our personality and

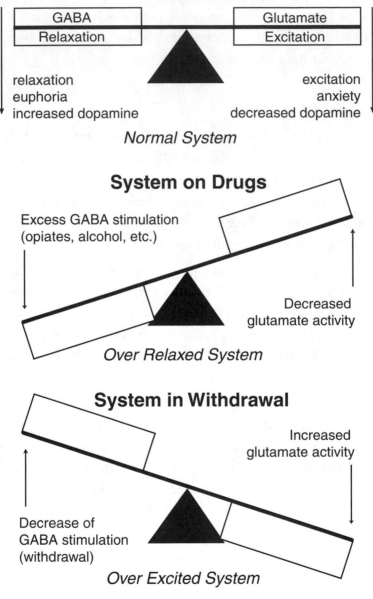

System in Balance

GABA	Glutamate
Relaxation	Excitation

relaxation   excitation
euphoria   anxiety
increased dopamine   decreased dopamine

Normal System

System on Drugs

Excess GABA stimulation
(opiates, alcohol, etc.)

Decreased
glutamate activity

Over Relaxed System

System in Withdrawal

Increased
glutamate activity

Decrease of
GABA stimulation
(withdrawal)

Over Excited System

8-3: The GABA/glutamate balance

determine our behavior and mood results. Since drugs are chemicals that affect the same pathways, people suffering from addiction undergo personality changes and are unable to think clearly about their situation.

These drugs also cause dopamine to be released in the pleasure centers of the brain. In some people, as alcohol is metabolized, the resulting chemicals combine with neurotransmitters to form compounds that powerfully stimulate receptors in a way similar to that seen with opiates. These compounds are themselves powerfully addictive.

Under normal conditions this system is activated by natural substances like endorphins. In normal (non-addicted) people, pleasurable events such as a fine meal, laughter, sex, and listening to music cause an increase in the dopamine levels. The part of the brain that is responsible for these feelings and emotions is called the limbic system. When dopamine is released in the limbic system, the person feels pleasure.

Alcohol, opiates, and even cocaine and methamphetamine, as well as the benzodiazepine ("benzos") class of drugs also cause the release of dopamine. Taking addicting drugs on a regular basis results in constant, strong, and direct stimulation of the GABA receptor. This eventually deprives the brain of its ability to feel good without this outside stimulation. Over time, this causes the receptors to become less sensitive and to actually change physically and decrease in number. When this occurs, the usual ability of a drug to cause a reduction of anxiety is greatly diminished. In addition, when there is no drug stimulation of GABA receptors, dopamine levels become low. Agitation, anxiety, and depression set in.

The drug that usually would bring relaxation is needed on an ever-increasing scale just to feel normal. This is addiction at its most basic level. The need for a drug to replace the natural brain chemicals is the cause of addiction. It soon takes more and more of the drug to get the same effect. This increasing need is called *tolerance* and is caused by physical changes in the brain.

The GABA and Glutamate System

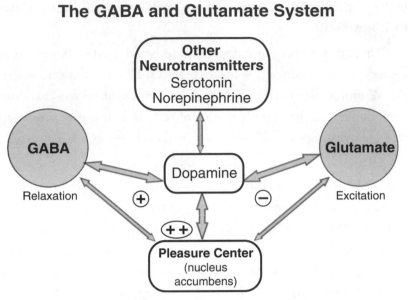

8-2: *The GABA and glutamate system*

Mechanism of Withdrawal

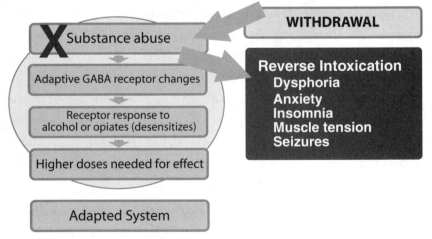

8-4: *The mechanism of withdrawal*

When the GABA receptor is unresponsive, it's like a car without brakes. The glutamate (or stimulant) system is the gas pedal and the car runs out of control. In this case the patient feels anxious. Since both systems are critical, the balance between them keeps us on an even keel, just as the arm muscles are never entirely relaxed or completely contracted. When one system fails, the entire mechanism suffers.

The damage might be permanent. Abstinence may only result in partial regeneration even after years. When the GABA receptor is chronically stimulated by drugs the number of receptors decreases and the cells' receptor areas become insensitive to normal neurotransmitters. Deprived of the drug, the receptor is underactivated and the glutamate system is overactivated. This creates the typical symptoms of withdrawal: anxiety, muscle aches, stomach cramps, sweating, agitation, and even seizures.

The altered receptors and receptor sites must be addressed before the cravings will subside. Although abstinence may create a gradual increase in normal GABA receptors, this may take a very long time. In some cases the brain may never return to normal. This results in long-term anxiety and cravings, and accounts for the frequent failures in programs where this critical issue is not treated.

For opiates, a medication like buprenorphine (Subutex/ Suboxone) is essential. It physically fills receptors and prevents cravings. For alcohol and stimulants there is the Prometa protocol, which we believe helps regenerate abnormal GABA receptor sites. Regeneration and normal brain function reverse anxiety and halt cravings, allowing the addicted individual to start down the path to a normal life.

The Two Forks of Brain Dysfunction in Drug Addiction

Sanjay Sabnani, Senior VP of Strategic Development at Hythiam, Inc., the company that licenses the Prometa protocol, conceptualized what I have just described as consisting of two separate forks.

First Fork: The Reward Circuit

The dopamine system, also called the rewards circuit, is responsible for stimulation of the pleasure centers in the limbic system. This circuit is modulated by GABA and glutamate, but is directly stimulated by addicting substances.

Another type of receptor called the NMDA complicates the situation. This receptor is activated by increased glutamate activity. It is also an important factor in the development of chronic pain. When stimulated, it causes increased pain and a variety of other symptoms. The NMDA receptor is also stimulated in drug withdrawal.

NMDA stimulation results in decreased activity in the reward circuit. Cravings for the addicting substance spring up as a direct way to calm this system and increase dopamine. Strategies to decrease cravings and drug dependence must modify NMDA activity.

Campral, used to treat alcoholism, is a chemical that blocks the NMDA receptor, decreasing cravings. Anticonvulsant medications are also used to decrease overall neuro-stimulation and irritability. Topiramate (Topamax) has shown positive effects in preventing relapse in alcoholism and smoking.

A common cough medication, dextromethorphan, also blocks the NMDA receptor. I have found this useful for the treatment of chronic pain.

Second Fork: GABA and the Neo-Cortex

GABA is very important in the neo-cortex, the part of the brain where judgment and emotional control exist. These behaviors are crucial to maintaining abstinence and being able to function comfortably in society.

While some level of anxiety can create a sharp focus and provide high-level energy needed for important situations, we must also be able to relax and rest. Too much GABA activity results in inattention, forgetfulness, and poor judgment. At even higher levels of stimulation, lethargy, sleep, and finally coma result.

In withdrawal, the GABA system is inhibited. The results swing to the opposite extreme and cause anxiety, panic, or even seizures. Persistent thoughts will not stop. There is no rest. There is also a disruption in the judgment areas of the brain, leading to poor decisions. When dealing with cravings and the ability or inability to resist them, sound judgment is critical.

Sabnani describes GABA's pivotal role in what he calls the Anxiety to Acquisition Circuit:

> Anxiety is your brain's way of making you acquire a solution. During times of stress you get agitated and worried, your heart rate increases, and sleeping becomes impossible. Take Sunday evening for example—a time that is stressful for many people. On Sunday evening…my mind focuses on the work I have to do beginning on Monday morning. Unfortunately it is too early for me to get started on my workweek, but my stress level starts to increase nonetheless…. GABA activity is decreased and my brain is hyperactive. Interestingly enough, if I "acquire a solution" to my worries by making a list of what I have to do the next week, or by sending out a few emails, my anxiety decreases and GABA activity increases so I can relax and sleep.

It turns out that the brain will accept a substitution as a solution if the actual solution cannot be found. The substitute it accepts is something it has filed away as a pleasurable memory in the limbic system—the brain knows that these are all good things that it values highly…. High up on the list you usually have sex, ice cream, chocolate, fried and salty foods. The brain accepts almost all of these as evidence that you have "acquired a solution" to what worries you, so in a strange way pigging out on a bag of chips makes your worries go away for the moment.

When the GABA receptor gets dysregulated through chronic drug and alcohol use, the brain is in a constant state of anxiety. "Acquiring a solution" becomes difficult because the pleasurable memories in the limbic system are no longer normal things like a glass of wine. Instead you have very highly potent memories of high intensity drug and alcohol use. A gram of cocaine with a beautiful woman, a fifth of scotch at a cool nightclub, shooting up heroin, or snorting meth have all replaced your previous experiences of pleasure. This is a no-win situation since long periods of anxiety are unbearable to people, but at the same time the only "solution" your brain is able to see is related to procuring and ingesting your drug of choice. As a result of this circuit, individuals get caught in a destructive pattern of self-medication to alleviate their anxiety. Restoring GABA receptor functionality bypasses this completely.[1]

The following diagram illustrates the GABA spectrum:

Coma-sleep-lethargy-anxiolysis-relaxed-alert-anxious-panic-seizure

More GABA stimulation   Less GABA stimulation

8-6: Spectrum of GABA activity

Genetic Factors

Receptor sites are coded on our DNA. Because each of us has our own genetic makeup, we each have different proteins on our brain receptors. For example, there are estimated to be about 100 different variations of the morphine receptor. This is why some people can take a given medication with good effect while others get nauseated, just like some of us have brown eyes and others have blue. These genetic variations are called single nucleotide polymorphisms (SNPs).

Opiates may fit one person's GABA receptor more easily than someone else's. If your GABA receptor only responds to high stimulation from an addicting substance, or if your pleasure center is relatively insensitive to dopamine, you have a greater chance of addiction. Note that this is true even though you need to take more of the drug to achieve the same results as others who consume less.

Someone who can "hold their liquor" is much more likely to become an alcoholic than someone who can only have one drink before getting ill. The low-response person is seduced into thinking that their drinking is not a problem because they don't feel drunk. Peer reinforcement often puts additional pressure on the individual to consume large quantities.

Genetic variation also impacts the way the liver detoxifies drugs and other substances. The complex cytochrome enzyme system processes these compounds so they can be excreted through the kidneys or stool. Many of the metabolites (substances created by the detoxification process) have active drug effects, sometimes more powerful than the original medication. At other times the drug itself is inactive while the metabolite is the active drug. Variations in this system are another reason for different responses to medications; they are also the cause of most drug interactions.

Effects on Depression

Genetic variation is also why depression is inherited. In fact, depression and drug addiction are interrelated, making it critical that both conditions be treated together. Depression itself is very complex and falls into two basic types.

The more typical major depression is common and affects up to 30 percent of the population at some time during their lives. It is treated with SSRI drugs, such as Prozac or Zoloft, and other medications, such as Wellbutrin. The less common type is bipolar disease, in which patients alternate between severe depression and a euphoric state called mania. This problem starts early in a lifetime and is probably the most common type of depression seen in teenagers. Some variations are not as extreme and have rapid cycling between the states. The manic state may also be seen as extreme irritability.

Bipolar disease may account for as many as 15 percent of all depressed people. This disease is not easily diagnosed. The average patient sees four physicians over a period of ten years before receiving the correct diagnosis—even though more than a third seek medical help within the first year of symptom onset. Over 20 percent attempt suicide at least once, and many of them succeed.

This distinction is important because treatment for bipolar disorder is very different than for unipolar depression. Using an SSRI to treat a depressed bipolar patient often triggers mania and may be the reason for the increased chance of suicide in younger patients taking these antidepressants.

In addicted patients, bipolar depression is common. They often use addicting substances to self-medicate anxiety, worry, guilt, fatigue, or pain. They eventually become physically dependent. If the underling bipolar syndrome is not properly treated, the chance of successfully addressing their substance abuse is very low. Bipolar disease and substance abuse are genetically linked. Family history of either problem is an extremely important factor in assessing risk for the other (please see the chapter on psychiatric disorders).

Future Treatments

The human genome has been completely mapped. The DNA site for each enzyme and process can be tracked. In only a few years we will know which type of enzyme or receptor site we have for any important site. With a DNA sample it will be possible to tell which medication will work for any given patient for any specific purpose. Perhaps more importantly, we will know which treatments to avoid.

It will not be long until we will know the physical and chemical reasons why a given person may suffer from depression and/or substance abuse. This knowledge, along with appropriate psycho/social treatment, treatment of underlying hormonal and nutritional problems, as well as dealing with legitimate pain issues, should yield much better long-term results.

---

[1] Sabnani, Sanjay, Private conversation with author

Chapter Nine
Opiates

You or someone you know has likely taken Vicodin, Norco, Percocet, or codeine after surgery. You may have had morphine in the hospital. We all have heard about heroin addiction and opium dens. These drugs are called opiates, meaning they are derived from the poppy plant. They are also known as narcotics. Used in appropriate dosages when prescribed by a doctor, opiates are vital painkillers that are safe and usually not addictive for a majority of users.

The opiates discussed in this section are:

- *Hydrocodone:* Vicodin. Lorcet, Lortab, Norco, Vicoprofen

- Codeine, aspirin and codeine, Tylenol and codeine, "T-3s and T-4s"

- *Oxycodone:* Oxycontin, "Hillbilly Heroin," OxyFast (liquid Oxycodone), Percodan/Percocet, oxycodone tablets (Roxycodone)

- *Morphine:* Avinza, Kadian, Oramorph, MS Contin, immediate-release morphine tablets, Roxanol (liquid form of morphine)

- Fentanyl: An opiate that is available as a skin patch that lasts from 48 to 72 hours (Duragesic); also available as a lollipop (Actiq) and a new fast-dissolving tablet (Fentora)

- Hydromorphone: Dilaudid, Pallidone (a 24-hour form of hydromorphone no longer available due to production problems and sometimes fatal interactions with alcohol)

- Methadone: a synthetic, inexpensive, long-acting opiate

- Heroin

Opiate Dependence–An Analogy

In this section opiates and their effect on the brain are described in an analogy. Although this chapter is not about buprenorphine, since the medication is so important in the treatment of the brain dysfunction caused by addiction, it has been included as part of this analogy. For more information on buprenorphine, please refer to the chapter titled The Cravings and the Cure.

An Important Introduction:

Before you can understand how opiates affect how you feel, you must first become familiar with brain systems and the receptors that affect them. Some systems create calm and others irritability and anxiety. How we feel at any time depends on the balance between these two competing systems. Another distinction is that some receptors *stimulate* activity in systems and others *decrease* it.

There are at least two opiate systems in the brain, one is called mu and the other kappa. The mu receptors stimulate the mu system, but the kappa receptors slow down the kappa system. This difference is important and if you grasp this concept it makes it much easier to understand how the brain reacts to different compounds.

The mu system causes relaxation, pleasure, and pain relief. The kappa system does the opposite, causing excitement, irritability, and anxiety. The complicated part is that if you stimulate the mu system you get the same effect as if you restrain the kappa system. When the kappa receptor is filled the kappa system is inhibited, resulting in relaxation. When the mu receptor is filled the mu system is stimulated, also resulting in relaxation.

The table below shows this same concept:

System Name	Action of System	Receptor Activity	Result
mu	Relaxation, pleasure, pain relief	Stimulates system	Relaxation
kappa	Excitement, anxiety, irritability	Restrains system	Relaxation

9-1: Mu and kappa receptors

The Analogy

Visualize a green meadow about the size of a football field, covered with soft grass. It is scattered with holes of two different sizes. The field represents the brain and the holes are two different types of opiate receptors.

The larger ones are the *mu* or morphine receptors, which when filled stimulate the mu system, giving relief from pain, increased pleasure (sometimes to the point of euphoria), and relaxation, thereby calming the field. When the mu system holes are filled we feel calm and relaxed. This is a feeling that we all know and love.

The smaller holes are *kappa* receptors, which when filled slow down the kappa system. The kappa system causes excitement as well as irritability. These receptors are also affected by opiates, but not as strongly as the morphine receptors. Opiates block the action of the kappa system. So the mu system is activated, or stimulated, by opiates while the kappa system is simultaneously inhibited, or slowed down.

Normal Opiate System Before Using Drugs

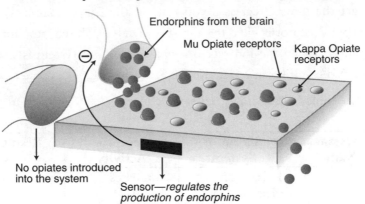

Normal system without drugs. Note that endorphins fill some of both the large Mu receptors and the small Kappa receptors. The sensor measures the number of balls on the field and regulates endorphin production to keep the system in balance.

9-2: Normal opiate system before drugs

When mu receptors are stimulated, the meadow stays calm and quiet. When the kappa holes are blocked the level of excitation is decreased, which also creates calm and relaxation. If the kappa system is too active, many of the symptoms of withdrawal, including muscle aches, depression, anxiety, and gastrointestinal symptoms appear. The same symptoms appear when the mu system isn't stimulated enough.

Together, the mu and kappa receptors regulate the relaxation and excitement systems in a way that keeps the body in balance. One of the ways this happens is by increasing or decreasing the release of dopamine in the pleasure center of the brain (the nucleus accumbens).

How Endorphins Work

Now notice that the entire meadow is mildly sloped. At the higher edge is a large tube; this is the endorphin factory. A steady stream of lightweight dark gray bowling balls (endorphins) is emerging from the tube. Our brains make endorphins, which act as the body's natural opiate. These balls roll across the field and drop into the holes. Some endorphins are large and others are small, to fit the two sizes of holes. They trigger relaxation or keep excitement at an appropriate level based on what a person is experiencing at any given moment.

We all need a significant percentage of these holes (receptor sites) to be filled to be comfortable. Since the gray endorphin balls are lightweight, they do not create new holes. Because they are slippery, they do not stay in the holes for long. After they slide out of the holes, they slip off the lower edge of the meadow.

Sensors under the meadow measure the weight and number of balls and the number of filled receptor holes. When there are more than enough balls, the sensors tell the factory to slow the production of endorphins. When there are too few, the factory is ordered to increase production. This way the number of receptor sites filled with balls is constantly controlled.

Under normal circumstances, pain creates an increase in endorphins. Exercise and pleasurable activities also increase endorphins. When many receptor sites are filled, one may feel a "natural high."

How Opiates Work

If s person takes an opiate such as heroin, morphine, methadone, oxycodone (Oxycontin), hydrocodone (Vicodin, Norco), hydromorphone (Dilaudid), or fentanyl (Duragesic), a large number of big, heavy, black balls are released suddenly, and dumped at the lower edge of the meadow.

These black balls fill in almost all of the receptor sites. Since they fit the mu receptors so well, they trigger relaxation, pain relief, and pleasure. Even though they are too large to fit into the kappa holes, they are so heavy that they sit on top of these holes and block the receptors. This blockage decreases the amount of activity in the kappa excitation system.

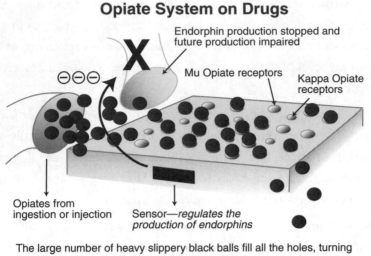

Opiate System on Drugs

Endorphin production stopped and future production impaired

Mu Opiate receptors

Kappa Opiate receptors

Opiates from ingestion or injection

Sensor—*regulates the production of endorphins*

The large number of heavy slippery black balls fill all the holes, turning off endorphin production. Because they are heavy they create new holes that have to be filled, and because they are slippery they rapidly roll off the end of the field.

9-3: Opiate system on drugs

This dual action has a powerful relaxing impact on the meadow, or brain. Used in the right quantities, the black balls fight pain. When too much is used, they can create the high associated with drug use, as well as over sedation and other side effects.

How Drug Abuse Changes the Meadow

Due to the fact that these black balls are so heavy, the sensors command the factory to stop endorphin production altogether. The sheer weight also means they make new holes all over the meadow. When these new holes are empty and no black balls are around, the factory must try to fill in both the original holes and the new ones to avoid withdrawal. Since it is now trying to fill in many more holes than normal, the factory simply can't keep up.

A new load arrives every time the drug is taken. Since the black balls are filling in all the holes, with persistent drug use there's no need for the factory to create the gray endorphin balls. The factory is shut down for so long that, eventually, it is virtually dismantled;

it loses its ability to manufacture any dark gray balls. Since the brain is constantly changing to find the most efficient way to operate, the pathways that enable the factory to function don't just lie dormant, they disappear. *It may take a very long time for the factory to regenerate. In some cases it may never be able to function at its former level.*

Opiate System in Withdrawal

Endorphins (still only a few released because production is impaired)

Mu Opiate receptors

Kappa Opiate receptors

No opiates ingested or injected

Sensor—*regulates the production of endorphins*

When the opiate is stopped (causing withdrawal), the field is empty and endorphin production, although not slowed by the sensor, is still impaired.

9-4: Opiate system in withdrawal

If the supply of black balls stops, the receptor sites sit empty and the endorphin factory cannot produce gray balls to fill them. The mu system (the larger receptor holes) is not stimulated, so there is no relaxation. Since the kappa system (the smaller receptor holes) has nothing to slow down the excitation, it runs wild. This results in a severe imbalance and creates the symptoms of drug withdrawal.

Anxiety and depression take over the brain. Muscle and joint aches, tremors, nausea, diarrhea, sweating, severe anxiety, and insomnia hit all at once. Hour after hour these sensations place the patient under attack. This experience is so painful that most people will do almost anything to make it stop. That's why many drug addicts will steal, prostitute themselves, or even kill for their fix.

How Buprenorphine Works

Now imagine that a man with a handcart approaches the field. He carefully rolls small, lightweight, light gray balls onto the meadow. Although these balls are small and very light, they are also very sticky.

This is buprenorphine. The small light gray balls are small enough to enter all the holes on the field, regardless of their size. Because they are so light, the grass begins to grow again. The new holes made by the heavy black balls start to disappear as the brain repairs itself.

Opiate System Initially on Buprenorphine

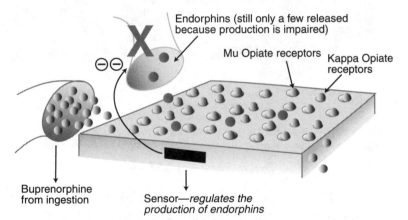

The buprenorphine fills both the large and small holes. Since the buprenorphine balls are lighter than the black opiate balls the field starts to repair and some of the holes created by the heavy black balls disappear. Although still impaired, endorphin production slowly restarts. Because the buprenorphine balls are sticky, they stay in the holes longer. The buprenorphine balls fit the smaller kappa receptor holes perfectly. They also fit in the larger Mu receptor holes, but because they are small, only partially stimulate them.

9-5: Opiate system initially on buprenorphine

Since the light gray balls are so sticky, they stay in the holes for a very long time, longer even than the natural dark gray balls. Even if another load of opiates returns, the light gray balls are so sticky that the black balls can't displace them. The black balls simply roll off the edge of the field and disappear.

Since the small light gray balls fit the smaller kappa receptors particularly well, they are especially effective at blocking this excitation system. In cases of prolonged drug abuse, the factory's natural endorphin balls are much decreased and cannot calm the overstimulation that is caused when the holes are empty. That's why simply stopping the drug use isn't enough. The brain has been wounded. Without buprenorphine, the patient will suffer and is likely to relapse.

Note that, since the light gray balls are so much smaller, they only partially fill the larger holes (the mu receptors). These small balls will displace any black balls on the field as they enter the larger holes and push the slippery black balls out of the holes so they quickly roll off the end of the field. The fact that the smaller light gray balls only partially stimulate the mu receptors will make the patient suffer withdrawal. It is important, therefore, to ensure that patients have no opiates (large, heavy, slippery black balls) in their bodies before administering buprenorphine. In other words, it is important to be sure that most of holes on the field are empty.

Opiate System on Buprenorphine Maintenance

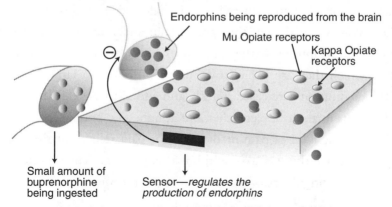

Endorphins being reproduced from the brain

Mu Opiate receptors

Kappa Opiate receptors

Small amount of buprenorphine being ingested

Sensor—*regulates the production of endorphins*

Over time many of the larger Mu holes and some of the kappa holes disappear. The buprenorphine fills many of the kappa holes, but because it is the right size and is so sticky, it only takes a small amount to fill them. The Mu holes are mostly filled by endorphins.

9-6: Opiate system on buprenorphine maintenance

Eventually the man with the handcart, the doctor, will find that fewer and fewer light gray balls are needed. The dose of buprenorphine will be lowered accordingly. The brain will reconnect the pathways to the endorphin factory, dark gray endorphins will once again be produced, and the system will get back into balance. This process usually takes several days to start to normalize, but it may take weeks or even months to fully stabilize.

Since the kappa receptors (the small holes) are so different from the mu receptors, they take longer to heal. This means that the excitation system can remain abnormal for a much longer time than the relaxation system. Fortunately, the little gray balls are so powerful and sticky that tiny doses of buprenorphine may be all that's needed to keep a patient comfortable over the months of healing the brain needs. For some individuals, though, the process may never be normal again.

Short- versus Long-acting Opiates

Short-term opiates create new and higher levels of tolerance. I call this "driving the dose." Although patients experience a short peak of euphoria and pain relief, it is followed by a dip when the effect wears off and then they are in pain again and they may feel withdrawal symptoms. If they take another pill before the prescribed time—which they are likely to do when suffering—a large portion of the medication is released quickly and added to the existing dose. This results in a jolt of pain relief *and* a high. The body still requires only the basic level of pain medication for pain relief, but the brain begins to crave those peaks. Without them, the patient experiences not only the original pain but also more pain from withdrawal.

With long-acting opiates, however, the original pain is treated for longer periods so that patients don't have to take medicine in a way that produces a high. It's not surprising that, when I first explain it, this often doesn't make sense to people who are fighting pain and addiction. I'm not recommending that they stop medication altogether. Instead, we want to supplant the short-acting drugs with

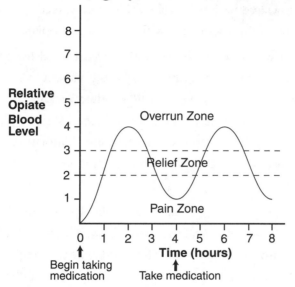

9-7: *Graph of short-acting opiates in a normal brain*

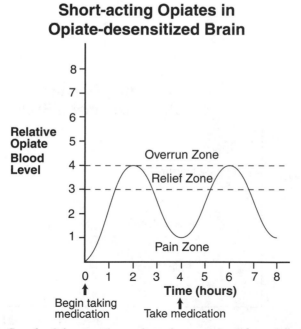

9-8: *Graph of short-acting opiates in an opiate-desensitized brain*

longer-acting maintenance drugs. The following graph shows you the zones associated with pain, relief, side effects, receptor desensitization and the high experienced with short-acting opiates.

Note that when dosage is above the level needed for pain relief (providing more stimuli than necessary), the patient is off balance. Tons of black balls are delivered when only a pickup truck-full of them was needed. The patient is in a heightened state of pleasure—he or she is high. This is the Overrun Zone. Unfortunately, these doses also cause more side effects and an increase in the number of holes in the meadow.

When the short-acting opiate leaves the system, the balance is again off, this time with too little medication. The drop plunges the patient back into the Pain Zone. The middle area is the place where the drugs treat the pain without creating a high. This Relief Zone is where both patients and doctors want the patient to be.

Now look at these next graphs:

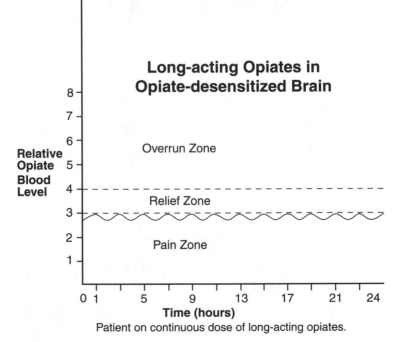

Patient on continuous dose of long-acting opiates.

9-9: Graph of long-acting opiates in an opiate-desensitized brain.

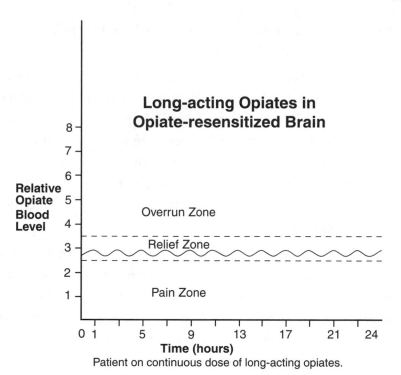

9-10: Graph of long-acting opiates in an opiate-resensitized brain

With long-acting opiates, patients experience fewer peaks and valleys (episodes of being in pain or being high). They also stay in the Relief Zone longer. These longer periods of relief allow the receptors to calm down, as the brain heals. As receptors become more sensitive, the body's natural chemicals are able to help. Pain naturally recedes and patients feel better overall.

Keep in mind that patients taking short-acting opiates or those addicted to opiates may be taking upwards of fifty pills a day. That level of receptor flooding puts an enormous stress on the brain and the body in general. Flooding followed by a lack of medication is why short-term opiates have such a high potential for abuse.

Moving patients to long-acting opiates such as long-acting morphine (Avinza, Kadian) or the fentanyl patch (Duragesic) means there is lower abuse potential. Patients experience long-term pain relief and a cessation of periodic cravings or withdrawal symptoms.

Often at this stage of treatment patients tell me that switching to long-acting opiates saved their lives.

If you think back to the meadow analogy, short-acting opiates dump tons of black balls on the meadow at once, shooting the patient into the Overrun Zone. Since the heavy balls make more holes that need to be filled, higher and higher doses are needed over the long term. And since the opiate is short acting, the balls all slide off the edge of the meadow before another dose can be taken, leaving the patient in the Pain Zone. The cycle only gets worse the longer the short-acting opiates are used.

With long-acting opiates, however, the black balls trickle onto the field. Enough holes are filled to put the patient into the Relief Zone, but not enough to send them into the Overrun Zone. The long-acting opiate lasts long enough that the patient doesn't slip back into the Pain Zone before the next dose. This creates a steadier, safer method of treating pain with much less chance of causing addiction.

The Problem

Short-acting opiates such as Vicodin, Norco, and Percocet are commonly prescribed for treatment of acute pain from injuries or after surgery. They are effective and well tolerated. If the pain persists over a month (or even much shorter for a genetically prone person), problems with tolerance and possible addiction must be considered when the physician decides what to prescribe.

Short-acting opiates last about three to four hours. The concentration of the opiate in the brain rises to high levels, and then falls rapidly. The pain returns, necessitating another dose. The cycle repeats. Many pain sufferers cannot sleep through the night without an extra dose. Disruption of sleep itself leads to more pain and, at times, depression.

Higher concentrations are also more likely to cause side effects, including sweating, nausea, and dizziness. These concentrations can also cause the high that is so addictive. Being in the Overrun Zone for too long causes the brain to become desensitized. When the drugs leave the system, the overstimulated kappa system cause nausea, sweating, swollen hands and ankles, constipation, and the host of other symptoms associated with withdrawal.

Drug levels in the Overrun Zone also desensitize the morphine receptors. At lower concentrations that create pain relief, the patient is in the Relief Zone. The Relief Zone offers freedom from pain with fewer side effects and little likelihood of receptor desensitization. In this zone less-sensitive receptors can also be rehabilitated, resulting in needing less medication for better, more effective pain control.

Short-acting drugs have more side effects, are more likely to lead to tolerance and addiction, and do not give reliable pain relief. This means that the Relief Zone shifts upward with time, reducing the period in which the patient experiences pain relief. It also reduces the time spent in the Overrun Zone and increases the time in the Pain Zone. This creates a desire for higher doses, what I call "driving the dose."

Driving the dose is not an effective treatment. Until recently there were no practical alternatives. Indeed, there was little or no awareness of the problem itself. Gracer Medical has coined the term as a way to help doctors understand why patients request more and stronger pain pills, and to facilitate open dialog and proper treatment for these patients.

The Solution

We now have several long-acting opiates. These maintain stable blood and brain concentrations, keeping the patient in the Relief Zone longer. Patients are almost always reluctant to change to long-acting opiates as they are used to the reliable and many times pleasurable effects of short-acting medications. Usually after a few days of somewhat increased pain and desire for the Overrun Zone, the pain gets much better. The Relief Zone resets at a lower drug level. The patient sleeps better because the medication level is maintained overnight. These changes create an improving upward spiral in overall health and attitude.

A recent study[1] comparing 24-hour release morphine (Avinza) to intermediate acting oxycodone (Oxycontin) showed a significant increase in pain control and in sleep time and quality. This improved over the eight weeks that the study lasted, also demonstrating the lowering of the Pain Zone in the patients who took the 24-hour release medication.

Ideally, the drug should maintain levels in the Relief Zone for at least 24 hours to allow pain control during the day as well as during sleep. Drugs that work in intermediate (8- to 12-hour) time frames are much better than short-acting or immediate release medications, but are still subject to variations in concentration over the day.

Hydrocodone

Hydrocodone is an effective antitussive (anti-cough) agent, and as an opiate it is also effective for mild to moderate pain control. Hydrocodone is considered morphine-like in all respects.

Over 200 products contain hydrocodone in the US. Usually hydrocodone is combined with acetaminophen (Vicodin, Lortab) but it is also combined with aspirin (Lortab ASA), ibuprofen (Vicoprofen), and antihistamines (Hycomine).[2]

Vicodin is a commonly abused version. Vicodin can be habit forming, causing dependence, tolerance, and withdrawal symptoms if not used as it is prescribed.

Common side effects: dizziness, light-headedness, nausea, sedation, vomiting, and constipation.

Less-common side effects: allergic reactions, blood disorders, mood changes, mental cloudiness, anxiety, lethargy, urine retention, urethral spasm, irregular breathing, respiratory depression, and skin rash.[3]

Since these side effects are common for all opiates, they will not be listed for the other opiates below.

Special Dangers of Hydrocodone

Hydrocodone is particularly sticky as it produces few side effects and induces euphoria in many patients. It is a short-acting opiate and fights pain extremely well. Addiction-prone patients seek the euphoria rather than just the pain relief.

Greg Critser of the *Los Angeles Times* wrote a fascinating article in October of 2003 called "Hidden Pain in Pain Pill." Critser traces the history of hydrocodone as it was championed to stop the epidemic of middle-class addiction to opium derivatives in major cough syrup brands.

The scientists who tested the compound back in the 1930s noted two particular effects. First, the heightened euphoria the drug could produce was unique from other opiates. Second, tolerance was built more slowly than with morphine or Dilaudid. Patients become dependent without realizing it. Even then, the scientists warned that hydrocodone had a high potential for causing addiction. Despite the warnings, the drug was approved for use. Now we're finally realizing that their predictions were right.

A newer formulation of hydrocodone, called Norco, is now available. Norco has a higher dose of the opiate and less acetaminophen. Since high doses of acetaminophen (such as Tylenol) can be liver toxic—especially if the patient also drinks alcohol—it is important to monitor doses. With Norco, the hydrocodone provides a quick high, plus patients feel safe because the amount of acetaminophen is lower. I still marvel at how some of my patients can still be alive while taking over fifty Norco per day.

Other brands containing hydrocodone include Tussionex, Tussend, Lortab, Lorcet, Hycodan, and Anexsia.

Codeine

Codeine is the most widely used, naturally occurring medicinal opiate in the world. This alkaloid is found in opium in concentrations ranging from 0.7 to 2.5 percent. However, most US codeine is produced from morphine. Codeine is also the starting material for the production of dihydrocodeine and hydrocodone.

Codeine is prescribed for moderate pain and cough suppression. Compared to morphine, codeine produces less analgesia, sedation and respiratory depression, and is usually taken orally. It is made into tablets either alone or with aspirin or acetaminophen. As a cough suppressant, codeine is found in a number of liquid preparations. Codeine is also used to a lesser extent as an injectable solution for the treatment of pain.[4]

Oxycodone

Oxycodone is a central nervous system depressant. People who take the drug repeatedly can develop tolerance. Thus, a cancer patient can regularly take a dose that would be fatal in a person never exposed to oxycodone or other opioids. Most individuals who abuse oxycodone seek euphoric effects, to mitigate pain, or avoid withdrawal.

Oxycodone has a high abuse potential and is prescribed for moderate to high pain associated with injuries, bursitis, dislocation, fractures, neuralgia, arthritis, and lower back and cancer pain. It is also used postoperatively and for pain relief after childbirth. Oxycontin, Percocet, Percodan, and Tylox are trade name rapid-release products. Oxyfast is a liquid form used for severe pain such as in cancer or after surgery.[5]

Oxycontin (Hillbilly Heroin)

Oxycontin is designed to be swallowed whole; however, abusers often chew the tablets or crush the tablets and snort the powder. Because oxycodone is water soluble, crushed tablets can be dissolved in water and injected.[6]

The fact that Oxycontin can be injected, along with its widespread use and abuse in rural areas of America (such as Maine, West Virginia, and Kentucky) has led to its current pejorative nickname of Hillbilly Heroin. The euphoria is so sudden and intense that users are hooked right away. Over and above the pain relief, many feel almost superhuman when using this drug.

Oxycontin is marketed as a long-acting drug, but since 30 percent of the dose is released immediately and often is completely released in less than eight hours, it is in fact an intermediate- to short-acting opiate. Generic formulations release the drug in variable time frames. This makes it difficult to regulate proper use when stable patients get a different brand.

Morphine

Morphine is the principal constituent of opium. Commercial opium is standardized to contain 10 percent morphine. Morphine is one of the most effective drugs known for the relief of severe pain.

Morphine is marketed under generic and brand name products including MS-Contin, Oramorph SR, MSIR, Roxanol, Kadian, Avinza, and RMS. Morphine is used by injection for preoperative sedation, as a supplement to anesthesia, and for analgesia. It is the drug of choice for relieving pain of myocardial infarction and for its cardiovascular effects in the treatment of acute pulmonary edema. Today, morphine is marketed in a variety of forms, including oral solutions, immediate and sustained-release tablets and capsules, suppositories, and injectable preparations.[7]

Remember that medications normally stigmatized (one patient calling morphine "The Big M," for instance) can be extremely effectual and safe under strict supervision by a doctor.

Avinza

Approved by the FDA in March of 2002, Avinza is a long-acting opiate that can provide pain relief for up to 24 hours. This medication has proven effective in the treatment of moderate to severe pain. Its long-acting nature helps keep patients from driving the dose and courting addiction.

The Action study, presented by Richard Ghalie, MD, at the February 2006 meeting of the American Academy of Pain Management, clearly demonstrates that use of Avinza instead of a short-acting medication leads to better pain control, better sleep, and an increased chance of returning to work. This is one of my top choices for the treatment of chronic pain.

Kadian

This is another long-acting morphine medication. In some patients it can be used every 24 hours, but in others it must be dosed every 12 hours.

Hydromorphone (Dilaudid)

Hydromorphone's analgesic potency is from two to eight times that of morphine but it is shorter acting and produces more sedation. The tablets are often dissolved and injected as a substitute for heroin.[8]

Pallidone

This medication contains a hydromorphone derivative. Severe side effects are possible if it is taken with alcohol. The FDA released an alert in July of 2005 to that effect, causing Purdue Pharma (Pallidone sponsors) to suspend sales and marketing of this medication. A new form of this long-acting medication should be available in 2007.

Methadone

Although chemically unlike morphine or heroin, methadone produces many of the same effects. Introduced in 1947 as an analgesic (Dolophinel), it is primarily used today for the treatment of opiate addiction. It is almost as effective orally as by injection. Chronic administration of methadone results in tolerance and dependence. Withdrawal develops more slowly and is less severe but more prolonged than heroin withdrawal.[9]

Methadone is a synthetic opiate that tends to be longer acting in many patients. It's used in methadone clinics for this reason, as it can be given out once a day. It's also prescribed as a chronic pain medication, typically by specialists.

Methadone is metabolized by the liver at a very specific rate and can build up in the system with long-term use. Secondary side effects due to this phenomenon make prescribing methadone a somewhat unpredictable process.

This drug is very dangerous when used for abuse. Methadone is increasingly being seen in ER patients with drug overdoses. Since the slow-acting effects take three to four hours after ingestion to fully develop, individuals trying to get high take more and more before the full impact hits. They then may fall into a fatal coma. This characteristic makes prescribing methadone a complex process that should be only be undertaken by a physician who is familiar with this drug.

Heroin

Heroin, an illegal opiate drug known on the street as smack, junk, brown sugar, dope, horse, skunk, and other names, is derived from the resin of the poppy plant.

The typical heroin user today consumes more heroin than just a decade ago, not surprising given the higher purity currently available. Injection is the most practical and efficient way to administer low-purity heroin. The availability of higher purity heroin has meant that users now can snort or smoke the opiate.[10]

Prescription drug addicts often use heroin because it is actually cheaper and the "high" is better. These people suffer all of the terrible problems that IV drug use brings: skin infections that can be fatal (necrotizing fasciitis), heart infections (endocarditis), hepatitis B and C, and HIV.

---

1 R. Rauck et al. *Journal of Opioid Management.* May/June 2006, 2:3.
2 Reprinted with permission from www.streetdrugs.org.
3 DEA.
4 *Ibid.,* www.streetdrugs.org.
5 National Drug Intelligence Center (NDIC), "OxyContin Diversion and Abuse," January 2001.
6 *Ibid.,* NDIC.
7 DEA.
8 *Ibid.,* www.streetdrugs.org.
9 DEA.
10 *Ibid.,* www.streetdrugs.org.

Chapter Ten
Stimulants, Benzodiazepines, and Marijuana

Cocaine and methamphetamine are both *stimulants*. They hit the pleasure centers so hard that it's like a barrage of bullets being shot into the neuroreceptors. Usually dopamine, the body's pleasure neurotransmitter, is stored in little bubbles at the tips of the neurons. These bubbles are called vesicles. The vesicles release the dopamine into the synapse, the space between neurons, in a controlled manner. To ensure that the dopamine doesn't end up anywhere it shouldn't and to carefully control the level in the synapse, tiny pumps retrieve the dopamine and store it back in the bubbles. This is called reuptake.

Cocaine and methamphetamine block the brain's ability to absorb the chemicals back into the neurons. This means there is more dopamine floating in the synapse than is needed. Since dopamine pleasurably affects how we feel, the cocaine or meth user feels euphoric.

But meth goes a few steps further. It also inhibits another enzyme called MAO that deactivates dopamine and may even stimulate the dopamine receptor sites itself. It also causes the vesicle to discharge dopamine *into the neuron*. This is toxic to the cell. Much

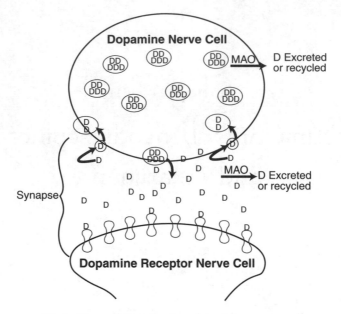

10-1: Normal functioning dopamine nerve cell

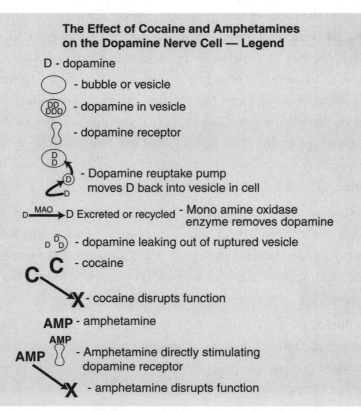

of the dopamine then leaks back out of the dead or dying cell, causing an extremely high level of dopamine to float in the synapse. This
has a long-lasting effect and therefore is more dangerous.

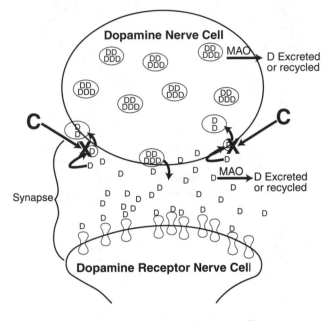

10-2: Cocaine-affected nerve cell

The damaged cells have a markedly decreased ability to reuptake
the dopamine, an effect that lasts even after the drug is stopped.
In time the remaining cells cannot provide even normal levels of
dopamine without meth present, thereby creating the basis for the
prolonged withdrawal symptoms so common for this drug, which at
times may never be corrected.

The combination of a highly addictive process and steady brain
damage is unique to meth. Compared to all the other drugs legal
and illegal, methamphetamine is probably the most dangerous.
Because of the brain damage, it probably also creates the most problems during addiction treatment.

Although the class of drugs known as *benzodiazepines* is not the
main focus of this book, they are so commonly abused by addicts

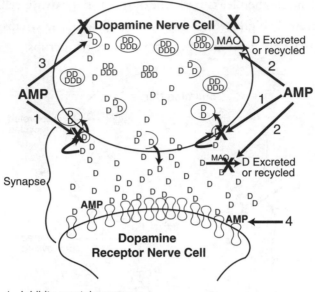

1 - Inhibits reuptake pump
2 - Inhibits removal of dopamine by MAO enzyme
3 - Releases dopamine from vesicles in cells causing cell damage
    and direct leakage of dopamine from cell into synapse
4 - There may be direct stimulation of dopamine receptors by AMP

10-3: Amphetamine-affected nerve cell

and used by the physicians who treat them that you should know how they work.

Marijuana is the most commonly abused illegal drug in the United States. It is usually found as the dried leaves of the hemp plant, *Cannabis sativa*. At times it is concentrated into a pure form called hash. The active ingredient, THC, is a potent compound with many effects on the brain and central nervous system. It is included here as well as in its own chapter in the second section.

Stimulants

Cocaine

Cocaine is a highly potent stimulant considered to be one of the greatest drug threats to the world because of the violence associated with trafficking and use, the physical and psychological effects associated with its use, and the costs to society as a whole.

There is great risk whether cocaine is ingested by inhalation (snorting), injection, or smoking. It appears that compulsive cocaine use may develop even more rapidly if the substance is smoked rather than snorted. Smoking allows extremely high doses of cocaine to reach the brain very quickly and brings an intense and immediate high.

Effects of Use

Moderate dose: disturbances in heart rhythm, increased heart and respiratory rates, elevated blood pressure, dilated pupils, decreased appetite, excessive activity, talkativeness, irritability, argumentative behavior, nervousness, or agitation.

Large dose: loss of coordination, collapse, perspiration, blurred vision, dizziness, feeling of restlessness, anxiety, delusions, heart attacks, chest pain, respiratory failure, strokes, seizures and headaches, abdominal pain, nausea, paranoia.[1]

Methamphetamine

Methamphetamine is a powerful stimulant that activates certain systems in the brain. It is closely related chemically to amphetamine, but the central nervous system effects of methamphetamine are greater. Both drugs have some medical uses, primarily in the treatment of obesity and ADHD, but their therapeutic use is limited. The effects from taking even small amounts include increased wakefulness, increased physical activity, decreased appetite, increased respiration, hypothermia, and euphoria. Other effects include irritability, insomnia, confusion, tremors, convulsions, anxiety, paranoia, and aggressiveness. Hyperthermia and convulsions can result in death.[2]

Methamphetamine is not a new drug. Created in 1919, it was taken by soldiers in World War II as a prescribed stimulant. In the

1950s housewives used it as a diet aid and anti-depressant. However, as documented in David J. Jefferson's *Newsweek* article, "America's Most Dangerous Drug," the use of meth has increased dramatically in the past few years:

Once derided as "poor man's cocaine,"...the highly addictive stimulant is hooking more and more people across the socioeconomic spectrum: soccer moms in Illinois, computer geeks in Silicon Valley, factory workers in Georgia, gay professionals in New York.

More than 12 million Americans have tried methamphetamine, and 1.5 million are regular users... Cops nationwide rank methamphetamine the No. 1 drug they battle today.[3]

Obviously meth also affects white-collar communities. It is easily available and encourages secrecy among its users. As Jefferson notes, soccer moms are not immune to the highly addictive substance. Many white-collar professionals are ensnared before realizing the devastating effects of the drug.

While genetics plays a role, meth is so addictive that a person with little or no risk of getting hooked on alcohol, marijuana, or opiates will become addicted to methamphetamine—and the way meth works in the brain is so powerful that addiction occurs quickly.

The key point with meth, as with all addictive substances, is the potency of the cravings. The cravings are intense and chronic, and leave patients depressed and feeling so poorly that they relapse rapidly. The post-acute withdrawal can last for years. Destruction of the brain can be so widespread that withdrawal symptoms may be permanent. Although there are other medications, such as modafinil (Provigal) that are being studied and may be effective, Prometa has the most promise to date as treatment for the severe cravings of meth and cocaine.

Benzodiazepines (Benzos)

Benzodiazepines work directly on the GABA receptors and are used largely as tranquilizers, muscle relaxants, and to control seizures. They can be addictive and rapid withdrawal can cause seizures. Although very high doses are needed, severe depression of breathing to the point of death is possible when ingested with alcohol. Here's a description from www.streetdrugs.org:

> The benzodiazepine family of depressants is used therapeutically to produce sedation, induce sleep, relieve anxiety and muscle spasms, and to prevent seizures. In general, benzodiazepines act as hypnotics in high doses, anxiolytics in moderate doses, and sedatives in low doses. Of the drugs marketed in the United States that affect central nervous system function, benzodiazepines are among the most widely prescribed medications.[4]

Benzodiazepines are classified...as depressants. Repeated use of large doses or, in some cases, daily use of therapeutic doses of benzodiazepines is associated with amnesia, hostility, irritability, and vivid or disturbing dreams, as well as tolerance and physical dependence. The withdrawal syndrome is similar to that of alcohol and may require hospitalization. Abrupt cessation of benzodiazepines is not recommended, as there is a high risk of seizures. Although a slow taper of the dose is safer, there are many long-time users who simply cannot get off the last 10 percent of the dose. They suffer from severe anxiety and insomnia, which can last for weeks. This is one of the most difficult situations to treat and many physicians opt to leave them on these small doses indefinitely. It's much better to avoid this situation by limiting the use of these medications in the first place.

Diazepam (Valium)

Diazepam is commonly used to relieve anxiety, muscle spasms, and seizures and to control agitation caused by alcohol withdrawal.

Stopping the drug suddenly can worsen [the original] condition and cause withdrawal symptoms (anxiousness, sleeplessness, and irritability).

Diazepam is also used to treat irritable bowel syndrome and panic attacks.[5]

Chlordiazepoxide (Librium)

Librium is a tranquilizer prescribed to treat anxiety and sleep disorders. It tends to be abused because of its sedating properties. With abuse, depressants cause tolerance and dependence. Withdrawal symptoms can be severe. Librium has a long half-life in the body, meaning its effects last longer.[6]

The long half-life of this drug makes is a good choice for detoxing from alcohol.

Lorazepam (Ativan)

Lorazepam is used to relieve anxiety.

Stopping the drug suddenly can worsen the original condition and cause withdrawal symptoms (anxiousness, sleeplessness, and irritability).

Lorazepam is also used to treat irritable bowel syndrome, epilepsy, insomnia, and nausea and vomiting from cancer treatment and to control agitation caused by alcohol withdrawal.[7]

Lorazepam's quick onset of action and the fact that is short acting make it very useful for acute anxiety, such as before an airplane flight. It is also used intravenously in the hospital and is safe and very fast acting in this context. Its short action is a problem at the same time because of possible rebound effects that can cause severe anxiety, making it very hard to quit using.

Oxazepam (Serax)

This medication has less abuse for potential than other benzos and may lead to limited physical dependence or addiction.[8]

Clonazepam (Klonipin)

This medication is used for muscle spasm after strokes and with multiple sclerosis. Its long action makes it a good choice for treating chronic anxiety in patients who do not respond to other more preferred medications.

Klonopin affects chemicals in the brain that may become unbalanced and cause seizures or symptoms of pain disorder. Physical and/or psychological dependence can occur, and withdrawal effects are possible if the medication is stopped suddenly after prolonged or high-dose treatment.[9]

Alprazolam (Xanax)

Alprazolam affects chemicals in the brain that may cause anxiety. This drug may cause drowsiness or dizziness. Alprazolam is habit-forming and withdrawal effects may occur if alprazolam is stopped suddenly after several weeks of continual use. It is a particularly addicting medication.[10]

Note that alprazolam is even more habit-forming than other benzos. Withdrawal from this potent drug must be done slowly. The entire process may take many months. Some patients find they can't get off the medication entirely.

Zolpidem (Ambien)

Zolpidem is used short-term to treat insomnia. It is often used for much longer periods. A recent new form of the medication called Ambien CR is longer-acting.

Despite the claims of the manufacturer, zolpidem can be habit-forming.

Since zolpidem acts on a different part of the GABA receptor than other benzos, it is less likely to be addicting. It can, however, be habit-forming. Recent reports also show that Ambien can cause a type of amnesia the day after use. I now stay away from this common medication, especially in addictive persons.

Eszopicione (Lunestra)

This popular sleeping aid is similar to Ambien and has lower chances for abuse than other benzodiazepines. Still, it should be taken in moderation, under close supervision by a physician. Next-day amnesia has not been reported to date.

Carisoprodol (Soma)

Although this drug is not a benzodiazepine, it is used so commonly along with other drugs that it must be included.

This drug is used as a muscle relaxant, but in reality it is a tranquilizer. It is converted into the drug meprobamate, which is the 1950s tranquilizer Milltown. Because it is more habit-forming and not as effective, this drug was displaced by diazepam (Valium). It is now a cheap medication marketed as a harmless muscle relaxant. Most physicians do not know about its background. In many addictive patients it is very dangerous. I avoid it when I can.

Marijuana

Marijuana is usually smoked but can also be ingested, most famously in brownies. Common terms for marijuana include grass, pot, dope, and hash. The major active chemical is delta-9-tetrahydrocannabinol, or THC. When smoked, THC rapidly enters the blood and then the brain.

According to the National Institute on Drug Abuse:

In 2004, 14.6 million Americans age 12 and older used marijuana at least once in the month prior to being surveyed. About 6,000 people a day in 2004 used marijuana for the first time. Of these, 63.8 percent were under age 18. In the last half of 2003, marijuana was the third most commonly abused drug mentioned in drug-related hospital emergency department (ED) visits in the continental United States, at 12.6 percent, following cocaine (20 percent) and alcohol (48.7 percent).[11]

Marijuana has detrimental effects with repeated and chronic usage. It is commonly seen as an "also used" substance of abuse. It is important to identify and then treat this problem if it is present.

Marijuana has several medical uses and is under study. There is a legal oral form available by prescription (Marinol). The medical use of this drug is legal in some states, but this practice is under court scrutiny.

These issues will be covered in detail in chapter 17.

---

1 www.streetdrugs.org.
2 DEA, "Drug Intelligence Brief: The Forms of Methamphetamine," April 2002.
3 www.streetdrugs.org.
4 www.streetdrugs.org.
5 The National Library of Medicine (NLM): www.nlm.nih.gov/medlineplus/druginfo/medmaster.
6 www.streetdrugs.org.
7 www.streetdrugs.org.
8 www.streetdrugs.org.
9 www.drugs.com.
10 www.drugs.com.
11 www.streetdrugs.org.

Chapter Eleven
The Trials and Tribulations of Joe

B elow is a fictionalized account of an average person's diary as he struggles with addiction. The entries show how many people feel when their therapy or twelve-step group pressures them to go public. Joe's wife is clearly near the end of her patience, as is his boss. Joe's drinking caused him to have an accident that left him with genuine pain issues, yet his doctor labels him a drug seeker.

Although he is seeking help, the treatment programs only give him buprenorphine for a short time. The medication helps his pain and the cravings for Norco, but does nothing for his alcohol cravings. When he tries to discuss this with his counselor, the response is "One thing at a time." But since all the "things" are hitting Joe at once, he returns again and again to the pills and the alcohol.

When his wife tells him to leave, Joe ends up living in a hotel. He can only afford fast food and is suffering mood swings worse than before he became addicted. Obviously Joe is having a pretty rough time. I assure you that his situation is commonplace.

Joe's Journal

Tuesday, May 7th

Played "Yellow Pages Roulette" again today and found a listing for a local twelve-step program. Took me an hour and a half to find the place, as it was in the basement of a synagogue. When I got there the other ten people in the room were nice but standoffish. It felt like they were already a clique and I was the new guy. So I did the, "My name's Joe and I'm a drug addict" thing so I could get the hell out of there right away. I downed a Vicodin while chugging some of their free coffee, which was the best part of the whole experience.

Wednesday, May 8th

Got a call from the leader of the twelve-step program I went to yesterday. Seems like a good guy. I lied to my wife and said he was a friend from work, which she knows is crap since I'm a hair's breadth from getting fired. Guy said he saw me take the Vicodin and wants to help. He seems genuine so I told him I'd meet for coffee or whatever. Hopefully he won't give me some useless motto to memorize. Still, I need help with the drinking problem. My wife still won't talk about the DUI I got a few months ago. All she could say when she brought me home from the police station was, "What if you'd killed somebody? What if somebody like you got drunk and killed our kids?"

When my car crashed into the median I smashed up my forehead pretty good and ever since the accident I've had severe migraines. That's why I got heavy into the pain meds. But when I went to my doctor to get something for the pain he thought I was a liar. I overheard him whisper "drug seeker" to his nurse.

But I guess he likes my money because he gave me a prescription for Vicodin.

Friday, May 10th

I turned 50 today. I celebrated by sobbing to my boss not to fire me after he caught me sleeping on my desk. The look of pity and disgust he gave me made me go in the bathroom and sneak a couple of Norcos I got from a guy I met in the emergency room yesterday. Then I got home and for a birthday gift after the kids went to sleep my wife gave me a brochure for a drug rehab clinic. I lost it, started yelling. Woke up the kids and they started crying. So I grabbed a bottle of Jack Daniels and sat in the car and downed it with a couple more Norcos. I swear to God I almost turned on the car and shut the garage door so I could take a permanent nap but I was holding a picture of my kids and crying and just couldn't do it.

Friday, May 24th

It's been a week now that I've been in the clinic. They put me on something called Subutex, which finally helped with my migraines, but it's not doing anything for the alcohol stuff. I keep telling them I want to stay sober but they say, "one thing at a time, one thing at a time." What the hell does that mean? I was shaky and I almost wet into DTs.

Monday, May 27th

Since they tapered and stopped the buprenorphine I'm going crazy. My headaches are worse than ever and I cannot think clearly.

Still, I lucked out and one of the other patients here got me some Oxycontin he got from a friend who smuggled it in on a visit. I feel better than I've felt in months.

Friday, June 14*th*

Got my Norco today. They sent it by FedEx right to my hotel room after I ordered it online last week. I made it to 10:30 this morning without taking any and tried calling Susan. She wouldn't pick up, actually had Stephanie say, "Mommy says you can't come home until you get clean and sober." Who the hell would tell a five-year-old to say that?

This new psychiatrist that I'm seeing today is way into drugs. Keeps trying different things on me. Doesn't even ask me about my drinking or whatever. It's like I'm a guinea pig for him. For the hell of it I asked him about acupuncture, see if that might help me at least quit smoking. I had a friend who tried it and hasn't smoked since. The doc looked at me and laughed. "Acupuncture?" he said. "Why don't you see a fortune teller while you're at it?"

He did send me to a therapist who's pretty nice. She's got a swanky office and big leather chairs. She keeps asking me about sex, though. Wondering if the drugs are making me impotent, which they are. She says I can take Paxil if I want to get "normal" again. I don't see the point, since my wife won't talk to me. Maybe she's hitting on me. Whatever the case, she seems to think my problems are all in my head. She keeps talking about my dad (who was an alcoholic) and saying until I resolve my issues with him I'll never get better. She also thinks I'm lying about my migraines. Thinks I use it as an excuse to take the drugs. But when I tell her about my recent drug rehab stay when I blacked out from pain after being off the meds for a week she doesn't believe me. "It's all mental," she says. "It's all in your mind."

Well, here's something that's not in my mind—I'm living in a hotel and my wife may leave me and take my kids. I'm scared to drive because if I get another DUI they'll take away my license and I could go to jail. I'm taking Norcos like they were M&Ms. My eating habits are for crap since I can only afford McDonald's. My mood swings are freaky, since I go from being suicidally depressed to feeling like everything is fine. That even happened before my life got so messed up. To top it all off, I dropped my pills this morning in the bathroom and threw my back out trying to pick them up. With my luck my lumbar problem is going to start up again and I can't afford physical therapy. Not that they'd give it to me anyway the way I look lately.

Nobody can help me. They throw these quick fixes at me but don't seem to give a crap whether I'm healed or not. I can't do this by myself and I have never felt so alone in my life.

Dear God, please help me. Please help me find someone who cares.

Part Two:
The Gracer Solution

Chapter Twelve
The Gracer Program

Introduction

"My life is better because Dr. Gracer listened, believed, and partnered with me to bring my health to the place it deserves to be."

"I feel very safe with Dr. Gracer. He listened to me and helped me find my way through my problem. He sincerely cares about me and has never treated me like I was a bad person, just someone who got into a serious problem. Being under his care has changed my life."

"Dr. Gracer's goal with his patients is not to just keep you on pills but to get you on a complete treatment program where you take the medication that you need. In other words, he helps you find the maintenance treatment that's best for you."

"I really feel like anyone who is in the 'hopeless' situation I was can be whole again if they just find the right doctor. Dr. Gracer has made the difference in my situation because he always believed in me and didn't give up. He saw me as a person worth helping, not just an addict as many doctors tend to do. And for that I will always be thankful to him."

These are not just actual quotes from my patients—they are the reason I've written this book. I am touched and pleased to know my patients feel that I am a partner and not just a prescriber of medication or advice.

Once I started thinking about the problems surrounding addiction and researching the types of support available, it became obvious that there was no comprehensive system that allowed for the accurate diagnosis of underlying factors. I had to develop a new method that treated not just the presenting problem—the chemical addiction itself—but also the wide range of related issues, such as genetic predisposition (family history and other drug problems such as smoking and alcohol), underlying psychiatric diagnoses (anxiety and/or depression, with an emphasis on bipolar symptoms), a history of drug abuse, a genuine pain problem, nutritional and metabolic factors, and emotional stressors. And that is just what we at Gracer Medical have done.

To best assess these factors, we evaluate a patient in three separate categories: biological, psychological, and social. We call this the Biopsychosocial Model of Substance Abuse and Dependency. This assessment provides a comprehensive view of a patient's overall health while demonstrating our commitment to treat them as an individual.

The Biopsychosocial Model of Substance Abuse and Dependency

Both abuse of and dependency on substances rely on a combination of biological, psychological, and social factors. Each plays an important role in substance use disorders. Moreover, each individual has their own blend of biopsychosocial factors that cause their disorder. Although the interplay among biopsychosocial influences is the key, let's examine each factor separately.

Biological Factors

Biological factors include genetic, prenatal, and brain dysfunction caused by chronic alcohol and drug poisoning. Substance abuse runs in families for genetic reasons. Prenatal factors also come into play when a mother who is drinking or using drugs passes on dependence to her child. Once born, the baby is in withdrawal and needs medical intervention.

A rule in chemical dependency treatment is once addicted, always addicted—so the child now runs an increased risk of having a chronic addictive disorder. The newborn certainly has to go through drug withdrawal directly after birth. Fetal alcohol syndrome (and most likely cocaine and methamphetamine use during pregnancy) leaves physical deformity and brain damage, as well.

Brain dysfunction from using alcohol and drugs can now be measured and scanned. The most common method is the PET scan, which measures blood flow as well as brain activity. As a clinician, I see the brain dysfunction in poor memory, learning, and concentration, which frequently causes poor decisions.

Psychological Factors

Psychological factors are plentiful. The key concepts are: 1) emotional management, 2) trauma, 3) self-concept, 4) sensation seeking, and 5) habituation. When most people explain what they get out of using, they generally talk about the sensation. Often they report the buzz or euphoria that enhances self-esteem and well-being. They simply feel better about themselves and the world in general. As use progresses, tolerance increases. The highs get shorter and their mood gets lower. The person uses drugs just to get rid of the bad feelings.

We refer to this as emotional management or self-medication. These people are medicating their pain, anxiety, and depression, which reduces their self-concept. They feel guilty and ashamed as they seek to keep their secret. As the consequences of drinking and using drugs increase, so do the feelings of sadness, guilt, and shame. A vicious cycle is now in place.

Many individuals abuse substances in order to cope with loss and trauma. The World War II and Vietnam veterans I have worked with drink and use drugs to suppress traumatic memories. People with a history of child abuse, neglect, domestic violence, and sexual assault also use to cope with feelings and flashbacks.

Habituation is another important psychological factor. It involves engaging in the same behavior until you no longer actively think about it. Once you've learned to ride a bike, you don't think, "Balance. Okay, balance. Pedal. Balance, pedal." Most drinkers don't think, "I'll walk inside, hang up my coat, and get a beer. I'll drink a twelve-pack and pass out on the couch." Drinking and drug use become an ingrained habit.

Social Factors

Social factors influencing substance abuse come from our environment. Families are the most notable influence. Social learning theory postulates that we learn from parents, family, friends, and others how to get along in this world—which is fine if those people are models of good behavior. If the social environment teaches that chemical use is a way to cope, people learn self-defeating patterns.

The workplace is a potent social influence as well. Many vocations lend themselves to the "work hard, play hard" philosophy. Trades such as carpentry and masonry have higher rates of smoking, drinking, and marijuana use. Stopping on the way home for a quick drink is normal. Other professions have similar high-risk patterns, including sales professionals, police officers, and office workers.

All these factors influence substance abuse. A person whose parents and grandparents all drank is affected in both the genetic and social learning domains. They may also have done a stint in the military, where drinking was both condoned and expected.

The Gracer Treatment Protocol

The Gracer Treatment Protocol is a comprehensive addiction craving management and recovery program. Our program provides the most complete examination of all factors surrounding addiction in any program today. Our unique protocol for individuals entering treatment involves:

A thorough history, including past treatments and their results, as well as other current problems and concerns.

A complete medical evaluation concentrating first on primary immediate medical concerns.

The proper diagnosis of real pain problems and a careful look at previous medical records.

Comprehensive laboratory testing.

A nutritional screening program.

The Gracer/Peterson Readiness Quadrant (RQ) evaluation.

Individual psychological and sociologic evaluation and therapy.

Participation in outside support group activities including twelve-step programs is encouraged. We also endorse other programs that empower individuals, such as SMART Recovery and Life Ring.

Treatment of any medical condition that impacts the substance abuse.

We do not consider relapses an automatic cause for discharge.

Treatment of cravings at all stages.

The following is a comparison of the Gracer program to traditional systems.

Flaws	The Gracer Solution
The most common treatment is drug detoxification (acute withdrawal) followed by a social/moral model (usually abstinence) for long-term support.	An integrative approach that designs treatments specifically for each patient for the best possible chance to succeed, thorough attention to a patient's holistic health in a caring and scientific environment without moral assessments or emotional stigmas.
Twelve-step programs are social programs.	The Gracer Program is based on science and incorporates substance abuse as a brain receptor disease. We treat legitimate psychiatric and pain issues that otherwise lead to dropping out of treatment and relapse.
Treatment is not evidence-based.	Our program is on the cutting edge of applied research and will be updated as new evidence-based approaches are developed.
Substance abuse is segregated from mental health, and/or substance abuse staff has little training in treating mental health problems.	In the Gracer Program we recognize that the biochemistry of addiction often coincides with psychiatric illness. Many times this problem is bipolar disorder, which must be treated differently from common depression and anxiety disorders. The Gracer Program recognizes that many people with addiction are self-treating for psychiatric symptoms.
Confrontation (shame or moral judgment).	The Gracer Program stresses empathetic treatment. Many people resist treatment that requires them to admit their addiction. Individual psychological and sociological evaluation and therapy is vital. We must treat people in a manner that is appropriate for them at their current stage of awareness.

Treating the manifestations of pain and/or addiction versus their underlying causes.	Just because people have an addiction, their best treatment may not be the same as another addicted person's. Treating the symptom does not treat the cause.
Prescribing medicines without regard to psychological or sociological issues that typically accompany addiction.	The Gracer Program supplies both medication and comprehensive evaluation and support.
No evaluation or treatment of nutritional problems.	The Gracer Program has a nutritional screening program for proper diet and supplementation. This aspect of treatment adds significantly to success.
No alternative medical approaches.	The Gracer Program includes many treatments based in alternative medicine. This includes acupuncture and Chinese medicine, herbal treatments, use of amino acids, and other functional medical testing and treatments.
No treatment or allowance for legitimate pain issues.	In the Gracer Program we treat any medical condition that impacts the substance abuse problem. We recognize that these are often the inciting reason for the addiction syndrome. If left untreated, they are an important factors for relapse. Patients with legitimate pain issues may also show signs of pseudo-addiction.
Not diagnosing and treating hormonal imbalances.	Subtle hormone deficiencies that are often overlooked by other doctors are evaluated and treated.
No evaluation of neurotransmitters.	Gracer Program patients undergo testing for neurotransmitter levels. The results are used to design specific supplementation programs to balance the brain's neurotransmitters.

No craving management.	The Gracer Medical Program is novel in treating dependence/addiction in that we use medications to treat cravings. Cravings are addressed at all stages of treatment.
Most programs (and general public mindset) just treat the substance abuse as the diagnosis.	The Gracer Program looks at the underlying factors and other problems that must be attacked as part of a successful addiction treatment program.
Programs don't always recognize social aspects of how the middle-class wants to be treated.	The Gracer Program recognizes the social differences that have an important effect on how we treat addiction. The Hidden need special outreach and private treatment options.
One-size-fits-all mentality.	Only by seeing the individual from many angles can we give each person the very best chance of success. The Gracer/Peterson Readiness Quadrant (RQ) evaluation allows for patient self-insight and helps the therapist choose the most effective treatment program.

12-1: The Gracer Program compared to traditional methods

Joe Revisited

Friday, June 28th

Today I met again with Dr. Gracer, who's been extremely cool to me. I knew right away that he was different, since he actually listened and didn't rush me out of the room. Then he asked a lot of questions, especially about my mood swings. He did some tests and told me I had bipolar disorder, which I guess makes sense.

He also asked me about my diet, which I totally didn't get at first. I told him about McDonald's and all the fast food I ate and he told me to stop if possible. He also pointed out that my tests showed I was hypoglycemic and that was typical for certain alcoholics. He said that through better nutrition and diet I could better fight my addictions. He also mentioned that my cholesterol level was high, so I told him about my family history with diabetes. He said this could affect something involving the metabolic syndrome and would also effect my treatment.

My head was sort of spinning at this point, since nobody had spent so much time trying to figure out what was wrong with me. I felt that I'd finally found a program that was different from all the rest.

Monday, July 1st

So Dr. Gracer tells me that the metabolic syndrome thing means I have high insulin levels. It also turns out that my testosterone levels are low (because of alcohol and other addicting drugs), so I wish my therapist hadn't pushed me to take more medications I didn't need. Plus the Prozac made my mood swings worse since I'm bipolar. Granted, my therapist didn't know that, but isn't she supposed to?

Thank God Dr. Gracer is treating my back pain with Suboxone. Since it'll also help my drug cravings I have to stay on the medication. Also, Dr. Gracer said that once I'm clean he could also treat my back with local ligament injections, which should really help.

Wednesday, July 3rd

So here's the good news, since tomorrow is July 4th and I couldn't find a better excuse to drink than that. Dr. Gracer prescribed this amazing protocol called Prometa that is treating my cravings so I don't walk around thinking how I could suck sap from a tree and convert it to beer or distill cough syrup for a quick shot.

I've been using the testosterone gel and taking vitamins to treat my metabolic syndrome. I'm also doing a low-carb diet and generally eating better. Dr. Gracer's also giving me a mood stabilizer for my bipolar disorder.

Wednesday, July 24th

Praise God—I'm back with my wife and kids. My wife is thrilled that I met Dr. Gracer and she usually comes with me to my appointments. I can continue working and still get intensive treatment at the evening and Saturday program at New Connections. We also hire a babysitter and, instead of a date night, have been visiting local programs recommended by New Connections. These are group settings with people who are supportive but understand that a one-size-fits-all mentality doesn't work with addicts.

I remember back when I started treatment with Dr. Gracer. Steve Peterson gave me the RQ evaluation. I realized that whether or not I was confident enough to change, I had to or I'd lose my family. I am also seeing Steve regularly to deal with these problems in private therapy.

Here's the thing—I know I have it (or had it) a lot worse than most people and got dealt some pretty bad cards in terms of my various conditions. It was only Dr. Gracer's willingness to dig deep and find out all of my history and circumstances that has led me to be addiction-free for almost a month. I know I may need treatment for quite some time, but I feel better than I have in years, even before I got into drugs and alcohol. I feel like a veil has been lifted and I can have a normal day without huge mood swings or cravings so bad they make my eyes water.

I've got my life back.

Chapter Thirteen

The Gracer/Peterson Readiness Quadrant Evaluation

Written by Steven M. Peterson, LCSW, CADC III,
with an introduction by Richard I. Gracer, MD

A s part of the research for this book and the development of our comprehensive treatment program, I asked experts in my community if they knew of a program or a person who could help me with this project. I soon received a call from Steven Mark Peterson, who had moved to the area after working at the Center for Addiction and Behavior Research at the Aurora Sinai Medical Center in Milwaukee, Wisconsin. He was the lead research therapist for numerous landmark studies as well as lead designer of intervention protocols, detox protocols, and therapist training. Steve is currently the director of the behavioral health portion of Gracer Medical's program.

I have asked him to write this chapter and the next, Empathy and Enlightenment, because of his experience and expertise in Motivational Therapy.

Gracer Medical's unique Gracer/Peterson Readiness Quadrant (RQ) helps both physician and patient recognize a patient's overall willingness and ability to alter behavior that has led to addiction.

This evaluation is a remarkable tool, and its success hinges on these four simple things:

As physician and patient use the tool, both parties are open to discovery.

The evaluation is remarkably easy to use.

It is empathetic in nature.

It encourages honesty without shame.

History

I have always been fascinated by the question of why some people change addicted behavior and others do not. Early in my training I was told that change was linked with "hitting bottom." The

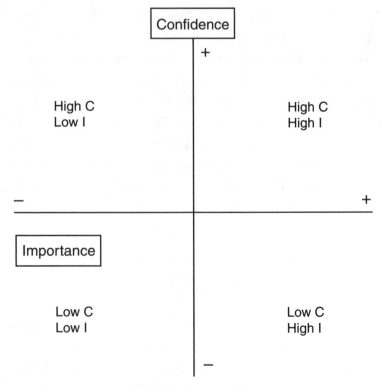

13-1: The Gracer/Peterson
Readiness Quadrant Evaluation

prevailing wisdom was that the individual must experience tremendous consequences. Treatment then focused on helping individuals break their denial. This never explained why some people hit bottom and still kept using until they died. Nor did it explain the people who voluntarily attended treatment because they were concerned about future consequences.

In the early 1990s I attended a conference on the Stages of Change Model presented by James Prochaska, PhD. He and Carlo DiClementi spent many years interviewing subjects who had changed their addictive behavior without formal therapy. Additional research by Steven Rollnick, PhD, and William R. Miller, PhD, yielded the now popular Readiness to Change concept.

Their work showed that changing addicted behavior is a dynamic yet measurable process. Current researchers evolved this model into the Readiness to Change concept. Our program harnessed this concept to evaluate patients and tailor interventions based on the patient's perception of both the importance of and their confidence to change.

Dr. Rollick believes that: Importance + Confidence = Readiness. This is the basis for our Readiness Quadrant Evaluation.

The Gracer/Peterson Readiness Quadrant Evaluation

We expanded these concepts and developed a new way to help patients and therapists rank both attitude toward change and confidence in ability to change. The subsequent treatment approach can be very different depending on these factors. Going through this simple exercise tells both the patient and the therapist "where it's at" and also can make a person much more ready to change. We have found that just going through this process can promote important changes.

Importance to Change

Importance to change involves the patient's perception that changing their drug or alcohol use is a priority, or at least deserving of focus. The individual may say, "If I don't quit using alcohol, my stomach isn't going to get better." Many have told me, "If I don't quit now, I'll be dead." Another common concern is based in relationships. "He'll leave me if I don't stop drinking," patients often worry, or cite the disappointment of family members. Giving up the role model status seems to really affect parents, as seen in the statement, "My kids think I'm a jerk when I drink."

On the opposite end, patients may say, "It sounds like a great idea but I've just got too much going on now to go into treatment," or, "I'm still young. How will I have fun without drinking?" Complicating the issue are patients who see the importance of changing alcohol use but who don't think changing marijuana use is important.

Our program evaluates importance to change in the first session. Here is a list of Importance Factors usually expressed by our patients:

- Legal concerns frequently lead people into treatment even when they don't believe they have a problem. Judges, probation officers, or parole officers are the enforcers. Others feel it is important to maintain abstinence so they do not go to jail or to recover a driver's license. Some parents are afraid that they might lose their children.

- Health issues. People have had accidents while high or drunk. One patient decided to quit when her hangovers were so bad she couldn't get the children up for school in the morning. Others have noted that opiates no longer help their pain and actually make them feel worse. Occasionally patients express concerns over future health consequences, even death.

- Relationship problems. One of the leading reasons couples go into therapy is abuse of drugs or alcohol. Friends, other family members, and co-workers are also motivating factors. What other people who are important in the person's life think really does matter and can be a motivating factor.

- Vocational and employment consequences can be as subtle as lowered productivity or as dramatic as being fired. For example, one patient, a welder, could easily have left his company for another and made significantly more money. He couldn't pass a pre-employment drug screen, however, so he remained at his job.

- Emotional importance. Self-perception, self-confidence, and emotional management are affected by drug use. One mother became ready to change when she neglected her children's need for food and clothing. Another important reason to change is that strong emotions such as anger can lead to rage when an individual is intoxicated.

- Positive results of quitting must be worth the effort. If a person believes that quitting cocaine will make their life better, they see it as important to quit. If the person thinks giving up drug use will result in a drastic reduction in their ability to have fun, the importance of changing is low.

Confidence to Change

Confidence is central to successful behaviors in general. How would any of us obtain employment if we didn't have the confidence to attend the job interview, fill out the application, and answer questions? This same variable applies to changing addictive behavior. When an individual decides it is important to change, they often run into the brick wall of low self-confidence.

In my experience, the primary issue affecting confidence is cravings. Early in the use history, people attempting to quit remember the positive feelings they got from alcohol or drug use. The craving, then, is missing the high. For the individual to have good confidence levels, they need to believe they can endure the absence of the drug and find an alternative behavior.

As the disease of addiction progresses, people attempting to quit have increasingly severe withdrawal symptoms. By this time, cravings create a desire to use drugs so the withdrawal symptoms will go away. These cravings keep the person hooked as they avoid the unpleasant withdrawal feelings. Moreover, for certain drugs, the acute withdrawal syndrome is potentially life-threatening and requires medical detoxification. Thus intensity of the withdrawal further promotes being stuck in the addictive cycle.

Below is our list of Confidence factors:

- **Self-efficacy (self-confidence).** This is the belief that change is possible and the person can implement a change plan. The helping professional can build on the person's belief that change is possible. If that belief is not present or is weak, treatment needs to focus on fostering this thought process. Self-efficacy is crucial for change to occur.

- **Past successes to instill hope.** When people come into the clinic and have already made other difficult changes, treatment can review and build on these successes. For example, some patients have stopped smoking and now want to quit drinking as well. The appropriate question is "How did you quit smoking and what skills that you developed then can you use this time?" Other past successes like returning to school or getting a better job can also be used.

- **Coping skills.** Abilities to cope with peer pressure and feelings of anger, to have fun, and so on are essential in behavioral change. Being aware of the skills is the first step, followed by practicing them in real situations. Often people report feeling empowered as they get better at recovery skills.

- **Level of social support.** Loneliness and boredom are probably the two main psychological triggers to alcohol and drug use. Being around supportive people can certainly ease these triggers. Social support can be found in many forms, including AA, NA, other support groups, family, friends, church organizations, and so on.

- **Cravings.** Cravings are triggered by physical and psychological factors. They significantly affect the person's confidence in the change process. Unless a careful craving management plan is developed, recovery is all but doomed. Integrating medications and behavioral change strategies seems to offer hope in the treatment of drug and alcohol cravings.

- **Psychological issues.** The field of substance abuse treatment is finally turning its attention to the crucial issue of co-existing psychological disorders. Confidence to change is hindered when patients see alcohol and drug use as a benefit in coping with depression, mood swings, anxiety, thought problems, and trauma issues.

Evaluation Factors

Our program measures and then evaluates these factors using the Readiness Quadrant, the results of which determine the best course of treatment for each individual patient.

Factors for Readiness

Importance	Confidence
Legal	Self-efficacy (Self-confidence)
Health	Past Successes or Failures
Relationship	Coping Skills
Vocational	Levels of Social Support
Emotional	Intensity of Cravings
Positive Results of Change (PRC)	Psychological and Mood issues

13-2: Factors for Readiness

Importance and confidence interventions build on strengths and move the individual forward in the change process. For example, people high in both importance and confidence have often undergone past successful changes, are able to manage their cravings, and have the support of others. They are ready to move forward rapidly and mostly need direction and basic support.

We have quantified these factors in the Readiness Rulers below. Place an X in the box that corresponds to the number you feel best describes how weak or strong each factor is for you or your loved one at this time. This is a "snapshot" of where you are at the time of the test. Remember that things may change and you may come up with different results as you develop and move forward with your plan. You can take the test again later to track your progress.

Importance Factor Rulers

Strongly disagree   Strongly agree

	1	2	3	4	5	6	7	8	9	10
I have serious legal problems due to my drug use.										
I have serious health problems from my drug use.										
I have serious relationship problems due to my drug use.										
I have serious vocational (job, career) problems due to my drug use.										

I have experienced serious emotional problems due to my drug use.										
I will get positive results from changing my drug use.										

13-3: *Importance Factor Rulers chart*

Confidence Factors

Strongly disagree   Strongly agree

	1	2	3	4	5	6	7	8	9	10
I am confident that I can change my drug use.										
I have experienced past success in dealing with my drug use issues.										
I have positive coping strategies to help me stay clean and sober.										
I have a high level of social support.										
I experience intense cravings for drugs.										
I have difficulties coping with my psychological issues (depression, anxiety, and thinking problems).										

13-4: *Confidence Factors chart*

Scoring:

1) For Importance: Add all six factor scores together. Any score above 30 indicates that the person has a high level of importance (scored as + on the Readiness Quadrant), although the higher the number the better. If it is less, then it is scored as a - on the Readiness Quadrant. Please note that a very high score on an individual factor, such as being diagnosed with cirrhosis of the liver or a beloved spouse leaving due to alcohol abuse, may itself be enough to push the person into a high importance category.

2) For Confidence: Add the scores for the first four factors: self-confidence, past successes, social support, and ability to cope. Subtract the scores from the total for the cravings and psychological issues. Any score above 15 is considered a high confidence number (scored as + on the Readiness Quadrant) and the higher the score the better. If it is less, then it is scored as a - on the Readiness Quadrant. Again please note that one factor, such as cravings or lack of a belief that change is possible, may be so overwhelming that it causes a low confidence score.

Use the results from these rulers to discover where you are on the Readiness Quadrant (RQ). The results will show whether you have high importance and high confidence, both are low, or one is high and the other is low. The exact number is not important. What matters is your sense of where you are. This process can help you clarify your readiness to change. Thus, this exercise is done therapeutically. The diagram below shows the Readiness Quadrant.

Outline for Readiness Quadrant (RQ) Evaluation

1. Use rulers to determine the readiness score for each Importance (I) and Confidence (C) factor.

Calculate I and C score totals.

Assign + or – to I and C.

Determine Quadrant.

The RQ is expressed as High C, Low I, and so on.

High Importance, Low Confidence (Case 1)	High Importance, High Confidence (Case 2)
Low Importance, Low Confidence (Case 3)	Low Importance, High Confidence (Case 4)

13-5: Outline for Readiness Quadrant (RQ) Evaluation chart

Case 1: High Importance, Low Confidence

These individuals are aware of the damaging consequences of alcohol and drug use; however, their self-confidence is low. Often they do not have support, reliable coping mechanisms, or a belief that they are able to change. More often than not, these individuals experience overwhelming withdrawal symptoms and cravings. They relapse once treatment is over.

Factors not identified or treated in many of these patients are co-existing mental health and physical illnesses, such as pain.

Therapeutic Strategy

The recommended procedure is to harness the motivation tied to the importance of change while building confidence. The most effective strategy is to treat the withdrawal, craving, mental, and physical symptoms. The therapist needs to partner with a competent physician or physicians.

Case 2: High Importance, High Confidence

People with both high importance and high confidence have a green light for change. They are aware that changing their drug and alcohol use is a priority and believe they have the tools necessary to change. A recent example is a patient who spoke about how his opiate use negatively affected his job performance and his finances. He noted previous periods of non-use and described several successful strategies to cope with cravings. He knew he needed to avoid certain situations and ask for help. He discussed his support system and how to access friends who cared.

Therapeutic Strategy

I reviewed his past success and coping mechanisms, and followed him in therapy until we both agreed that he was on the right track. I find that occasional booster sessions are helpful to maintain change and avoid relapse.

Case 3: Low Importance, Low Confidence

These patients have both low confidence that they can change and feel little need to do so. These patients are the most difficult to treat and are the first to drop out of treatment or almost as commonly, be dropped from treatment.

Therapeutic Strategy

By exploring barriers, the person gets a chance to re-evaluate both factors. For example, once the person sees that their cravings can be managed with a combination of medical and behavioral interventions, their confidence is enhanced. At the same time we give the individual personalized feedback on how their use affects them.

By integrating biological intervention (withdrawal and cravings) with behavioral intervention (improving importance and confidence), the heart of addiction as a biopsychosocial illness is revealed. Moreover, as people learn coping skills like assertiveness, mood management, and having fun without chemical use, their attitude improves significantly. The same feeling of empowerment comes from managing high blood pressure through medication, diet, and exercise.

Proper treatment must be provided for any psychological or psychiatric issues that cause low importance and low confidence. One individual said, "I'm getting better at dealing with what happened to me in Vietnam. I see that drinking doesn't help the flashbacks. I no longer blame myself for my friend's death."

Case 4: Low Importance, High Confidence

These individuals think other life issues take priority over change. An example is the person who sees drug use as a way to cope with difficult feelings or problems. They might say, "Drinking is my reward for getting through a stressful work week." Self-medication leads to the thought that, "I need this drug use to deal with my crummy life," and, "This is all I deserve."

Others have overwhelming stressors, such as losses, unemployment, abusive relationships, or their own or a loved one's physical illness. Here the thinking is, "I've got way too much going on to make changing drug use my top priority." Another example is the person who has had some legal consequences but rationalizes their use as long as they do not get caught.

They might also overestimate their confidence level and state, "I can change whenever I need to," or, "When things settle down, I'll consider changing." The individual often doesn't see that drug use is causing many of the problems. Others may have good reason to be confident in their ability to change due to past successful change efforts, high levels of support, and helpful coping mechanisms.

Therapeutic Strategy

In these types of cases the clinical response is to encourage the person to compare the reasons to change with the reasons not to change. Sorting out what he or she gets from drinking or drug use often reveals that costs vastly outweigh the benefits. One person proclaimed, "It isn't even close. Drinking is related to all these problems and all I get is a buzz."

Often by pointing out the discrepancy between a person's self-image and reality can shift their attitude. For example, "If drinking is not a problem for you, how did you get a DUI?" (or lose your job, or end up in the hospital, or so forth).

Another approach is to shift to a topic the patient does consider a priority. Often, by starting the change process in one area the person becomes more aware in general. This can lead to rethinking the need to change their drug or alcohol use. At the same time, the therapist needs to maintain the high confidence levels and highlight them as strengths.

Note: The empathetic philosophy utilized in conjunction with the RQ is of paramount importance. The therapist and physician's role is to act as a counselor and reinforce a patient's efforts.

The Change Plan Worksheet

The questions on the following Change Plan Worksheet[1] are meant to galvanize your thoughts and commitment to change. This worksheet can also be downloaded from the Gracer Medical website.

Change Plan Worksheet

The most important reasons why I want to make this change are:

My main goals for myself in making this change are:

I plan to do these things in order to accomplish my goals:

Specific action   When?

Other people could help me with change in these ways:

Person   Possible ways to help

These are some possible obstacles to change, and how I could handle them:

Possible obstacle to change   How to respond

I will know that my plan is working when I see these results:

Drinker's and Substance User's Checkup

This four-session program, which we offer at Gracer Medical, quickly determines substance abuse problems and related factors unique to each individual, and then formulates a proper intervention plan. It is included here to demonstrate steps you can take in evaluating whether you or a loved one may have a drinking or drug use problem.

Research has shown this method to be very effective in increasing self-awareness and motivation for change. This approach, delivered in a confidential medical setting and supplemented by a workbook, has been shown to promote rapid change of substance abuse behavior. In fact, patients going through this short-term program have significantly reduced their drug and/or alcohol use even without further therapy. After completion, each participant also has a specific roadmap along with the support needed for its implementation.

The sessions are set up as follows:

Session 1–Pattern Evaluation

Specific alcohol and drug use patterns are examined. Careful attention is paid to the motivation and readiness to change levels. Triggering factors are explored.

Session 2–Objective Measures of Use

The individual is given assessment tools to determine the extent of the alcohol and/or drug use. The person then evaluates their support system and relationships. Session 2 concludes with the RQ evaluation.

Session 3–Feedback Session

Personalized feedback is given on the diagnosis, comparison to normal drinking patterns, problematic behaviors, triggering factors, social support, and readiness to change.

Session 4–Treatment Plan Formulation

A change plan and treatment roadmap is developed. If possible, a supportive significant other is involved. The change plan may include a recommendation for craving management treatment with medical procedures. Booster sessions are available to support long-term change.

Medical consultation is also available, although it is not a part of the checkup. Test results from patients' own physicians are also used for part of the evaluation.

---

1 Reprinted with permission from Miller & Rollnick. *Motivational Interviewing.* (2002) New York, NY: The Guilford Press.

Chapter Fourteen
Empathy and Enlightenment
Written by Steven M. Peterson, LCSW, CADC III

O ur goal at Gracer Medical is to create an atmosphere of trust and care in which patients can feel motivated for change. Note that the same attitude of supportive, nurturing care can help you help a loved one struggling with addiction. The empathic model presented here fits very well with the RQ results from the last chapter.

A History of Empathy

I'm an addiction counselor. I first got into the field working with children in Wisconsin's alternative schools, where students wound up after being kicked out of regular schools. About 80 percent of the kids I worked with had addictions (cigarettes, alcohol, and so on). If I was going to be effective, I had to become an expert on addiction. I started my training in chemical dependency at the University of Wisconsin at Madison, and then got a job at a treatment center working with adolescents.

One thing that's different about me is that I'm not a recovering alcoholic or drug addict. About 75 percent of my colleagues are in recovery. In fact, 75 percent of therapists and 50 percent of doctors who specialize in addiction have struggled with addiction. Because I've never had my patient's experiences, I've had to be incredibly empathetic and try to put myself in their shoes. Fortunately, research has discovered that being empathetic is very effective for the treatment of addiction. Therapists who are confrontational don't have the positive results that empathetic therapists do.

In the confrontational model, doctors or therapists typically tell people, "If you don't change you're going to die, go into an institution, or go crazy." In essence, they are telling their patients what to do, which sets up a me-versus-you scenario. It is not a collaboration. Patients who really want to change might say, "Fine, I'll do whatever it takes." But other patients will likely say, "I'm going to do what I think I need to do, not what you tell me to do."

In the empathetic model, we support and collaborate with another person who happens to be our patient. We feel that this is the most effective way to treat addiction. Many patients suffer low self-efficacy, which means they don't believe they can change. But it's not that they can't change—it's that they don't believe they can change. Oftentimes people feel defeated and ashamed while struggling with addiction, so the last thing they need is their therapist or doctor telling them what to do in an overly authoritative manner. Instead, building up their confidence is critical to a positive outcome. If a person is trying to get clean and has a relapse, rather than telling him or her they haven't hit bottom yet, the empathetic therapist will find a way the patient can cope. Flexibility, collaboration, and therapeutic alliance are all crucial steps in the empathetic process.

Gracer Behavioral Health Solution

We have developed a counseling style that uses many of the most modern and proven methods. In addition, our personal experience has allowed us to expand on them with new, innovative techniques.

Although some of these have already been alluded to in previous chapters, it is worth noting them here to get a big-picture sense of how all of the techniques fit together in the empathic model. Our overall approach includes:

- Our *Readiness Quadrant (RQ) evaluation,* which helps patients and therapists find the best way to approach the initial interview and decide on the best treatment.

- Motivational Interviewing techniques that develop and enhance a person's desire to change. By collaborating with the therapist, the patient becomes *part* of the change process rather than just the subject. Our counselors use empathic techniques that allow patients to change without the usual anger or conflict.

- Solution Focused Therapy that builds solutions for practical, real-life situations. This uses the patient's past successes instead of focusing on their failures.

- Skill building to help individuals cope with high-risk situations, such as attending a cocktail party, as well as talking with their pain doctor and dealing with life's inevitable conflicts.

- Building a support system so that the individual has encouragement and a peer group that supports change.

- Coordination with pain and other medical treatment.

- Integration with treatment of depression, anxiety, and bipolar disorders.

Patient Program

- No matter what, the therapist works on engagement, or what we call treatment *compliance.* This means working with the client/patient on staying involved with the program instead of getting frustrated and giving up.

- We foster an environment of supportive collaboration.

- We foster and nurture empathetic responses.

- We look at the root causes of dependence/addiction issues.

Along with these, we assess biological, psychological, and social factors. Not only are these essential to the diagnoses, the process is unique to our program.

Motivation

The other main things we're concerned with are issues related to patient motivation. Rather than thinking of motivation as a trait (as in, "he's a motivated individual"), we think of motivation as a state of being. For instance, I'm motivated to get my license back if I've lost it because of drunk driving. It's active, not passive.

So we try to find out where a person's motivation lies regarding their potential treatment. We do this through the use of a type of therapy known as Motivational Enhancement Theory, or MET. This is where the Gracer/Peterson Readiness Quadrant Evaluation comes in, as described in the last chapter.

Empathy Explained

As I look back at my twenty-plus years of working with patients with addictions, I am struck by how much this field has changed. One of the constants, however, is that certain therapists have more positive outcomes with patients than others do. Therapists with the more positive outcomes have several key characteristics in common. Most obvious is that therapeutic empathy (the ability to put oneself in another person's situation) differs greatly from sympathy, or feeling sorry for an individual.

I learned about empathy early in my career. My first assignment for college practical studies was at Malcolm Shabazz High School in Madison, Wisconsin. Within the first fifteen minutes of my first day,

I had to break up a fistfight. These were rough kids, most of whom used drugs and alcohol.

We initiated support groups so the kids could talk about their troubled family lives and drug use. In these sessions, I expressed unconditional positive regard. To my astonishment, the kids opened up. Many even agreed that their drug use interfered with their schoolwork.

Upon graduation, I started working at a chemical dependency treatment center at Kettle Moraine Hospital, near Milwaukee. The program there blended the twelve-step model with basic counseling strategies. This, the so-called Minnesota Model, was the foundation of my early professional training and therapy experience.

Much of the understanding about addictive behavior at that time focused on the idea that addiction was a disease of denial. We were told that breaking down the denial, often with confrontational methods, was critical. Group, individual, and family sessions routinely became loud. The patient was told, "If you don't have a problem, why are you here?" Smart patients quickly figured out how to say whatever the therapist wanted to hear in order to be discharged quickly.

The confrontational approach didn't work for me. How could I be taken seriously when I told my patients they were in denial if I had not had personal experience? My colleagues described my method of listening, exploring feelings, discussing resistance, and direct support as too soft and even enabling. But the outcomes spoke for themselves. Patients often thanked me for listening and caring about what they thought. Parents wrote letters about the changes in their family members. After two years at Kettle Moraine Hospital, even my peers acknowledged my work. Empathy really did facilitate change.

Motivational Interviewing

By the time I was thirty-four I had worked in several inpatient and outpatient treatment centers. I had been a student assistance coordinator at a local high school where drug and alcohol use were prevalent. I had even started a private practice specializing in substance abuse treatment. I trained intern students and was asked to teach college courses on addiction treatment. The supportive, empathic approach worked in every setting.

A graduate student offered me a copy of a book she had been assigned in an earlier class. *Motivational Interviewing,* by William Miller and Stephen Rollnick, gave a name to what I had been practicing for ten years. It also gave me many more strategies. I have since been personally trained by Dr. Miller and participated in several large research studies that had Motivational Interviewing at their foundation.

The technique helps people weigh the reasons they want to change against the reasons they don't want to change. The therapist keeps their personal views to themselves unless the individual specifically asks what they think. The patient then gets a chance to really examine what they want to do without being pushed into something they aren't ready for.

Many traditionalists doubt this approach, however. They say, "How can a person make a decision for themselves when their life is totally unmanageable and their body is full of drugs?" But this motivational enhancement approach harnesses the person's own strengths and resources. I do agree that the decision is best made when the individual is stabilized from acute withdrawal symptoms. After the withdrawal symptoms have been treated, though, the patient and the therapist can take time to sort out where things stand. At this point, many individuals reflect on the damage incurred and conclude that they need help.

Several researchers, including William Miller, PhD, who cofounded Motivational Interviewing along with Stephen Rollnick, found that if counselor's empathic responses were recorded, the data could be compared to drinking outcomes. Sure enough, the higher the therapists scored on expressing empathy, the better the drinking outcome was after one year. By contrast, the more the therapist confronted the patient, the worse the drinking outcomes were. More confronting also caused more dropouts.

Expressing Empathy

In reviewing successful treatment programs of the 1970s and 1980s, Miller and Rollnick found that these programs had the foundation of expressing empathy. Listening, asking open-ended questions, and reflecting the answers prompted meaningful exploration of factors impacting change.

Patients who are ready for change can be educated about their disease as a way to promote acceptance. If the patient needs to sort out whether using alcohol is a problem, then exploration is warranted. One man I worked with did not believe that his daily pot use was a problem until he got caught smoking in the company bathroom and was fired. We worked together for many months. Empathy and alliance kept the patient in treatment until he was ready to change.

The following are some common open-ended questions that express sincere concern, build a therapeutic alliance, and explore motivation for change. These must all be delivered with positive regard for the patient.

- How can I help you?
- What are some things you like about drinking? Drug use? What else? Please tell me more.
- What's the other side? What are the not-so-good things about drinking? What are the not-so-good things about drug use?
- What's helped in the past when you tried to change something about yourself?
- What are some strengths you can build upon if you decide to change your drinking/drug use?

Developing Discrepancy

Motivational Interviewing (MI) theory states that a desire for change is created when a discrepancy is noted between present behavior and the patient's values or future goals. For example, one patient's desire to not break the law conflicted with a driving while intoxicated (DWI) arrest. In a supportive way, I helped her take a look at how her drinking had violated her values. This prompted a change in her drinking behavior.

Another man experienced his turning point when he said, "If I keep smoking crack, I'll lose my marriage." Empathy kept him open as I helped him explore how his present behavior would lead to a divorce. Now I could have easily confronted his behavior by saying, "What did you think was going to happen to your marriage if you kept using crack?" It might have worked…or he might have become defensive and dropped out.

The following are some reflections MI therapists use as they listen carefully and then turn a mirror toward what they have heard. The discrepancy is created when the patient realizes that addictive behavior conflicts with important goals.

- Your daughter is the most important thing in your life, and when you drink she says you embarrass her.

- You really value being productive at work, but recently you've noticed you aren't as sharp because you're hungover.

- You're worried about your health because your doctor told you about your liver being adversely affected by your alcohol use.

Avoiding Argument

Defending leads to defensiveness. Early in my career I found myself arguing with patients about their disease. With empathy, I foster an exploration of both the reasons they like using drugs and the not-so-good things about using drugs. This open discussion leads to an awareness that their drug use will negatively affect their life, if it isn't already. Today, when I find myself wanting to argue, I know it's my signal to change the therapeutic direction.

"I'm gonna keep getting drunk no matter what you or my parole officer thinks. This is B.S. I don't have a drinking problem," said one patient. Many traditional alcoholism therapists would respond, "Here's a great example of your denial. You're not getting that you have a disease."

Expressing empathy and rolling with the patient's resistance, instead, leads to several other possible responses. For example, "You don't see this as problem in your life," or, "You don't want to be told what to do about your drinking." By reflecting the patient's thoughts, the therapist reduces the level of resistance. As Socrates said, "I learn what I believe as I hear myself speak." Patients get a chance to hear their thoughts. In Motivational Interviewing, one of the main goals is to increase the number of "change talk" statements. These statements come in many varieties:

- **Concern about self:** "Drinking is wrecking my health."
- **Concern from others:** "My kids hate when I drink."
- **Intention to change:** "I need to quit right away."
- **Optimism about change:** "I believe I can quit."

MI therapists listen for change talk and reflect it back to the patient. Hearing their own words seems to harness their motivation for change. On the other hand, resistive statements such as, "I don't drink any more than any of my friends" are a signal that the person is not ready for change. Instead of confronting, we suggest further exploration of the person's perspective.

Supporting Self-efficacy

Albert Bandura, a psychologist famous for his theories on Behavior Modeling, found that people who believed they were competent were able to change a behavior much more easily than those who did not. As mentioned in a previous chapter, this belief in personal competence and ability to change is called self-efficacy.

An empathic therapist leads the patient to discover hidden strengths and supports the belief that change is possible. This is done by reviewing past successful changes and by looking at present positive coping behaviors (such as, "You're here and talking about this honestly. It's a great start!"). The therapist can also shape the patient's change behavior with verbal reinforcement. I regularly find myself saying, "Just one month ago, you didn't think you had a problem. Now not only do you attend AA meetings, but you also have a sponsor and avoid drinking situations. That's great progress!"

How Does Therapist Empathy Work?

First, empathy facilitates honest sharing about concerns as well as a discussion of what the patient enjoys about drug use. The patient takes a guided tour of the pros and cons of change. "If I quit drinking I can get my driver's license back but I won't have my friends at the bar," said one patient. This ambivalence is common and therapist empathy can help sort it out.

Secondly, empathy supports treatment compliance and adherence. Much of the research has shown that patients need the proper "dose" of treatment to benefit. Dropping out is a chronic problem in chemical dependency treatment. Treatment compliance is measured by tracking the patient's follow-through on specific tasks, such as taking medication for cravings, attending group sessions, and completing assignments. Empathy increases treatment compliance and creates a better chance for long-term success.

One recent example is a patient who seemed ready for change. However, he missed several sessions and was not available by phone. Empathy helps the therapist realize that change is difficult under the best circumstances, let alone when the patient's entire family drinks. Handwritten letters expressing concern, giving different contact options, and letting patients know that even if they have used it's okay to return to treatment have significantly reduced my dropout rate.

Finally, therapist empathy works by not turning the patient away from treatment. Several patients have said, "I really don't want to go to treatment. I can't stand people yelling at me. They act like they know me better than I do."

Patients have the right not to change. If a patient is not ready now, they may be ready later. If a patient believes that they will be listened to and supported in treatment, they are more likely to one day become "help seekers."

One of my mentors, Lance Longo, MD, is a proponent of the empathetic model. I asked him to relate some thoughts on addiction in general and the successful intervention theories he's been using lately. Here's what he had to say:

Treatment has to be based on an individual's characteristics— their motivation, their support system, their resources, and their needs. Initially the most important thing to do is ascertain how ready a person is to make changes in their life and to help them match their desire and their resources to treatment opportunities.

Motivational Enhancement Therapy helps a patient by demonstrating that the consequences of their behaviors have outweighed the benefits of their behaviors.

New Connections

When patients need intensive outpatient treatment, we work in conjunction with an award-winning nonprofit organization called New Connections in Contra Costa County, California. We've formed this alliance to care of our patients that need more concentrated treatment.

This program, which is accredited by the Commission on Accreditation of Rehabilitation Facilities (CARF), runs on weekday evenings and Saturday mornings. This allows patients with nine-to-five jobs to remain in the mainstream of their lives. This unique schedule fits perfectly with our philosophy to tailor our program for the middle-class Hidden.

Named as one of the top twenty programs in the United States by the National Association of State Alcohol and Drug Abuse Directors and the National Prevention Network, their work in peer/family support for recovering addictive/dependent patients rounds out the Gracer Program's biological, psychological, and social tiers.

Jeri Stegman, MA, RAS, the director of programs and services for New Connections, employs a cognitive approach known as The Matrix Model to help patients create peer relationships and ties to counselors in an effort to build self-esteem. As he describes it,

> The Matrix model helps clients to re-examine their belief systems regarding drug use, much of which is subconscious or unconscious... Substance abusers develop belief systems that allow them to continue using despite negative consequences. You have to replace them with beliefs that support recovery.

When people have the courage to come into treatment they are quite fragile and have little self-esteem. They develop a relationship with the agency that is able to help them, and they develop a comfort level. If they are able to get all or most of their needs met in one place it makes the changes much easier.

Chapter Fifteen
The Cravings and the Cure

The buprenorphine helped, but I was only on it for a few days before it was tapered and stopped. Then the cravings took over.

At first I was so excited that I wasn't on drugs that I didn't think about getting back on the Oxycontin. But when the cravings hit I wanted to get high again. I kept thinking how much better it would feel to get high than to cope with the intense pain of reality. I crushed some hillbilly heroin and injected it in the bathroom. My four-year-old daughter caught me and when she asked me what I was doing I told her I was taking medicine the doctor gave me.

I lied to my daughter.

So I tried even harder to deal with the cravings but I missed the euphoria after shooting up. I'd felt like crap for so long, and it felt so good to get high again. Plus, nobody tells you what cravings are really like when you're trying to get off drugs, alcohol, or even cigarettes. They tell you they're bad, but words can't express how hard it is. Everything makes you think about your fix—I see kids laughing and I remember the time I shot up and laughed at myself in the mirror for two hours. Golf clubs remind me of needles. Stupid stuff.

Then the cravings kick in and you know that it's physical, not just mental. My new doctor, Dr. Gracer, told me about dopamine and the GABA receptor. I didn't really understand most of it except to realize that the battle I'm fighting is as much physical as it is mental. But now I'm back on the buprenorphine to control the cravings, in a twelve-step program for counseling and support, and have used the Prometa protocol to deal with my alcoholism. All of these pieces are coming together to take care of my problems—like they're different articles of clothing suiting me for life.

So remember, if you quit your drug of choice, great. But deal with the cravings or you'll be back with the pill, needle, or bottle before you can take any steps, let alone twelve.

* * *

Cravings are the primary cause of relapse from addiction. They are the result of both the physical changes in the GABA and dopamine systems in the brain that have been discussed earlier in this book, and psychological responses that are conditioned through repeated social interactions. Even if the "brain disease" is treated with medications or nutritional intervention, these non-medical cravings can lead to relapse. Likewise, if the physical cravings are not dealt with, most patients will sooner or later succumb.

When a craving hits, it typically lasts less than an hour or two before abating. This is why patients are urged to call a sponsor (as in a twelve-step program) for the accountability and support they need to make it past the craving. This is also why patients are urged to stay away from the people and environments that could trigger cravings (for example, alcoholics should avoid bars).

In order to successfully stay clean, a patient needs to understand how cravings are triggered in the first place. The cognitive aspects of managing cravings can be impossible to grasp while dealing with the chemical side of the experience. This is why Gracer Medical deals with the chemical side along with the other factors that fuel addiction.

This chapter will first describe the most modern and revolutionary medical treatments available to treat the "brain disease" of addiction and then show you how to avoid the pitfalls of ongoing psychological cravings. Later chapters will describe important nutritional factors and treatments that can make a huge difference in cravings and general health. Together these methods are powerful help for your recovery.

Treatments

The initial success of protocols such as Prometa show how resetting or regenerating the brain receptors can lessen addictive or dependent behavior. It can even lead to the normalcy enjoyed before drugs were ever taken. Other medications, such as monthly injectable naltrexone (Vivitrol), camprosate (Campral), and buprenorphine decrease cravings and are an important part of modern treatment programs.

Different addictions, of course, require different treatments. The following are some of the most cutting-edge in use today.

Primary Medical Treatments

- Buprenorphine–Opiates
- Prometa Protocol–Alcohol and the stimulants cocaine and methamphetamine
- Naltrexone (Vivitrol), monthly injection–Alcohol and opiates
- Camprosate (Campral)–Alcohol

Other Medications

- Nicotine replacement (gum, patch, inhaler), buproprion (Wellbutrin), new strategies to reset receptors–Nicotine

- Modafinil (Provigil)–Cocaine and possibly methamphetamine

- Topiramate (Topamax)–Alcohol and probably nicotine

- GHB/Xyrem–Alcohol, cocaine, and methamphetamine

The Promise of Prometa

It became obvious to me early on that the Gracer Program needed to include patients addicted to substances such as alcohol, nicotine, marijuana, cocaine, and methamphetamine, as the treatments available for these substances were as dysfunctional as those for opiate addiction. Fortunately, it was around this time that I read about the Prometa protocol.

After a clinical conference with David Smith, MD, the chief scientist at Hythiam, the company that licenses Prometa, I began using it at our clinic. Prometa treats alcohol, cocaine, and amphetamine abuse by dealing with the severe cravings that usually cause relapse. This is the first process I am aware of that actually affects cravings caused by stimulant withdrawal. Here is some specific information from Hythiam's website:

> Hythiam's Prometa treatment protocols treat individuals diagnosed with dependencies to alcohol, cocaine, or methamphetamine, as well as combinations of these drugs. The Prometa protocols address both the neurochemical imbalances in the brain and some of the nutritional deficits caused or worsened by substance dependence. The protocols also provide for psychosocial or other recovery-oriented therapy chosen by the patient in conjunction with their treatment provider. As a result, Prometa represents an innovative approach to managing alcohol, cocaine,

or methamphetamine dependence that is designed to offer patients an opportunity to sustain their recovery.

Amongst the numerous important aspects of the Prometa protocol is the focus on social and psychological factors as well as nutritional supplements. Prometa is also discreet and doesn't require long periods away from home or work, which means that middle-class patients feel comfortable with this treatment. Finally, the medications used in the protocol are not habit-forming or addictive.

Although the precise way that the Prometa protocol works is not known, it appears to reset GABA and perhaps other receptors in the brain. An intravenous medication (flumazanil) combined with two other oral medications is delivered following a specific protocol. Although we cannot be absolutely sure of the true clinical effect of the Prometa protocol until the double-blind clinical studies that are underway at UCLA, Cedar Sinai Hospital in Los Angeles, and at the University of South Carolina are available, the results we have seen in our clinic are excellent, as are the findings of numerous studies included in the following tables:

Completed Studies and Pilots		
INSTITUTION / INVESTIGATOR	# OF PATIENTS	DESCRIPTION
Harold Urschel, M.D. Research Across America	50	Open label study testing efficacy treatment of methamphetamine * STUDY COMPLETED
Gary Indiana Justice System	30	Drug court pilot for cocaine and crack cocaine offenders * PILOT COMPLETED
State of Washington (Pierce County Alliance)	40	Pilot for methamphetamine and cocaine dependent offenders * PILOT COMPLETED

15-1: Completed Studies and Pilots Table 1

Remember that most addiction treatment programs have only a 15 percent success rate, probably less for methamphetamine addiction. Nothing comes close to the results that have been reported using Prometa.

INSTITUTION / INVESTIGATOR	# OF PATIENTS	DESCRIPTION
Dr. Joseph R. Volpicelli/ Dr. Jenny Starosta	60	short-term double-blind placebo-controlled study of PROMETA's Addiction Research Institute acute and immediate effects on cravings and cognition in alcohol dependent subjects
Dr. Harold Urschel	84	short-term double-blind placebo-controlled study of PROMETA's Research Across America acute and immediate effects on cravings and cognition in methamphetamine dependent subjects
Fulton County Justice System	20	Pilot for stimulant dependent criminal justice population
Walter Ling, M.D. UCLA	90	Randomized; multi-site double-blind, placebo controlled clinical study testing efficacy for treatment of methamphetamine
Jeffrey Wilkins, M.D. Cedars-Sinai Medical Center	80	Randomized controlled clinical study testing efficacy for treatment of alcohol dependency
Raymond Anton, M.D. Medical University of SC	60	Double-blind, placebo controlled clinical study testing efficacy for treatment of alcoholism
Parallax Center	100	Alcoholism Pharmacoeconomic
Southern University	30	Open label study testing efficacy treatment for alcohol and substance dependent offenders accepted for drug court
State of Idaho	30	Pilot for methamphetamine dependent offenders; successful outcome will result in statewide adoption
Donald R. Wesson, M.D.	750	Prospective, open label, observational study of patients who are treated according to PROMETA™ Treatment Protocol

15-2: Completed Studies and Pilots Table 2

Physicians' Experience with Prometa

As of April 2006 more than 450 patients had been treated with Prometa by physicians in the US. Two physicians have performed retrospective reviews.

A Florida licensee reported that 92 percent of his patients experienced remission when he combined the Prometa treatment with 90 days of intensive psychosocial therapy.

Of 36 patients, 33 who completed this treatment had immediate, dramatic gains in functional improvement. The doctor felt this constituted remission of the disease.

A California licensee reported that of 63 patients, 73 percent were in remission 90 days after initiation of the Prometa treatment.

That's 92 percent and 73 percent remission rate at ninety days after treatment. These numbers are much higher than those seen with traditional treatments.[1]

Prometa and Meth

America is suffering a methamphetamine epidemic. According to federal estimates, more than 12 million Americans have tried it and 1.5 million are regular users. Up until now, there have been no viable treatment options. Prometa's potential ability to reset brain receptors, however, targets the physiology of the brain instead of the morality of the individual.

Harold Urschel, MD, presented his study of 50 methamphetamine patients treated with the Prometa protocol in June 2006. He found that the protocol created a statistically significant reduction in methamphetamine cravings and use. The positive effect was seen almost immediately, usually within the first three days, persisted more than two months after treatment—even without other therapy or social support. The study reported that cravings were reduced in 97 percent of patients. Eighty-five percent stayed in treatment and 80 percent reduced their meth use.

Dr. Urschel also noted that "...the Prometa treatment resulted in immediate improvement in our subject's cognitive functioning, including memory, alertness, and concentration. Additionally, we saw improved sleep patterns and a decrease in anxiety,"[2] which can help patients learn the coping skills they need for long-term abstinence.

Case Study: Ed

Ed was a thirty-year-old "boy-man" who lived in a single-room, converted shed in his parents' backyard. He had started taking drugs when he was fourteen and used almost every type of drug you could think of, but it was the meth that had ruined his life. Although he was a member of a major trade union, Ed had not worked in over five years.

His days consisted of finding meth and using. As is the case with most meth heads, he would go for days without sleep and then "crash" and sleep for days. When he woke up he would feel depressed, tired, and achy. The only way to relieve the feeling was to use again. Whenever he tried to stop, the withdrawal became intolerable.

Ed's parents were middle-class, educated folks who did not use drugs and barely drank. They were at the end of the line. Either he needed to make a change or he was out. Ed loved his parents but felt very distant and ashamed. He would not eat with the family and was a very lonely person.

Ed's mom heard an ad on the radio about Prometa. She called and was referred to our clinic. When Steve and I met Ed, he was skeptical that anything could take away the severe withdrawals that had enslaved him for so many years. After a thorough evaluation we agreed to treat him with the Prometa protocol.

Ed was treated with a three-day IV protocol the first week. By the second day his mood improved and he slept better than he had for years. After the third day he was elated and had minimal if any withdrawal symptoms. Over the next three weeks Ed saw Steve regularly. I treated him for depression and he continued to do well. The second two Prometa treatments came after the third week. By that time, Ed was sleeping well and his mood had leveled out. He got to work re-establishing his life.

A closer analysis of Ed's psychological condition showed that he suffered from attention deficit hyperactivity disorder (ADHD) and was probably bipolar. ADHD is often treated with stimulants, including amphetamines. Ed had treated himself, and because of addictive genetics he got hooked. I started him on atomoxetine (Strattera), a non-stimulant treatment, and he responded beautifully. Quitiaprine (Seroquel), a mood stabilizer, helped him to sleep even better.

Since his treatment over three months ago, Ed has had no cravings. He has been in regular therapy with Steve and has worked out most of the problems with his folks. The latest news is that he is returning to work, but not to his previous job, as that is where many of his drug connections were. The initial elation has receded, but his depression is well controlled and we are monitoring his condition carefully. Although the last time I saw Ed he told me he was ready to return to life, his prognosis is still guarded due to his bipolar problems and his impulsiveness. Prometa surely helped him over the cravings, but his social and psychiatric problems remain.

The Prometa Treatment and the Gracer Program

It is important to stress that the Prometa protocol is not a stand-alone treatment. By this I mean that it is used as an important part of our comprehensive program.

The Prometa treatment protocol includes:

- A full multi-factor evaluation
- Nutritional supplements and medication for the first month

- Either the Prometa alcohol or stimulant intravenous therapy protocol

- Professional counseling following the initial treatment

There are, in fact, two Prometa treatment protocols. Prometa for alcohol dependence involves two or three days of intravenous treatment, depending upon the patient's specific clinical condition. Prometa for stimulant dependence (cocaine or methamphetamine) includes a second medically supervised treatment of two visits about three weeks after the initial treatment.

The intravenous treatment takes about one hour. It is painless and virtually without side effects. Most patients go home and relax for the rest of the day. Many take a nap. Patients usually sleep very well and feel rested the next day. Often the physical cravings and/or withdrawal symptoms rapidly resolve. They usually do not return.

Four important aspects of Prometa are:

- Patients receive treatment in a private setting.

- Patients receive initial treatment quickly (in two to three days).

- Treatment is essentially painless and non-invasive.

- It is vital to treat the underlying psychiatric issues and address the social triggers, as these can cause relapse even without the physical cravings.

Buprenorphine (Subutex/Suboxone)

Two of the medications used in the Gracer Program to combat cravings are Subutex and Suboxone. Both contain buprenorphine, and Suboxone also contains naloxone, a drug that will cause severe withdrawal if a patient uses the medication incorrectly (for example, by grinding it up and injecting it). The Gracer Program advocates the use of buprenorphine to help patients detox or wean off of opioids. Although our goal is to get patients completely off drugs, many need to stay on buprenorphine to control cravings for a protracted period of time.

The benefits of buprenorphine are:

- Suppresses withdrawal symptoms and drug cravings.

- Avoids the strong effects caused by prescription painkillers, heroin or methadone.

- Sticks to the brain's receptors for several days, making it difficult for other opioids to attach.

- Partially stimulates morphine mu receptors, dramatically decreasing withdrawal and post-acute withdrawal.

- Only stimulates these mu receptors up to a point, so increasing doses eventually have no further effect.

- Blocker of kappa receptors, giving it a unique antidepressant and anti-craving effect, often at tiny doses.

Buprenorphine is called a partial agonist, or stimulator, for the opiate receptor. Opiates are full agonists. A partial agonist occupies the receptor site but only partially stimulates it. After a certain amount of buprenorphine is present, adding more has no additional effect. This is called a ceiling effect.

Buprenorphine eliminates withdrawal and treats pain to a certain extent. It is therefore important that its use be timed correctly. The first dose should be taken just as withdrawal starts. If taken too early, acute withdrawal can be induced; administering the first dose too late causes needless suffering.

Buprenorphine allows the endorphin process to slowly regenerate. For most people the buprenorphine dose can be gradually reduced. However, many individuals will never completely recover their ability to make endorphins or their receptors will never completely regenerate. For them it may be necessary to continue treatment indefinitely. Buprenorphine is a far better alternative than opiates and can help these people lead normal lives.

Here's what Kathleen Thompson-Gargano, of the National Alliance of Advocates for Buprenorphine Treatment (NAABT) and co-founder of NAABT.org, says:

> Buprenorphine is unique. My patients categorically refer to it as a miracle drug and they do so within the first hour of taking their first dose. Because of this I am befuddled that buprenorphine is not yet a household word. Patients who have experienced the difference between buprenorphine and any other treatment are not interested in the non-buprenorphine alternatives.
>
> I have had the privilege of working with more than 400 opioid-addicted patients in our studies at Yale. At the onset of buprenorphine treatment patients tend to ask how long they will have to be on the medication. By the end of the study they are trying to get help to remain on the medication, not because they have switched addictions, but because they have accepted the physiological fact that they need help.

In an editorial that appeared in the *American Family Physician* on May 1, 2006, David A. Fiellin, MD, of the Yale University School of Medicine noted that:

> Nearly 10 percent of high school seniors have experimented with prescription drugs.
>
> Detoxification through opioid withdrawal is not an effective treatment for most patients with opioid dependence. This finding has been demonstrated in a wide spectrum of patients, including highly motivated patients, and reflects the disruption of normal brain function that occurs with long-term use of opioids and the need for ongoing treatment. *The relapse rates approach 90 percent at six months after detoxification through withdrawal.* [Emphasis mine.]

It's clear that, without buprenorphine, the results in even the best circumstances are dismal.

For an easy-to-understand analogy describing how buprenorphine eases cravings and post-acute withdrawal, please see the mechanics of addiction section in Chapter Eight titled The Addicted Brain.

Buprenorphine and Depression

In some people, buprenorphine has a unique relation to depression. Many patients with chronic pain who have been on opiates for a long time may develop addiction issues. It is often necessary to wean them off opiates to see if their pain will be tolerable or even disappear without medication. The Gracer Program uses buprenorphine for this. However, while it is easy to start patients on buprenorphine and get them off opiates, weaning and stopping the buprenorphine can be difficult.

Some of this is because the opiate addiction has created changes in the brain. Another reason is that buprenorphine seems to have powerful antidepressant properties. Opiates stimulate different receptors, mainly the mu receptor. This receptor is responsible for pain relief and for the GABA stimulation that leads to opiate-induced euphoria.

Another receptor activated by opiates is the kappa receptor. Selective stimulation of this receptor under laboratory conditions shows that kappa stimulation causes moodiness, depression, edginess, and nausea. Selective blocking of kappa sites can help depression. Buprenorphine is a powerful blocker of the kappa receptors, and even at tiny doses can eliminate these symptoms.

The combination of partial mu stimulation and kappa blockage is probably what makes buprenorphine an effective antidepressant. Several patients have told me that, since being on buprenorphine, they feel better than they ever have. These patients have a very difficult time stopping buprenorphine.

Many of them only require a tiny dose to maintain their feeling of wellbeing. For example, a common dose when switching patients from opiates to buprenorphine is from eight to 24 milligrams per day.

It is quite easy to gradually decrease this dose to about 6 milligrams per day. At this point, symptoms may arise. Several patients now taking as little as one milligram daily feel fine. When they stop, though, they feel edgy, depressed, and achy. These feelings can persist for weeks. Some of these patients eventually feel better, but many others have to return to taking buprenorphine in tiny doses.

Post-acute withdrawal syndrome (PAW) is characterized by similar symptoms. Many of these patients probably suffer from this problem. It is also possible that they have a form of depression that has been left untreated after detox.

A study done at Harvard showed buprenorphine to be effective in the treatment of treatment-resistant depression in ten patients.[3] Another study[4] showed the same result. In addition, they state that the kappa receptors are in overdrive after opiate addiction. This is probably a major cause of PAW. Kappa overactivity may also be why these patients respond so well to buprenorphine for depression that is resistant to other treatments. This may be an important factor in the cravings that cause relapse.

Another issue worthy of consideration is that many addicted people self-select the substances they abuse. Someone with severe anxiety is not likely to seek out cocaine or amphetamines, but may self-medicate with alcohol. Those with depression and pain may seek out opiates to relieve their depressive symptoms. It's important to treat a patient for every aspect of their addiction (physical, therapeutic, and social) and to understand how their various symptoms interrelate.

GHB/Xyrem

GHB (gamma hydroxybutyrate), or Xyrem, initially got a bad reputation as the date-rape drug when individuals used it for its intoxicating effects. However, the medication has since been FDA approved for treatment of narcolepsy, a rare sleep disorder. The medication, manufactured by Jazz Pharmaceuticals, has also been recently approved in Europe for treatment of fibromyalgia. A large, multi-center study is under way in the US for the same application. Xyrem also decreases cravings and has been studied for use in alcohol and cocaine withdrawal.

GHB is close in structure to GABA and acts on those receptor sites. It also affects dopamine levels in the brain. Patients who take this medication feel relaxed and sleep well, as it is dosed at night. The sleep architecture changes with GHB, delaying dopamine release until morning. Then it is released in increased amounts. This combination of effects increases daytime alertness and decreases cravings and depression.

In studies on alcohol detox, GHB has been found to be safe and effective. It also helps patients stay abstinent. We use GHB off-label for fibromyalgia, drug cravings, and sleep problems. In other patients it can help treat specific forms of depression.

GHB can only be obtained through a specialty pharmacy.

Modafinil (Provigil)

Modafinil (Provigil) is a unique and interesting drug. It is a stimulant, but is not related to amphetamines, methylphenidate (Ritalin), or cocaine. Modafinil works on the histamine system rather than the dopamine system. While it makes the patient more alert, the shaky, edgy sensations that the other stimulants bring are not present. Research has shown that there are no withdrawal symptoms after nine weeks of constant use.

Modafinil was first approved by the FDA for treating narcolepsy. Since then, it has been approved for use in sleepiness from obstructive sleep apnea and for evening or night workers (or anyone who works rotating shifts) who have problems staying up during work and sleeping when they should (this is called "shift work sleep disorder"). The National Institutes of Health (NIH) are now conducting a $10.8

million research study to see how effective the drug is in treating cocaine addiction. Modafinil may also be helpful in treating ADHD and depression. The drug is available over the counter (OTC) in some European countries and the manufacturer has an application with the FDA to make it OTC in this country.

Gracer Medical is using this medication in a variety of circumstances with excellent results. It can be used in combination with many of our other treatments. In addition to reducing cravings, modafinil might also help the brain to heal. Study results from on this subject could be ready in 2007.

Dr. Nora Volkow, director of the NIH's National Institute on Drug Abuse, says that the medicine is the most promising therapy for cocaine addiction. It may help restore proper dopamine function and also appears to block the high associated with cocaine use.

Dr. Charles Dackis of the University of Pennsylvania led a pilot study that suggested Modafinil more than doubled an addicted person's chances of staying off cocaine for at least three weeks. The main side-effect found in all the research is insomnia.

Modafinil also improves a person's mood, energy levels, and ability to concentrate. As seen in prior chapters, the ability to think rationally and get back to a normal life supports the efforts to break free of addiction.

Non-Prescription Approaches to Cravings

As described in Chapter Fourteen on Empathy and Enlightenment psychosocial (non-prescription) treatments have a proven positive effect. The four principles Carpenter/Brooks listed as important in facilitating behavioral change are:

- Coping skills
- Competing reinforcers
- Clinician-patient verbal interactions
- Social networks

These principles also apply to patients suffering from cravings. Patients must know the triggers that might lead them to relapse, such as an alcoholic going to a bar. The concept known as "recognize, avoid, and cope" can be employed here. Once a patient and physician understand the specific triggers, they create a list to help the avoidance/coping process. For instance, a patient who suffers from cocaine addiction can write down all the places they formerly purchased or used cocaine:

- Alley behind supermarket (met dealer)
- O'Doolin's Pub (snorted coke in the back room)
- The bathroom in my apartment

As you can see, some places are easier to avoid than others. It's possible that a patient might shower at their local gym. However, this measure is extreme and might only work over a short length of time. When someone can't avoid using their own bathroom, distraction can help them stave off temptation. They might purchase a waterproof radio and listen to inspirational music while they shower. Anything that keeps them from falling into typical using behavior can help them recover.

Some patients experience success by actually facing their cravings. The idea here is to prepare for the craving and experience it by analyzing where or how it affects them. Compare the experience to "hitting the wall" while running. Although physical discomfort will be unavoidable, recognizing and moving behind the pain provides a great sense of satisfaction. In the case of cravings, it helps patients readjust their mindset toward social triggers that used to bring them pleasure.

Another helpful tactic is to recall negative experiences. Some patients place photographs of their children in the medicine cabinet or other places where they'd normally keep their Vicodin or other prescription. They might write down a particularly painful experience and read it when tempted to use. Note that this tactic also is a form of distraction. Whichever method is used, it's important to keep away from the drug during the initial, most intense part of the craving.

Journaling is also very effective. Worksheets can be created between a physician and patient with a simple table like the one below:

Date	Time	Intensity	What I Did to Cope
5/16	Noon	8 on a scale of 10. Lasted 20 minutes.	Put on my running sneakers and sprinted around the block.

15-3: Journal sample

I highly recommend that patients discover multiple non-medication ways of dealing with cravings. These pre-planned alternatives can prevent relapse in the heat of the moment.

---

1 Hythiam.com, News Release, June 2006.

2 Urschel, H. News Release, *Research Across America*. June 2006.

3 Bodkin, J. A., et al. 1995. "Buprenorphine treatment of refractory depression." Consolidated Department of Psychiatry, Harvard Medical School, Belmont, MA, *J Clin Psychopharmacol* Feb; 15(1):49–57.

4 Fudala, P. J., et al. "Office-based treatment of opiate addiction with a sublingual-tablet formulation of buprenorphine and naloxone." *New England Journal of Medicine*. 2003. 349(10):949–958.

Chapter Sixteen

Alcohol

Written by Steven M. Peterson, LCSW, CADC III,
with an introduction by Richard I. Gracer, MD

Alcohol-related issues fill the pages of thousands of books and medical journals. As you read this chapter, please note similarities between alcoholism and addiction to opiates and stimulants, even smoking. Many of the physiological components are the same or similar for any substance. As with other forms of addiction, leading scientists agree that alcoholism is a disease, rather than a moral failing or lack of self-control.

Some non-traditional approaches for the treatment of alcoholism have started to convince the medical community and society at large that addiction to drinking stems more from physical issues than those of the psyche. In fact, Joan Larson, PhD, describes four physical types of alcoholics, which we will discuss later in this chapter. The Gracer Program uses this information along with other cutting-edge methods to evaluate and treat patients.

* * *

Case Study: Robert

Robert has been my patient for over twenty years. He has had severe neck pain and headaches, and for many years he took opiates. I was able to get him off opiates and he did well for over five years. Then he needed to have two vertebrae fused. After this he never got off of opiate pain medications no matter what I tried. He was employed at a high-paying job and functioned well. Although his dose was high, it was stable for years. I saw him every month and did his yearly examinations. He denied alcohol use and his labs were normal.

I was very surprised when he was admitted to the hospital with severe abdominal pain. He had been drinking for a long time and had escalated over several months when he ran into problems with his girlfriend. We stopped his opiates and stabilized his medical condition. He had pancreatitis, a life-threatening condition usually caused by alcohol that inflames the pancreas. When he was finally released, he was still experiencing severe abdominal pains and was so weak he could not work. His girlfriend broke off their relationship.

I tried to treat his depression, but he resisted medication, would not talk easily about his problems, and resisted psychotherapy. The abdominal pain, neck pain, and headaches, along with severe cravings, drove him to start drinking again.

Within a few days he was in very severe pain. He started taking high doses of aspirin and other anti-inflammatory medications. I simply would not give him more opiates. The GI specialist was unsure of the diagnosis. If he drank again, he would die.

This is when I basically mandated the Prometa program for him. He had been reluctant to undergo this type of treatment, saying he could deal with his own problems. Now it was life or death. Robert underwent the three-day Prometa alcohol protocol. By the second day he felt better, his mind was clearer, and his mood improved. He no longer craved alcohol. The problem simply disappeared. Robert became interested in getting psychotherapy and made real progress in understanding the problems in his relationship.

Robert told me that he could go to the supermarket and didn't even think about going to the liquor department. He no longer needed opiate medications for his continuing neck pain.

Robert's abdominal pain turned out to be an ulcer caused by the aspirin and anti-inflammatory medications. He almost died again when the ulcer perforated. Even with all of the stress, he has never thought about alcohol again. It has been over seven months since his Prometa treatment. He is back to work and his girlfriend is now his fiancé.

Prometa saved his life; of that I have no doubt.

The Dangers of Alcohol

After caffeine and nicotine, alcohol is the most widely used and abused drug in the United States. Alcohol is completely intertwined into our culture. From wine-tasting events in California to beer-chugging contests on college campuses, alcohol affects our lives in multiple ways.

Recently, much has been written about the beneficial use of alcohol for lowering cholesterol levels. This is certainly in contrast to the vast damage alcohol does to American culture. The information presented here is designed to document the fact that alcohol is an extremely damaging drug for individuals, families, communities, businesses, and society.

Although many of us consume alcohol in moderation, approximately 10 percent drink in problematic ways. This includes the 4 percent who become alcohol dependent. Hereditary factors appear to prime the pump for addictive use. Individuals who are not particularly sensitive to alcohol's influence due to genetics tend to drink more and sustain more damage.

Biological Damage

The immediate effect alcohol has is that of a general anesthetic. It depresses the central nervous system. Alcohol turns off parts of the brain, causing our biological computer to malfunction and eventually

The Cerebellum

The cerebellum of the brain in a normal person

The cerebellum with habitual alcohol use

The Ventricles

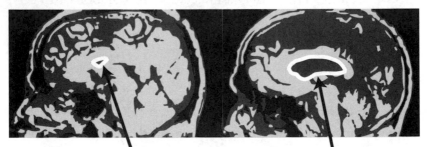

Ventricles of the brain in a normal person

Ventricles of the brain with habitual alcohol use

16-1: Shrinkage in the brain as a result of habitual alchohol use

shut down. The more alcohol consumed, the greater the malfunctions. Even relatively small amounts (one to three standard drinks) shut down the cerebral cortex enough to impair the judgment centers: Jokes are funnier. We no longer worry about the overdue mortgage.

Additional consumption results in emotional mismanagement. We may overreact by doing and staying things we would never have dreamed of while sober. All the while the person experiences euphoria because the pleasure centers of the brain are being stimulated.

When people binge (18 shots on their eighteenth birthday, for instance), they risk shutting down vital functions like breathing and blood circulation. This results in many deaths on college campuses each year, as well as the street deaths of chronic alcoholics.

Binge drinking is defined as consuming five or more standard drinks in one sitting for men and four or more drinks in one sitting for women. Around one-third of drinkers report binge drinking in any given month. Binge drinking is closely related to drunk driving and accidents such as drowning.

Moreover, binge drinking plays an important role in brain damage. The long-term damage of chronic alcohol poisoning can be documented with CT scans. This so-called "alcohol dementia" results in loss to permanent judgment and memory along with cognitive damage.

The National Institute of Alcohol Abuse and Alcoholism's 1993 report to Congress states that heavy alcohol use either directly or indirectly affects every organ system. Most susceptible are the brain, liver, heart, and the immune system. Prior to severe diseases such as jaundice (yellowing of the skin), we are often able to detect damage with liver enzyme tests like the GGT, ALT, and the AST. Unfortunately, doctors do not just ask enough questions after enzyme tests come back. If they did, it could lead to earlier intervention.

Drinking and accidents go hand in hand. One college fresh-
man in our practice underestimated the distance from her balcony
to the cement below. She broke her foot and remained in a cast
for most of the semester. Alcohol abuse accounts for roughly
35 percent of emergency room visits each year,[1] and in 2000 alone there
were approximately 85,000 deaths attributable to either excessive or
risky drinking in the US, making alcohol the third leading actual
cause of death.[2]

For women, there seems to be a telescoping effect. If a man
and woman drink the same amount, the woman is more harmed.
This is due to many factors, mostly related to women being smaller
than men are. For women of childbearing age, the consequences of
excessive alcohol consumption, particularly binge drinking, includes
unintentional injuries, domestic violence, risky sexual behavior, sexually transmitted diseases, unintended pregnancy, and alcohol-exposed
pregnancies.

Psychological Damage

Because the mind and body are joined, as alcohol damages the
body the mind is also affected. As the consequences mount, guilt and
shame overwhelm the drinker. In one of my cases, a father's shame
was so intense that he avoided his children. Many individuals report
negative worldviews when their emotional needs go unmet, making
alcohol use even more attractive.

Alcoholics report feeling isolated. They learn that intense feelings like anger, guilt, shame, fear, and loneliness can be numbed
with alcohol. A negative feedback loop is perpetuated as more drinking creates more depressive feelings, necessitating more drinking to
numb the depression.

Because of this, however, the risk of suicide increases exponen-
tially. Approximately 23 percent of suicide deaths are attributable to

alcohol.[3] We often hear about suicidal thoughts from patients who are intoxicated. When you feed a chemical depressant into an individual who feels depressed, the feelings are exacerbated. The treatment community calls this "double trouble."

Individuals who meet the criteria for alcohol abuse and alcohol dependence have a significantly increased risk for developing mental health disorders. The opposite is also true: individuals with mental health issues are more likely to abuse alcohol. We call this phenomenon, when alcohol abuse and mental health issues occur together, co-morbidity disorders.

The following diagram is taken from the National Co-morbidity Survey.[4] It shows the odds ratio for a given percentage of people who have alcohol dependence to experience certain psychiatric disorders, compared to those without alcohol dependence.

Psychiatric disorder	Individuals with alcohol dependence			
	Men		Women	
	%	Odds Ratio	%	Odds Ratio
Anxiety	35.8	2.2	60.7	3.1
Mood	28.1	3.2	53.5	4.4
Drug depend.	29.5	9.8	34.7	15.8
Antisoc pers.	16.9	8.3	7.8	17.0

16-2: Co-morbidity of alcohol and psychiatric disorders

Social Damage

The most significant damage from abusing alcohol occurs inside the family unit. Neglect and abuse influenced by parental drinking are daily topics in individual and group therapy. Nearly half of reported cases of child abuse and neglect are associated with parental alcohol or drug abuse. The pain of living in a family affected by alcoholism is well described by Claudia A. Black, PhD, in many of her books, such as *It Will Never Happen to Me* and *Changing Course: Healing from the Loss, Abandonment, and Fear.*

In addition to child neglect and abuse, other significant social problems like crime, drunk driving, sexual assault, and unemployment are closely correlated with excessive drinking. Many of the most heart-wrenching stories I've ever heard were told by women who became victims of sexual assault while intoxicated. Most of these patients blamed themselves, even if they were children or teenagers when the assault occurred. Other women who were sexually assaulted as children not only blamed themselves, but they used alcohol to numb the flashbacks. There is evidence that this type of abuse, especially at an early age, causes permanent physical damage to brain function that may result in addiction with other psychiatric illness.

Additionally, in 2002, 17,419 people in the United States died in alcohol-related motor vehicle crashes, accounting for 41 percent of all traffic-related deaths.[5] One elderly man I worked with several years ago told me that he had never gotten over killing a girl while driving intoxicated when he was in his thirties. The really frightening thing is that most people admit drinking and driving for years before being pulled over. Far more people are driving drunk than are being caught.

Young People and Alcohol

Drinking behavior starts at a young age. In 2003, 28.3 percent of 9th through 12th graders reported binge drinking at least once during the past thirty days.[6] I started my career working with adolescents and college students who had issues with alcohol and other drugs. The pain and difficulty these young people face is tragic. I have seen several situations in which young people have been killed as a result of their use. One boy I worked with actually froze to death on a train track after he passed out from drinking.

Each year in America approximately 5,000 young people under the age of 21 die as a result of underage drinking. This includes about 1,900 deaths from motor vehicle crashes, 1,600 homicides, 300 suicides, and hundreds from falls, burns, and drownings.[7] And those are just the deaths—approximately 72 percent of rapes on college campuses occur when victims are so intoxicated that they are unable to consent or refuse.[8] Other adverse consequences of underage drinking include risky sexual behavior and poor school performance.[9]

Our Basic Approach

People's relationship with alcohol goes back thousands of years. For most of us alcohol is not a concern. Those of us who work with people with alcohol problems, however, see the devastation to the mind, body, and soul that alcohol can bring. The fact that the treatment of alcoholism and mental health problems is so fragmented, combined with the lack of treatments for cravings, keeps treatment failure rates extremely high. This is why the methods we describe in this book are so important.

As with all disorders, we perform a comprehensive holistic evaluation before initiating treatment. Alcohol works differently in different groups of people. This is mostly dependent upon genetic factors, but is also influenced by social factors. For some, alcohol combines with other substances and acts as an opiate. In others it creates nausea and headaches. Some are allergic to it and others use it to raise their blood sugar.

While each of these types must be approached differently for optimum results, the basic nutritional strategy remains the same: stop the toxins, decrease the cravings, and rebuild the body's healing system. Replenishing what the body needs makes all the difference.

When an addicted person stops drinking, a cascade of events similar to those described in the opiate section occurs. These include over-excitation, anxiety, nausea, vomiting, muscle spasms, and even seizures. Post-acute withdrawal may last for years. Until recently, there has been little help. We now have new, potentially paradigm-shifting

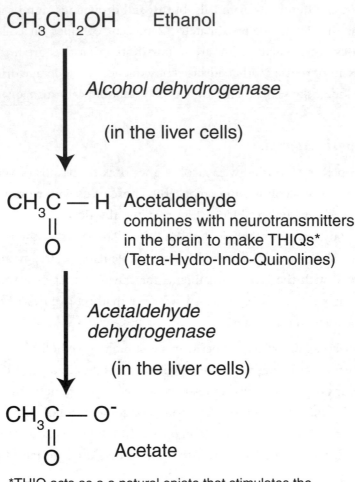

CH_3CH_2OH Ethanol

Alcohol dehydrogenase

(in the liver cells)

CH_3C — H Acetaldehyde
$\quad\ \ \|$ combines with neurotransmitters
$\quad\ \ O$ in the brain to make THIQs*
$\qquad\qquad$ (Tetra-Hydro-Indo-Quinolines)

**Acetaldehyde
dehydrogenase**

(in the liver cells)

CH_3C — O^-
$\quad\ \ \|$
$\quad\ \ O$ Acetate

*THIQ acts as a a natural opiate that stimulates the
opiate receptors in the brain the same way as a drug.

16-3 Alcohol metabolism

treatments such as the Prometa protocol and Vivitrol monthly injections. The difference this makes in patients' lives is remarkable.

Still, this in no way means that psycho/social treatment is not needed. A holistic approach is vital. This is why we also offer effective nutritional and hormonal treatments to help address this complex problem.

Alcoholic Types

Joan Mathews Larson, PhD, describes four physical types of alcoholics in her groundbreaking book *Seven Weeks to Sobriety*. The four types are:

- ADH II /THIQ
- Allergic/addicted
- Reduced EFAs (essential fatty acids) in the brain
- Hypoglycemic

The ADH/THIQ-type Alcoholic

Alcohol is metabolized by the liver in two separate steps. The first is the conversion of ethanol to acetaldehyde by the enzyme alcohol dehydrogenase (ADH). The second is the conversion of acetaldehyde to acetic acid by aldehyde dehydrogenase (AldDH). This product is used by the body to create fats or to burn for energy.

Acetaldehyde is toxic in high concentrations. It causes nausea, diarrhea, and abdominal cramps. The drug disulfiram (Antabuse) blocks the AldDH enzyme from working. This results in an accumulation of acetaldehyde in the body if the patient drinks. The unpleasant toxic effects act as a strong deterrent.

At the lower but still elevated levels common in alcoholics, acetaldehyde attacks the liver, heart, and nervous system. Unfortunately, toxic effects on the liver result in further deterioration of the liver's ability to process acetaldehyde. Even higher and more toxic levels of this compound are therefore produced.

Acetaldehyde also prevents the normal conversion and release of neurotransmitters in the brain, which may play an important role in alcohol addiction.

Since alcohol provides calories without any nutritional value, the liver, stomach, and pancreas are compromised. The absorption of vitamins and other nutrients suffers. Acetaldehyde also directly prevents activation of many vitamins.

Specific and well-known genetic differences affect how an individual's body responds to alcohol. For example, the efficiency of the enzymes in an individual depends upon genetics. Alcoholics with the gene for ADH II (a variant of the normal alcohol dehydrogenase enzyme) convert alcohol to acetaldehyde at twice the normal rate but then slowly convert acetaldehyde to acetic acid. This results in the ability to drink large amounts of alcohol without as much intoxication, only to suffer increased toxic effects.

In addition, acetaldehyde combines with some of the neurotransmitters to form THIQs (tetrahydroisoquinolines), which act as powerful opiates. The GABA receptors are affected by both the alcohol and the opiate-like THIQs and morph into the addicted, less-sensitive type.

The Allergic-type Alcoholic

We usually think of an allergy as hay fever or getting hives from bananas or penicillin. In my practice I have found many allergies are quite subtle with effects that are not easily connected to the offending substance. This is the case with most food allergies. For example, if you are allergic to wheat it is very difficult to connect feeling poorly to eating, as wheat appears at almost every meal.

Additionally, the allergic reaction can induce a burst of endorphins that initially makes us feel better. Then we suffer a letdown when it passes. The low-grade inflammation set up by this type of reaction can cause depression, pain, or other physical symptoms such as headaches, abdominal pain, and diarrhea. Eating the offending food temporarily helps, so it is common for people to crave the exact thing that causes the problem.

Dr. Larsen feels that many alcoholics have this type of allergy to alcohol. At first they have problems with drinking, but eventually they overcome their intolerance. They find that drinking decreases depression, and then later have a terrible hangover. They go back to alcohol to escape the pain. Many are binge drinkers. They may have severe mood swings when they drink and can be abusive. This problem can be complicated by additional allergies. These patients need a full nutritional evaluation to detect these and other metabolic imbalances.

Alcoholics with Reduced EFAs (Essential Fatty Acids) in the Brain

Other genetic factors influence the effects of alcohol. One governs the production of hormones called prostaglandins. These molecules regulate the most basic functions of our cells. Some cause inflammation and others decrease it. Prostaglandin E_1 (PGE1) is one of the most important anti-inflammatory compounds. If the level decreases, you can lack energy, feel depressed, and have a high risk of degenerative arthritis and heart disease. What we eat makes all the difference.

Alcohol stimulates the release of PGE1 in the brain. Since the amount is limited, the effect is short-lived. These patients feel relief with drinking only to have their depression recur soon after. They have to use increasing amounts of alcohol to maintain the effect. Many have significant psychiatric problems, including schizophrenia.

With these people the trouble often started in their teens. They may suffer from eczema, irritable bowel disease, premenstrual syndrome, or be diabetic. David Horrobin, MD, studied the effect of gamma-linolenic acid (GLA), an essential fatty acid, on PGE1 levels. He found that supplementing GLA could create major changes in PGE1 levels. His studies showed a significant reduction in alcoholic withdrawal symptoms, maintenance or sobriety, and even in liver disease in groups that took GLA. Barry Sears, PhD, has found that the addition of high-dose, highly refined fish oil that contains eicosapentanoic acid (EPA) greatly enhances this effect. (Please see the Nutrition chapter for more detail.)

At our clinic we evaluate our patients for this risk factor and supplement when indicated with oils from different natural sources. These supplements are inexpensive additions to a patient's holistic approach to breaking free of addiction.

The Hypoglycemic-type Alcoholic

Some hypoglycemic patients crave alcohol when their blood sugar gets low. Alcohol acts like sugar in the brain and relieves the symptoms quickly. These people have a low tolerance to alcohol and often get ill after a couple of drinks, yet the cravings are so intense that they drink even though they know they will suffer later. When the hypoglycemia is treated, the drinking stops.

This is only a brief overview of the alcoholic types. For more specifics and for tools to help you determine what type of alcohol problem you might have, please get a copy of *Seven Weeks to Sobriety*. Detox suggestions, a list of supplements, and dietary suggestions are included toward the end of this book.

You may also access more detailed information on our website. For individuals who wish to create lifestyle changes that will support their freedom from addiction over the long term, Gracer Medical has a book dedicated to nutrition and supplements in the works.

Treatment for Alcohol Cravings

Fortunately, today we have several medical treatments that we can use to combat alcoholism. These medicines drastically reduce or even eliminate cravings in an extremely short period of time. Gracer Medical uses the Prometa protocol, Naltrexone (Vivitrol), or camprosate (Campral) as needed. Below you'll find a description of each, along with a discussion of disulfiram (Antabuse) and topiramate (Topamax).

Prometa for Alcohol Cravings

Two US physicians reviewed their case histories and found that Prometa allowed up to 92 percent of patients to stay alcohol-free ninety days after treatment. Although double-blind university studies on the full efficacy and effect of the treatment are still underway, the protocol is so unique that we decided to offer it to our patients now.

Meanwhile, patients who undergo this treatment are astonished to find their cravings rapidly decrease within the first few days. Because Prometa is also used to treat cocaine and methamphetamine cravings, a detailed discussion of this protocol is found in Chapter Fifteen.

Naltrexone (Vivitrol)[10]

Of the more than 18 million Americans who abuse or are dependent on alcohol, approximately 2.2 million seek treatment. Unfortunately, with most currently available treatment approaches, more than 75 percent of these patients relapse within the first year.

Monthly injection of naltrexone (Vivitrol), a treatment recently approved by the FDA, offers new hope. The once-a-month injection means that patients don't need to take medication every day, thus helping to more consistently control cravings that lead to relapse. It works well for alcohol-dependent patients who are able to abstain in an outpatient setting and are not actively drinking when initiating treatment.

At Gracer Behavioral Health Services, we use naltrexone in combination with counseling and group therapy. This drug binds to opioid receptors in the brain. Although the mechanism is not entirely understood, preclinical data suggests that the binding action blocks the neurotransmitters involved with alcohol dependence.

As mentioned earlier in this chapter, alcohol is metabolized by conversion into acetaldehyde and then into acetic acid. Many alcoholics have the genetic predisposition to build up acetaldehyde in the brain. This combines with the brain's opiates, causing the same relaxation and euphoria of taking opiate drugs.

Monthly naltrexone injection works by taking away the euphoria. While Prometa and camprosate remove the negative aspects of withdrawal, naltrexone removes the "reward" that comes from consuming alcohol: it blocks the high.

Naltrexone injection is therefore very effective for people who struggle against the social triggers for drinking. Since social cravings occur separately from physical cravings, even someone who has successfully broken their physical addiction is still susceptible to social triggers. By blocking the opiate receptors, naltrexone takes away the reward, leaving the individual with no reason to drink.

Because naltrexone is an antagonist for opiates it is also used in ERs to treat opiate overdoses. By blocking the effect, it negates the euphoria and reward that drinking usually brings. The need to drink lessens and people can stop drinking more easily. Unlike disulfiram (Antabuse), naltrexone does not make you feel sick if you drink alcohol while taking it.

Garbutt and his group published a study of over 600 patients[11] that showed that patients who could abstain for seven days and then start Vivitrol had over 90 percent fewer drinking days than the placebo group. Those who were abstinent for at least four days were also much more likely to be abstinent. These findings show great promise for this treatment.

Key Benefits of monthly injection of naltrexone (Vivitrol)

- Reduces opiate-like effects of alcohol, blunting or removing the "reward" for drinking

- Helps patients remain abstinent and avoid relapse

- Decreases the tendency to drink more if a recovering patient slips and has a drink

- Requires only a once-per-month injection instead of a daily pill

Camprosate (Campral)

Camprosate is a medication that the Gracer Program has used with great success to decrease cravings. Like Prometa, the makers of Campral also recommend counseling or support groups in conjunction with the prescription. We have found that camprosate works well in conjunction with all of our other treatments. As two tablets must be taken three times a day, it is more difficult to use than naltrexone. It has minimal side effects, however, and works well with Vivitrol, as the combination blocks cravings and also decreases the high that many alcoholics experience.

The following information is taken from Campral's website:

Campral is the first new medication approved for the treatment of alcohol dependence, or alcoholism, as it is commonly referred to, in a decade.

Campral helps reduce the physical distress and emotional discomfort (e.g. sweating, anxiety, sleep disturbances) associated with staying alcohol-free... In several clinical trials, Campral was shown to help up to three times more people stay alcohol-free than placebo pills (sugar pills). In addition, for patients who did experience a slip, or relapse, Campral prolonged the periods of abstinence and reduced the number and severity of relapses.

Disulfiram (Antabuse)

This medication can prove effective but oftentimes leaves patients feeling nauseous. It blocks the full metabolism of alcohol leading to a buildup of acetaldehyde, which causes nausea and diarrhea. The problem with this treatment is that it is very easy to stop the medication in anticipation of drinking. While disulfiram decreases drinking in those who take it, it is not effective for most alcoholics. For a long time it was the only medication available for alcoholism. Now, with all the other treatment options available, it is not being used as much.

Topiramate (Topamax)

Topamax is an anti-convulsant medication that is particularly helpful for migraine headaches. In trials of patients with migraine problems, it was noted that it also decreased alcohol consumption. A research study done at the University of Texas Health Science Center at San Antonio[12] proved that the effect is real. It also decreased smoking in those treated.

It probably works by stimulating the GABA receptor at a different site than the usual drugs, and by increasing dopamine levels. Topamax also decreases appetite and is therefore very commonly used in overweight patients.

1 SAMHSA, 1999. Substance Abuse & Mental Health Services Administration.
2 Mokdad, 2004. Actual causes of death in the United States, 2000, *Journal of the American Medical Association.*
3 Smith, 1999. Fatal non-traffic injuries involving alcohol: A Meta Analysis, *Annals of Emergency Medicine.*
4 Kessler, Crum, Warner, Nelson, Schulenberg, & Anthony, 1997. Lifetime co-occurrence of DSM-III-R alcohol abuse and dependence with other psychiatric disorders in the National Co-morbidity Survey, *Archives of General Psychiatry.*
5 NHTSA, 2003. National Highway Traffic Safety Administration.
6 SAMHSA.
7 SAMSHA.
8 Mohler-Kuo, M., Dowdall, G. W., Koss, M. P., Wechsler, H. Correlates of rape while intoxicated in a national sample of college women, *Journal of Studies in Alcohol,* 2004, vol. 65, 37–45.
9 CDC, YRBS, 2001, Center for Disease Control, *Youth Risk Behavior Surveillance System report,* 2001.
10 Volpicelli, J., Watson, N., King, et al: Effects of naltrexone on alcohol "high" in alcoholics. *American Journal of Psychiatry* 152(4): 613–615, 1995. Note: Dr. Volpicelli has also completed much of the initial work on combining medication for cravings and behavioral therapy. For more see his book: *Combining Medications and Psychosocial Treatments for Addictions, The BRENDA Approach,* Guilford Press, 2001, ISBN 1-57230-618-1.
11 Garbutt, et al. "Efficacy and tolerability of long-acting injectable naltrexone for alcohol dependence: a randomized controlled trial." *Journal of the American Medical Association, 2005.*
12 Barclay, et al. *Archives of Internal Medicine, 2005.* 165:1600–1605.

Chapter Seventeen
Marijuana

We all know that marijuana affects memory and ambition. I recently heard a lecture given by Timmen Cermak, MD, a psychiatrist in private practice in the San Francisco Bay Area who has studied the effects of marijuana on brain function. Dr. Cermak elegantly described how marijuana acts in the brain and why its effects create the various symptoms we see in its users. Much of what follows comes from this insightful physician.

Effects in the Brain

THC (delta-9-tetrahydrocannabinol), the major active chemical in marijuana, acts on specific brain receptors called cannabinoid receptors. These are found in many areas of the brain, especially those dealing with memory, learning, concentration, pleasure, time perception, coordination, and emotions. THC is also active in areas that regulate appetite.

Why are there so many receptors for cannabinoids? After all, THC is not found naturally in the body. To answer this question, let's review how opiates work. Opiates activate the morphine receptor found in many parts of the brain. For our purposes, it is most important in pain regulation. The naturally occurring compounds that stimulate these receptors are called endorphins. Opiates are drugs that hyperstimulate these receptors.

The same pattern is seen for cannabinoids. The naturally occurring compound in this case is called anandamide. While it is not a true neurotransmitter, it does affect brain function. This type of chemical is called a neuromodulator because it modulates, or affects, neurons.

The Hippocampus–The Memory Center of the Brain

When we remember something it is first placed in our short-term memory, also called our working memory. Important facts are then deposited in our long-term memory, which functions somewhat like the hard drive in a computer. When we need it later, we can access it fairly easily.

Some things we know and use every day, such as language. Other memories are used sporadically and usually for certain tasks, like knowing which street to turn onto when visiting a friend. How long something stays in short-term memory and how efficient we are in copying it to our hard drives determines how easily we learn and how we function in our daily lives.

Scientists often use rats to study the effects of drugs on the central nervous system. Although humans are nothing like rodents, rat behavior mimics basic human behavior in many ways. Drugs often have very similar effects on both species.

When adult rats are placed in the same cage with younger rats they've never met, a sniffing ritual takes place. After the rats "get to know" each other, sniffing is not necessary even if they are separated for several hours. If they are separated for more than a few hours, however, the process has to be repeated.

When rats are given marijuana, the length of time they can remember the other rats is much shorter. This phenomenon is seen in marijuana users who forget the first half of a sentence before they finish the second half. THC blocks the creation of normal memory. Although this does not appear to affect prior long-term memories, people under the influence of marijuana have a much-reduced capacity for learning and retaining new information.[1] This is caused by a disruption of normal GABA function in the hippocampus.

The Amygdala–The Emotional Center of the Brain

The emotional content of our experiences is regulated in the amygdala. These effects determine how we feel about the information we draw from memory or current input. This directly affects our appetites (not just for food), painful memories, pain perception, anxiety and fear, and how our thoughts relate to our emotions.

Marijuana changes the emotional content of our thoughts. It decreases our inhibitions and makes us less critical. Dr. Cermak calls this drug effect "virtual novelty." When under the effects of THC, everything seems new. The impact on our senses is heightened. Unfortunately, users usually do not remember the experience! Meanwhile, the emotional effects of bad memories may be decreased. The ability to concentrate is impaired. The amygdala also stimulates appetite, so it's common for this to occur in marijuana users.

Over time, with ongoing marijuana use, the number of cannabinoid receptors in the amygdala decreases. This decreases the ability of the body's own version of THC, anandamide, to stimulate the brain's receptors. When they are not intoxicated, chronic marijuana users therefore have less ability to experience novelty and therefore are less interested in the world. In addition, the effects on short-term memory can linger for many months. This is not a good combination for high school students.

The Cerebellum–The Coordination Center of the Brain

Marijuana also modulates the cerebellum, the part of the brain that controls coordination. The impact slows reaction times. When combined with time distortion and decreased short-term memory, the result is lack of coordination and increased danger while driving and performing other manual tasks. It is interesting to note that while driving impairment for marijuana is less than for alcohol, marijuana users' driving impairment still exists the next day, although the effect is much reduced.

The Nucleus Accumbens–The Pleasure Center of the Brain

We experience pleasure when higher levels of dopamine are released in the nucleus accumbens. This effect is very important in all substance abuse. THC increases dopamine release. A decrease in the number of receptor sites also occurs in the pleasure center. There is some evidence that THC works through the same system as opiates, in part explaining its positive effect on pain.

The Prefrontal and Frontal Cortex–
The Executive Center of the Brain

The prefrontal and frontal cortex areas, along with our emotions, are what make us human. This is where our social skills and judgment reside. THC decreases blood flow to this area and also decreases the amount of glucose utilized, indicating that this part of the brain is not used as much as usual. Since glucose is the primary substance the brain uses for energy, poor judgment, poor planning, and a decreased ability to deal with complex situations results.

Cannabinoids modulate almost all of the critical functions of our brain. Because of the decrease in the number of receptors from chronic use, serious consequences may result along with withdrawal and long-term impairments.

Why Teens Smoke Marijuana

Teenagers in general, especially modern teens, have to be constantly entertained. They have cell phones, they text message, and they are always surfing and instant messaging on the computer. Without constant stimulation, they get bored. Since they are jaded, they don't experience any sense of awe.

Marijuana heightens their sensory experiences. They feel that they are funnier, happier, and less anxious. Other teens may self-medicate for anxiety and even for attention deficit hyperactivity disorder (ADHD). As an occasional escape, this may seem harmless. But because of the potentially serious brain changes described above, they soon have significant problems finding enjoyment and sensing the novelty in daily life. Their motivation is decreased. They become anxious, irritable, and depressed. Their solution is to get high again. Withdrawal may last up to six weeks, and maybe even longer, after discontinuing marijuana.

Marijuana is an addicting substance. Just as with the other addicted people, marijuana users continue smoking despite negative consequences. They are often in denial about having a problem because they are preoccupied with getting high.

Marijuana's withdrawal symptoms include anger, decreased appetite, irritability, anxiety, problems sleeping, and strange dreams. Plenty of data demonstrates that chronic marijuana users do much more poorly in school and graduate less often than their "straight" friends.

Other Effects of Marijuana Use

According to the National Institute on Drug Abuse (NIDA):

> Workers who smoke marijuana are more likely than their co-workers to have problems on the job.... Employees who tested positive for marijuana on a pre-employment urine drug test had 55 percent more industrial accidents, 85 percent more injuries,

and a 75 percent increase in absenteeism compared with those who tested negative for marijuana use. In another study, heavy marijuana abusers reported that the drug impaired several important measures of life achievement including cognitive abilities, career status, social life, and physical and mental health.

Research has shown that some babies born to women who abused marijuana during their pregnancies display altered responses to visual stimuli, increased tremulousness, and a high-pitched cry, which may indicate neurological problems in development. During the preschool years, marijuana-exposed children have been observed to perform tasks involving sustained attention and memory more poorly than non-exposed children do. In the school years, these children are more likely to exhibit deficits in problem-solving skills, memory, and the ability to remain attentive.

Another serious consequence is that marijuana smoke contains just as many cancer-causing substances as tobacco. The main difference is that marijuana contains THC while tobacco smoke contains nicotine. Marijuana users hold the smoke in their lungs longer, increasing their toxin exposure. Chronic users get chronic bronchitis just like cigarette smokers do. There is even evidence of an increased risk of lung cancer and heart attack in chronic marijuana users.

Interactions

Marijuana increases pleasure in the brain through a mechanism similar to opiates. Research also shows that stimulation of the cannabinoid receptors may trigger cocaine relapse. When laboratory rats are given cannabinoids, they increase their alcohol consumption. The fact is that many of our patients use marijuana along with other drugs. It is important to treat this addiction along with other substance problems.

Treatment

The same psychosocial techniques used for alcohol and stimulant addiction work for marijuana abuse. A clear explanation as to the effects and results of marijuana use and the benefits of stopping helps an individual get through withdrawal. Treatment of underlying psychiatric disorders, such as depression and anxiety, is also important. Helping users get through their denial and helping them to develop normal relationships is also effective.

One study of adult marijuana abusers, most of who had smoked for at least 10 years, found that a 14-session cognitive-behavioral group treatment had similar benefits as a two-session individual treatment. The shorter, personalized treatment sessions included motivational interviewing and advice on ways to reduce marijuana use. Education, awareness, and help with practical ways to avoid triggers were most helpful.

For many of these patients, symptoms and social problems improved for over a year. At the end of the study, 30 percent still did not use.[2]

Medical Marijuana

Several states have legalized the medical use of marijuana. Good evidence shows that cannabinoids decrease pain, anxiety, and nausea, especially after chemotherapy. Many people suffering from HIV/AIDS use marijuana to stimulate their appetite and to ease their suffering. There's some evidence that it also decreases the elevated eye pressure of glaucoma. Much of this may be due to the interdependence between the cannabinoid system and opiates.

Marinol is an FDA-approved oral medical form of marijuana that has been available for many years. It is very expensive and, according to a few of my patients, not as effective as the smoked form. For others, it seems to work well. Because of the controversy between federal and state governments (I live in California), I opt for the prescription form. I do, however, have a handful of patients who prefer to buy medical marijuana and who claim significant benefits with its use.

Rimonabant (Acomplia) is a medication under development that blocks the action of cannabinoids in the brain. It promises to help patients lose weight and also may be effective in smoking cessation.

Help is Here

At Gracer Behavioral Health Services, we evaluate all of our patients for marijuana abuse. Proper treatment can significantly decrease use of this drug. Stopping marijuana use entirely can significantly increase mental clarity and mood in substance abuse patients. In addition, there's evidence that marijuana use makes relapse for other substances much more likely. Parents should read Dr. Cermak's book, *Marijuana: What's a Parent to Believe?*

---

1 Terranova. "Improvement of memory in rodents by the selective CB1 cannabinoid receptor antagonist, SR 141716." *Psychopharmacology,* 126:1655-172. 1996.

2 Stephens, R.S., Roffman, R.A., Curtin, L. "Comparison of extended versus brief treatments for marijuana use." *Journal of Consultations in Clinical Psychology* 68[5]:898–908, 2000.

Chapter Eighteen
The "Cut Out Smoking" Craving Management Program

As this book deals with the major problems caused by substance abuse, it would not be complete if it left out the most common addiction of all: nicotine. The US Department of Health calls tobacco "the single greatest cause of disease and premature death in America today," with over 430,000 deaths each year. Nearly 25 percent of adult Americans—46 million people—are addicted. Every day, 3,000 children and adolescents take up the habit.

More than 70 percent of smokers want to stop. Fewer than 10 percent succeed. Think of how severe the addiction to nicotine must be if that many smokers want to quit, yet only a tiny fraction can.

Nicotine–An Introduction

Nicotine is rapidly absorbed through the mouth lining, not just through the lungs. Those who smoke pipes and cigars or chew tobacco get a large dose without inhaling and are also subject to its addicting effects. It appears that a gene makes an important enzyme that breaks down nicotine in the brain. This gene is less active in some persons than in others.

Research has shown that smokers with the less-active enzyme are more likely to smoke and that they have a harder time stopping. The theory is that when these people smoke, nicotine stays in the brain for a longer time, increasing the effects of the drug and the chances for addiction.[1]

Other work has shown that the brains of younger people are more sensitive to these effects. Although most teens try smoking because they think it's cool, genetics determines who gets hooked.

Another area of research shows that a common byproduct of smoking is acetaldehyde, the same compound formed when alcohol is metabolized. As with alcohol, acetaldehyde combines with endorphins to form compounds that activate GABA and morphine receptors. This gives a feeling of relaxation and, at times, euphoria and is apparently a major factor in the development of smoking addiction.

It is interesting that the acetaldehyde comes from smoking, not directly from nicotine. This may be a major factor in the limited effectiveness of nicotine patches, gum, and inhalers. It also may be the reason that smoking and other addictions reinforce each other.[2]

It is not a coincidence that twelve-step meetings for alcohol, opiates, gambling, or obesity have large numbers of people who smoke. Nicotine and smoking addiction work in the same areas of the brain as the other addictive drugs. Nicotine can also make the brain more sensitive to the effects of other addicting drugs, an effect that can last for some time after nicotine exposure.[3]

Additional studies show that liver enzymes must metabolize the various toxins associated with smoking. As they also metabolize drugs, these compounds are excreted much more rapidly. This means that higher doses of medications, especially pain medications, are needed for smokers. This adds to smokers' problems with many common diseases, such as coronary artery disease; their medication doesn't work as well.

How Nicotine Works in the Brain

Nicotine acts as a neurotransmitter, stimulating the same receptors used to activate skeletal muscles and the parasympathetic nervous system. While these receptors are found in many parts of the body, the most important ones in terms of smoking increase dopamine levels. Increased dopamine levels help treat depression and decrease anxiety.

These receptors rapidly get desensitized. The fact that nicotine is rapidly eliminated causes almost constant withdrawal because

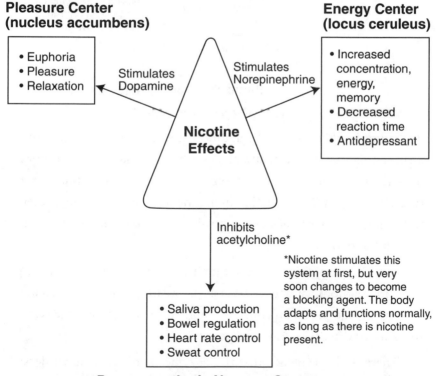

18-1: Effect of smoking or other nicotine use

Nicotine Withdrawal

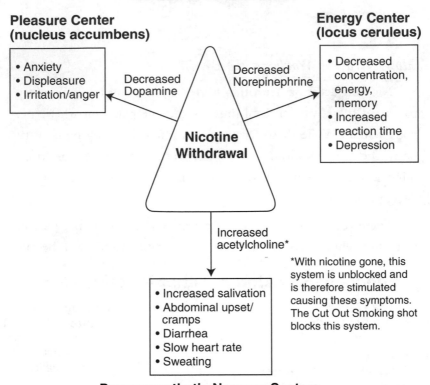

18-2: Nicotine withdrawal

dopamine levels decrease. In addition, there is evidence that after a short time nicotine actually blocks many receptor sites. To compensate, the brain produces more of a specific neurotransmitter (acetylcholine). When a smoker quits, the nicotine is no longer there to block the chemical messenger, resulting in overstimulation of neurons in the mid-brain.

Specific symptoms are created by this overexcitement, including salivation, abdominal cramps, diarrhea, sweating, increased irritability, anxiety, and problems concentrating. Note how close these symptoms are to drug withdrawal in general.

There is also evidence that the enzyme that breaks down dopamine in the brain is decreased in smokers. This results in more dopamine in the mid-brain, alleviating depression and anxiety. Then, when smoking stops, you end up with overstimulated neurons and decreased dopamine. This effect is so rapid and strong many smokers suffer if they don't smoke for just a short time. No wonder smokers have so much trouble quitting.

Perspective: Pack Mentality

Smoking makes other drugs more potent in the brain, while its effects on liver metabolism eliminates drugs more quickly. Addicted smokers get a more potent high from other drugs but need more frequent doses to maintain the effect. Since the withdrawal from nicotine is caused by almost the same mechanism as withdrawal from other medications, it can actually compel an addicted person to use more drugs. This is a deadly combination.

The fact that cigarettes are legal and easily available makes the problem almost insurmountable. Because people addicted to smoking can function normally in society, we usually leave smoking alone when we deal with the more serious and immediate problems of substance abuse. Since a majority of persons in recovery smoke, it's impossible for a patient to avoid temptation, a common treatment strategy.

Still, it is important to stop smoking. Nicotine addiction is an enormous public health problem. Fortunately, we have found a method of dealing with nicotine cravings that can allow patients to conquer their addiction.

The "Cut Out Smoking" Program

Many effective behavioral treatments are available to help you stop smoking. They include educational methods and psychological techniques to deal with that aspect of cravings. Some medical treatments, such as the nicotine patch or gum and the antidepressant buproprion (Wellbutrin, Zyban), also have a positive effect. All

cessation programs, including those that rely on psychosocial techniques, average a 20 to 25 percent success rate, with a maximum of
30 percent success when they are combined. These percentages prove
their value.

Yet telling adults that smoking is unhealthy is useless. Who
doesn't know that smoking is deadly? It is important for children
to learn this in school and to ensure that this information remains
common knowledge, but lecturing people can create frustration
and anger.

Since people commonly become addicted in their teens, we
must stop it before they start. Efforts should be made to make it less
appealing to young people. The best analysis I have read is in *The
Tipping Point,* Malcolm Gladwell's recent bestseller. The just ask philosophy applies to smokers as much as it does to those suffering from
medication addiction. People may understand some of the dangers
but likely aren't aware of increased drug potency on the brain and
other complications.

A colleague of mine who was a heavy smoker and finally quit
shared an important fact: the worst cravings occur the first day. *Many
smokers actually experience their worst cravings before they quit.* They
light up in response to cravings. They suffer these feelings many
times a day. If they can get past the first two to three days, things get
easier. The affected brain receptors readjust in about two weeks.

How to Stop Smoking

The initial step to Cut Out Smoking is an analysis of a person's
Readiness Quadrant (RQ). As with any addiction, the physical impact
of cravings is profound. However, a person's confidence and willingness to change are also of paramount importance.

The Smoking Shot–Blocking the Cravings

Many people have tried repeatedly to quit smoking using nicotine treatments plus buproprion or other medications. For those who still can't stop, Gracer Medical now has an effective way to markedly decrease or even eliminate cravings for the first two weeks or so, when they are the most intense. We first stress the more traditional ways to quit and always institute a behavioral program as part of any treatment. We also use buproprion and nicotine replacement. In those patients who have failed these methods, we use the following protocol.

Nicotine is eliminated from the body in about three days and the physical effects on the brain last about two weeks. It is important to block the system for a short time, and then keep it in check until it normalizes. By blocking the desire and allowing the receptors to be reconditioned, the hardest part of quitting becomes much, much easier.

On the first day our patients see a video outlining the treatment. After an appropriate medical history and physical examination, the physician gives the "smoking shot." These injections block the targeted brain receptors. For two weeks, patients take two types of pills to maintain the effect. According to three published studies, about 80 percent of patients treated this way are still successful after two months. Many stay off smoking for the long term.

The medications block the receptors in the mid-brain that would otherwise trigger the symptoms of nicotine withdrawal. In addition, the dry mouth that is a common side effect of this treatment makes smoking less enjoyable. The anticholinergic medications we use are common and safe, although they are not approved by the FDA for smoking cessation. This common type of medication usage is called "off label."

Note that this method has not been studied completely. A double-blind controlled study is currently underway. In addition, Gracer

Medical is conducting its own study. More definitive results will be available in one to two years. For now, the results from several doctors who have used this protocol on over a thousand patients have been excellent, with at least 75 percent of those treated staying off at least two months and some reports up to 60 percent after one year. We are in the process of carefully analyzing this data and will have it available on our website soon.

By this time, most people are over the physical addiction, so behavioral and psychosocial treatments are used to help them stay off. I want to stress that you should quit any way that you can. You should try again if you fail. Most patients try several times before they finally quit.

Behavioral Interventions

Medication alone will not create a successful long-term outcome if the patient is not ready to change. The medications also work much better when used with more traditional smoking cessation methods, such as behavioral changes. Behavioral interventions can be easily integrated with the medical protocol detailed above for the best chance at success.

Step 1. See yourself as a non-smoker.

Step 2. Find a support person or group.

Step 3. Remove and avoid triggers.

Step 4. Disrupt smoking-related behaviors.

Step 5. Substitute new non-smoking behaviors.

Step 6. Reward yourself.

Motivation for Change in Nicotine Dependence

Motivation is the key ingredient for a successful outcome in any change process. This is especially true for nicotine dependence because of the tremendous reinforcement to the brain that smoking provides. As one smoker put it, "I would rather have a cigarette than have sex." We start the motivational process with the worksheet on the next page.

After the worksheet has been filled out, we ask, "What do you make of this?" The individual gets a chance to sort out the pros and cons of cutting back or quitting. This helps the patient explore important benefits while being aware of the very real barriers.

These often appear under the Not-So-Good Things. Here the person confronts what they give up if they quit. For example, a smoker gives up the euphoria of nicotine as well as a coping strategy for anxiety and boredom. Moreover, many women smokers see gaining weight as a significant not-so-good thing.

Other important factors include:

- **Health:** What are the health consequences of continuing to smoke?

- **Relationships:** What does your family think about you smoking?

- **Positive Benefits to Change:** What's in it for me?

Self-confidence about one's ability to change can be a potent barrier, which is why we focus so much time on craving management and behavior. Most people think, "It's not that I don't know it's important to change, it's that I don't think I can change." The belief that change is possible is central to success. We build confidence by strengthening the following:

- **The ability to cope:** Skills to deal with intense emotions and other smoking triggers.

- **Past successes:** Review past successful changes like getting into school or learning a new job.

- **Treating underlying psychiatric disorders:** Anxiety, depression, and so on.

- **Social support:** Develop a support system of friends, family, and support groups.

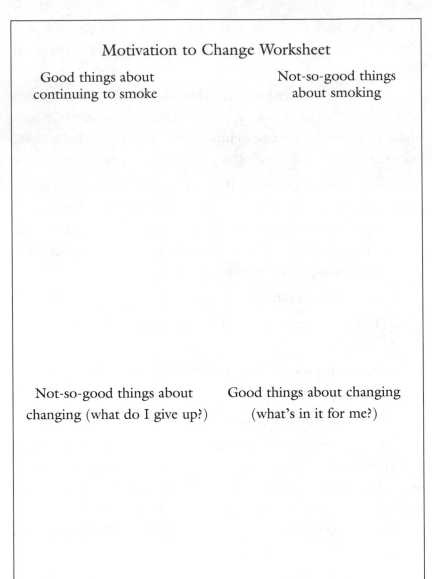

Motivation to Change Worksheet

Good things about continuing to smoke	Not-so-good things about smoking
Not-so-good things about changing (what do I give up?)	Good things about changing (what's in it for me?)

Cognitive Behavioral Therapy and Smoking

The way a person thinks and feels about their emotional issues, and how they deal with social pressures, can cause them to smoke, help them abstain, or cause or prevent relapses. Cognitive behavioral therapy can help them examine the emotional issues behind why they abuse nicotine and looks at how that affects their quality of life.

Some of the techniques and skills used to fight the temptation to smoke are:

- Relaxation

- Forming and maintaining healthy relationships

- Substituting a healthy behavior for an unhealthy one

- Dealing with social pressures

- Dealing with interpersonal conflict

- Dealing with negative emotions

- Identifying high-risk situations and avoiding them

These skills can help a person develop a greater sense of control, which enhances self-esteem and well-being.

The Relaxation Response

Many times when we experience stress the body tightens, breathing becomes shallow or we hold our breath, our muscles ache, and we clench our jaws. Our bodies can suffer a serious toll from stress.

Different cultures and belief systems use deep breathing and/or meditation to quiet the mind and relax the body. Scientific studies have shown that focused breathing and body relaxation can help manage stress and stress-related conditions by soothing the mind and calming the nervous system. Physiological changes that occur during relaxation include:

- Lower blood pressure and heart rate

- Reduced stress hormones

- Reduced or diminished cravings

- Balanced levels of oxygen and carbon dioxide in the blood

- Improved immune system functioning

- Increased physical energy

- Feelings of calm and well being

A Simple Technique to Reduce Cravings and Stress

Sit comfortably in a chair with your spine straight and your feet flat on the floor.

Place both hands on your belly. Imagine filling your abdomen with air, rather than your lungs. Inhale deeply, then exhale. Your hands should rise and fall.

Draw you attention inward. Listen to the sounds around you or notice the sensation of air passing through your nostrils.

With each breath, tighten and release all your muscles, starting at the feet and ending at the head.

Spend this quiet time with yourself as often and for as long as you need to relax.

Additional Coping Skills

- For the first 10 days or so, cut white straws in half. Hold them in your hands whenever you feel the need to smoke. The straws will keep your hands and mouth busy while the habit is being extinguished.

- Crunch on baby carrots and celery sticks when you feel angry, frustrated, or bored.

- Distract yourself by vacuuming a room in your home.

- Call a friend, family member, or person in your support group when you think about smoking.

- Take a brisk, ten- to fifteen-minute walk.
- Play with a pet.
- Engage in a hobby like painting, knitting, or pottery.

Remember that the urge to smoke is a time-limited event. Wait it out for 10 to 20 minutes and the urge will weaken.

Importance of Support

Support groups and supportive people are a crucial aspect of successful recovery from addiction. When a habit that may have been in place for decades is given up, patients may find themselves afraid to hang out with old acquaintances in their usual places or participate in old activities. Part of living a lifestyle without nicotine may include having new friends, going to new, places and participating in new activities. This does not mean that dear friends should be abandoned. Instead, it calls for you to examine your friendships and acquaintances to assess how supportive they are of your decision to quit.

Ask yourself the following questions about the people around you:

- Who can I always go to for help?
- Who is a good listener when I feel upset?
- Who supports my decision to quit?
- Who tells me I can have just one?
- Who in my life do I admire and what do I admire about them?

Ask yourself the following questions about the places you go:

- When I am feeling lonely, where do I go?
- In what places am I most likely to smoke?
- Where do I go to celebrate?

Ask yourself the following questions about your activities:

- What do I do to keep my body healthy?

- How do I feel about exercise?

- What activities make me feel good about myself?

- What activities make me think about smoking?

These questions should help you gain insight about the people and places in your life and about the things that you do. If some of the questions were hard to answer or seemed troubling, don't worry. People who give up a major habit sometimes feel empty and lost. Knowing how to create a strong support system and healthy activities is the key to a fulfilling, healthy life without smoking.

Building a Support System:

- Start working out. Swim, practice yoga, or get a personal trainer. Join a gym or a dance class.

- Throw a party or barbecue, or take friends to lunch.

- If you have one, take your pet for walks or hikes. A dog park is a good place to meet new people.

- Volunteer your time at a community center, hospital, temple, or church. You can form strong connections when you work with people who share a mutual interest.

- Join a support group for others who are quitting smoking.

- Join a group. Find people with similar interests, such as hiking, biking, running marathons, playing music, community gardening, knitting, or a book club.

- Join a cause for a goal you believe in, such as animal rights, forest preservation, or ending homelessness.

- Take a class or two at your local college to meet people with similar interests, or go for another degree.

Other Methods to Deal with Cravings

Nicotine replacement is an effective way to deal with some of the cravings. It is available as a patch, gum, nasal spray, or inhaler. Remember that at least some of the addicting properties of cigarette smoke are not due to nicotine. These methods are mostly available without a prescription.

The other major treatment is buproprion (Wellbutrin or Zyban), a common and very effective antidepressant. This medication increases the dopamine in the brain. Clonidine, a drug used for high blood pressure and to decrease opiate withdrawal, is also effective. Nortriptyline, another antidepressant, may also help. Many studies show that a combination of behavioral therapy, nicotine (often in more than one form), and buproprion is the most effective strategy.

Topiramate (Topamax), a drug for migraine headaches, is effective for alcoholism. Studies have also proven that it allows smokers to quit. In one study, the group who took the topiramate for alcohol addiction was 4.46 times more likely to stop smoking than the group that did not[4]. This drug is not easy to use and has significant side effects, but in the right situation it may be the best way to treat a complicated patient.

Acupuncture has also helped smokers quit. We use it for addiction and it helps many patients. It is simple and effective, and it certainly causes relaxation. While more research needs to be done to prove its efficacy, since it is safe and easy, why not try it?

---

1 Lerman, C., et al. "Pharmacogenetic investigation of smoking cessation treatment." *Pharmacogenetics* 12(8): 627–634, 2002.

2 Belluzzi, J. D., Wang, R., and Leslie, F. M. "Acetaldehyde causes laboratory rats to self-administer nicotine." *Neuropsychopharmacology* 30[4]:705–712, 2005.

3 Mansvelder, H. D., Keath, J. R., and McGehee, D. S. "Nicotine itself directly induces stimulation in the brain reward areas." *Neuron* 33[6]:905–919, 2002.

4 Barclay, L., et al. Univ. of Texas, San Antonio, *Archives of Internal Medicine, 2005.* 165:1600–1605.

Chapter Nineteen
Pain Issues

I stare at the long, blue mat ahead of me. Thirty feet away is the horse I'm supposed to vault in front of five hundred people. It's a good thing I love gymnastics so much because sometimes I'd rather be playing with dolls or boys...or whatever other ten-year-old girls do when they're not at school.

It's my turn. I pick up speed and jump—but I aim wrong. Normally my feet hit just behind the thick, white line on the board. Today they hit halfway up the board, which means I won't get the spring I need to do both my turns.

Midair I make the second mistake of looking into the stands instead of keeping my focus on one point so I won't get dizzy. I make both of my turns but now I'm coming down and I have to stick the landing or my coach will yell at me. But my feet don't have time to get all the way under me and my right foot buckles under my thigh and I feel something rip inside my ankle. Then I lurch forward and get the wind knocked out of me so hard I feel like I'm going to puke.

Then I feel the pain in my ankle. It hurts worse than anything ever has before. It hurts so bad I see stars and tears well up in my eyes. Coach runs up to the mat. He looks pissed. He starts yelling at me, calling me a quitter, doesn't even ask me if I'm okay. Apparently he wants me to do the vault over, says the judges will let me take another shot.

I'm not sure if I can stand up, let alone vault again. But my coach is screaming and the rest of my team is looking over wondering what's going on. It's our last meet of the year and they need my points to win.

I get my coach to shut up long enough to tell him to help me up. He helps me hobble back to the starting position. Every time my foot hits the mat I see white dancing balls around the corners of my eyes and feel like I'm going to faint.

Then I'm running again and I feel like I'm running barefoot in snow because my hurt foot feels ice cold. But I hit the board in the right place and the pain keeps me from looking around. I make both my turns really fast and stick my landing on one foot, which is cool except my other ankle is turning blue.

We win the match. My ankle is the size of a baseball and they can't find enough ace bandages to fit. I know I won't be able to run for a while now, maybe even walk. But we won. I hope it was worth it.

* * *

This account is from a patient of mine who still suffers from chronic regional pain in her ankle—not surprising considering the depth of the trauma. I've included her story because a major issue is that many patients with substance abuse problems have legitimate pain issues. Patients on chronic pain medications have a 15 percent chance of substance abuse, about the same as the general population.

When we evaluate these cases, we find that sometimes the pain condition and physician-prescribed opiate treatment started the patient on drugs. If these genuine pain issues are not treated, ongoing suffering will likely cause a relapse and will certainly increase the patient's daily agony.

The other side of the coin is that sometimes increasing doses of medication won't alleviate pain. Perhaps the patient has neuropathic pain, caused by inflamed nerves rather than an injured body part, that is not responsive to opiates. But when doctors prescribe ever-increasing doses in an attempt to "capture" the pain, some patients become addicted.

Doctor "Dealer"

When doctors prescribe medication to a patient without knowing their full medical/therapeutic history, they may be unknowingly acting as the chief catalyst for a patient's ensuing addiction.

As part of our comprehensive program we evaluate and treat the neuropsychiatric disorders that are commonly found with substance abuse. We also evaluate and treat any other underlying pain or medical problems that may have triggered the original abuse.

One of my patients, Kent, suffers from bipolar disorder. He abused amphetamines in his teens. His father and sister also have addiction problems. The first doctor to work with Kent was unaware of his psychological disorder and prescribed opiates for chronic pain. It didn't take long for Kent to become addicted.

In the doctor's defense, the medication would have likely been fine in most patients. However, not knowing that a patient is bipolar and not working to become aware of prior substance problems and family history before prescribing addicting medications is dangerous. This does not mean that these types of people cannot be treated for pain; it just takes skill and care to avoid serious problems.

Kent actually feels that this doctor got him hooked. He believed that since his doctor was giving him the medications, they were safe. He trusted his doctor and now feels betrayed.

Another patient had a cyst in her foot that was extremely painful. Her initial doctor prescribed Vicodin, to which she became addicted. She also feels tricked. She feels that doctors have sent her the wrong messages regarding medications and pain and she doesn't know where to turn.

I know of many patients struggling with meth or alcohol addiction who don't receive appropriate treatment for pain, and may not receive adequate treatment for addiction. Many doctors pass off their meth or alcohol patients as solely opiate drug seekers without providing proper evaluation or treatment for pain disorders. Part of this reaction comes from the recent string of lawsuits filed against physicians who prescribe opiates for pain. Although I feel for my fellow physicians, it's the patients who suffer the most.

You may also remember Joan, who struggled with alcoholism until she started the Prometa protocol. It's essential that programs like Prometa and the use of drugs like monthly naltrexone (Vivitrol) be introduced to the public as quickly as possible. This is of special importance to doctors, so that they have the resources for referral and proper care for their patients.

These unfortunate relationships provide yet another reason why both patients and doctors have to just ask each other about addiction issues. Without full disclosure on both sides of the examining table, confusion and regret will be inadvertently prescribed in heavy doses.

Guidelines for Opiate Prescription

Every doctor should ask these questions before prescribing opiates, even for acute problems:

1. Do you have a history of drug or alcohol abuse?

2. Do you have a history of bipolar disorder or depression and/ or anxiety problems that started at a young age or that did not respond to the usual antidepressants?

3. Is there a family history in siblings, parents, grandparents, uncles, or aunts of alcohol and/or drug addiction and/or serious depression or bipolar disorder?

4. Have you had any problems in the past with using or stopping opiate medications?

Any positive answers to these questions should increase the level of scrutiny before prescribing opiates to these patients. It does not mean that they should not be used, however:

- Long-acting opiates (such as Avinza or the fentanyl patch) should be used as early as possible.

- Alternate non-opiate therapies should be maximized.

- Opiates should be stopped as soon as practical, comfortable, and safe.

The physician must be on the alert for:

- Increasing dosage requirements without corresponding results.

- Lack of efficacy at the usual doses.

- Aberrant behavior such as losing medication, early refills, and evidence of doctor shopping either at ERs or other medical offices.

- Inability to decrease the dose as the primary condition improves.

If any of these occur, the physician should consider stopping the medication (if appropriate to the clinical situation) or refer to a pain or addiction specialist. In any case, he or she should avoid simply increasing the dose of short-acting opiates, which fuels addiction in many patients.

When these guidelines aren't followed, the patient-doctor relationship may change without either the physician or the patient knowing. Things get worse and often spin completely out of control, with the patient landing in the emergency room for medication or even with an overdose. Many patients start buying drugs over the Internet. The physician is usually surprised. At other times the patient will be referred to a pain specialist who can take corrective action earlier. Patients are incensed that the trust they've given their doctors has led them to become addicted.

Many of these patients have a condition called pseudo-addiction, the result of inadequate pain control. They suffer genuine pain but don't get the treatment they need because their behavior marks them as addicts due to their frequent requests for refills and visits to the ER. It may not be possible to tell the difference between pseudo and actual addiction without a full evaluation and a careful medication treatment trial.

Pseudo addiction "resolves" with adequate pain management, meaning the aberrant addictive behavior goes away. Physicians very often aren't treating pain issues because patients who ask for increasing doses of medication are automatically labeled "drug seekers." Only a full understanding of all the issues by physicians and patients alike will break the cycle.

Pain–The Fifth Vital Sign

Pain in general is undertreated in our society. Only recently has it been dubbed the "fifth vital sign" by the medical community. In hospitals, nurses now record their patients' blood pressure, pulse, respiratory rate, temperature, and pain level. There have been recent successful malpractice lawsuits and even medical board actions brought against physicians who did not treat pain appropriately.

While this is a vital issue for many patients, once a person is diagnosed with a substance abuse problem, their pain is often no longer considered important. Under the traditional paradigm, the substance abuse needs treatment, not the underlying problem. Often, in strict abstinence programs, patients with a history of alcohol abuse who have never abused prescription opiates are not treated for pain.

In his recent memoir *A Million Little Pieces* by James Frey, this problem of undertreated pain is graphically depicted. Despite the controversy surrounding this book, it dramatically describes the experiences of many people treated under the traditional addiction paradigm. In the book, Mr. Frey wakes up on an airplane unaware of how he got there. He has multiple injuries including broken teeth and facial lacerations.

He is taken to a renowned inpatient rehab facility where he is detoxed and sent to a dentist nearby. Under the rules of the program, his teeth are fixed without local anesthesia. As a drug addict, his treatment dictated that he must be totally abstinent.

He describes the absolute agony of the procedure. I cringed when I read it. I was also angry to think that anyone should be treated with such disregard for his or her suffering. In his case, Mr. Frey was a poly-substance abuser and it was a good idea not to give him opiates. However, he was not even allowed lidocaine during the procedure. He was also not given even a non-opiate pain reliever like ibuprofen or acetaminophen afterwards, all in the name of abstinence.

This is an extreme example of where the treatment of substance abuse ignores the person and their specific needs. It also doesn't go under the surface to see why someone has a substance abuse problem.

Types of Painful Conditions

The comprehensive diagnosis of painful conditions is beyond the scope of this book. Suffice it to say that many of these problems are not diagnosable with routine objective tests such as x-rays and laboratory tests. The same problem exists here as for substance abuse: the symptom, pain, is treated without knowledge of the underlying causes. In many cases, it is treated without the thorough evaluation found in Gracer Medical's program.

This problem is especially common for two types of medical conditions: The first is the diagnosis and treatment of musculoskeletal and spinal pain. The second is for painful conditions that do not have clear-cut, objective findings, such as headaches and fibromyalgia.

Chronic Spine Pain

About 80 percent of the population will suffer back pain at some point in their lives. The usual diagnosis made when someone hurts his or her back is "lumbar strain." Since this condition most often resolves in a short time, an exact diagnosis may not be important. Unfortunately, when the pain continues and then becomes disabling and severe, the diagnosis often continues to be obscure.

Many chronic back pain patients have no specific diagnosis because most physicians do not know the biomechanics and common pain generators of the spine. Most back pain is attributed to nonspecific strain or disc protrusions. The disc is the source of much low back pain, but the sacroiliac joints and other ligaments are also common sources of pain. Effective treatments exist for these conditions and I help many patients with "untreatable" back pain.

When pain persists for more than a few weeks, the brain starts to change. In fact, there is evidence that this process starts in a few days. The brain becomes more sensitive to pain and pain spreads to areas that were not previously involved. Stimulation that is usually not painful, such as joint movement, becomes painful. This is called allodynia. When mildly painful stimuli hurt severely, it is called hyperdynia.

In many cases, the problem that originally caused the pain becomes insignificant. Many of the neurological chemical changes that have occurred are, remarkably, the same as seen in drug withdrawal. This type of pain does not respond well to opiates and many patients are given increasing doses without good symptom control. Many develop physical dependence and drug addiction. Many of them also self-medicate with alcohol, marijuana, cocaine, or meth-amphetamine.

My approach is to make a proper tissue diagnosis and then evaluate and treat the whole person. Chronic pain is treated with medications aimed at the central nervous system dysfunctions, and may include a variety of nutritional and hormonal regimens. Many patients with these conditions have total or very significant pain relief.

Non-specific Pain Problems

A good example of a non-specific painful condition is fibromyalgia. Medically this condition is known as a "diagnosis of exclusion." This means that if the physician cannot find another medical cause for a specific set of symptoms, the diagnosis is fibromyalgia. This condition has pain and sleep disruption as well as multiple tender spots on the neck, chest, back, arms, and legs.

Chronic Fatigue Syndrome, a related disorder in which the patient feels tired with flu-like symptoms and lack of energy, is also often present. Other disorders seen in this group of patients include interstitial cystitis (IC), a painful bladder condition common in women, irritable bowel syndrome (IBS), and chronic pelvic pain. All these conditions are dysfunctions of the central nervous system. Their specific causes are as yet unknown.

Problems may start as an abnormal response to stress or after severe emotional trauma such as sexual abuse. The triggering event may be a traumatic physical, emotional, or financial event. It may start after a viral illness such as the flu or Epstein-Barr (infectious mononucleosis). These patients have a number of abnormalities in the hormones present in their brains and in their responses to stress. This may make them more susceptible to pain. These diseases affect women more than men. There is also evidence that many of the affected women have suffered emotional or sexual abuse.

When I see a patient with these problems, I look for many of the same conditions outlined in this book. The problem is often with the body's system and not with any specific tissue that would show up on an x-ray. This means the tender spots themselves are not abnormal but that the most likely cause of the pain is with either the brain or any of the body's organ systems, such as the thyroid or adrenals. It may even be a result of toxic exposure or allergy. By evaluating and treating these areas, as well as improving the patient's general nutritional status, many regain normal health.

Many of these patients are anxious and/or depressed. Some of them suffer bipolar disorder. While treatment may help or even fully relieve the pain, it does not correct the underlying cause for most patients. At other times this pain is so intense that it must be treated with opiates. These patients have a higher than normal risk of developing drug dependence, as many causes of fibromyalgia and system dysfunctions are also present in patients with substance abuse.

Treatment Methods

Before I see these patients, their family physicians have usually treated their pain with short-acting opiates such as Vicodin or Norco. They still have significant pain that does not get better despite increasing doses. Even after a full evaluation and treatment of all abnormalities, many still require opiate-type medication. The dilemma is to reach a level of medication that gives adequate symptom control with the fewest side effects. Another complication is the fact that many of these patients have not done well on high doses of pain medication in the past.

When confronted with a patient who has poor pain relief despite high doses of opiates, I consider whether they might feel better when taken off this medication. Often the pain is much better off the opiates. In other cases, after a period off opiate medication (often called a drug holiday), I can restart the pain medication later at much lower doses and with much better efficacy.

I insist that these patients use long-acting opiates to eliminate the tendency to "drive the dose" and to avoid euphoria (for more details on this, refer to the discussion of short- versus long-acting opiates in Chapter Nine, entitled Opiates). Their medication intake is carefully monitored and they keep detailed pain diaries to document their progress. All of my patients sign a pain agreement that outlines my specific requirements and conditions for proper pain medication treatment.

Buprenorphine has been invaluable for these patients. They are often fearful of withdrawal and have had prior unpleasant experiences either running out of their medications or with well-intentioned physicians rapidly tapering and stopping opiates without other treatment or support.

Buprenorphine usually makes this process comfortable and successful. Since it is long-acting and blocks the opiate kappa receptor, it effectively eliminates many of the symptoms that make this process so difficult. Many patients feel better than they have in years. Their pain is often controlled with very small doses.

Patients with substance abuse can have legitimate pain problems that may have originally triggered their addiction. Co-existing nutritional, hormonal, and psychiatric conditions must be treated, which often results in significant improvement or even resolution of their pain. This allows successful treatment of their addiction. Pain that is not responsive to opiates should be treated with other types of medications.

Many of these patients suffer from sleep problems that make their problems worse and may even be an important cause of the problem. These must be diagnosed and treated.

Pseudo-addiction is often the problem and must be recognized before assuming that a patient is a drug seeker. For others, careful use of long-acting opiates or buprenorphine with strict accountability, frequent office visits, and appropriate social and psychological support is effective.

The Importance of Treating
Sleep Problems in Addiction and Pain Patients

A good night's sleep is important for good health. Sleep problems are common in addiction and pain patients for many reasons. Although many of these people have other primary problems such as depression, attention deficit disorder (ADD), headaches, obesity, heart disease, restless legs or periodic leg movements, and pain, the drugs they use and abuse are a major cause of insomnia.[1, 2, 3] Sleep disruption is also a major component of chronic fatigue syndrome and fibromyalgia. The proper diagnosis and treatment of these problems can make a big difference in the outcome of addiction and/or pain treatment, as well as increase longevity and well-being. This type of sleep problem is called a secondary disorder, meaning that it is due to one of these other causes and is treated by correcting the actual cause.

There are also primary sleep problems, the most common of which is sleep apnea. Over 6 percent of the US population suffers from this problem, with about one third undiagnosed. That's over 5,000,000 Americans. The percentage of addiction and pain patients who suffer from this condition is probably much higher. In sleep apnea a sufferer stops breathing in his or her sleep for up to a minute at a time, several times each hour. In mild cases this happens over five times per hour, while in severe cases it can occur up to 20 times per hour, a situation that can be fatal. These episodes result in decreased oxygen in the blood to a critically low level, which triggers the body's alarm system, releasing adrenalin and spiking blood pressure, causing an increase in breathing effort that kick-starts the system again, bringing much needed oxygen into the lungs...until the next episode a few moments later. This occurs again and again with repeated acute stress on the heart, brain, and other organs. This leads to increased risk of heart attacks, irregular heartbeat, strokes, and probably many other chronic medical problems.[4] The most common symptoms of sleep apnea are morning headaches, fatigue, and episodes of daytime sleeping. High blood pressure, depression, decreased sexual function, and a decrease in intellect are other common symptoms. It's no wonder that these people are tired and depressed.

About 80 percent of patients suffer from this problem as a result of obstruction or constriction of the nasal passages or throat, a specific condition called obstructive sleep apnea (OSA). These patients usually snore and some are obese. Often the diagnosis is made after a sleeping partner observes periods of non-breathing. OSA often develops in women after menopause. Smoking and alcohol make the situation worse—smoking because of its direct effect on the bronchial tree, and alcohol because it directly depresses breathing.

Another group of patients have a failure of the normal brain signals that trigger breathing. This much less common condition is called central sleep apnea (CSA). Most of the time CSA is of unknown cause, but it can be the result of stroke or other brain damage, heart failure, or low thyroid function, as well as being secondary to drug use. Opiates, alcohol, and benzodiazepines all are well-known breathing depressants, making this type of sleep apnea prevalent in drug-intoxicated addiction patients. There is even evidence that patients on methadone maintenance treatment for opiate addiction have a high risk of CSA, even with doses of the drug that do not cause direct respiratory effects. Additionally, patients often suffer from both types of apnea. This is called mixed sleep apnea.[5, 6, 7, 8]

Even when doctors take a careful patient history, up to 50 percent of sleep apnea sufferers can be missed. This makes testing imperative for high-risk persons. The diagnosis is usually made at a sleep lab, where an overnight sleep study is used to make observations of brain-waves, respiration, and blood oxygen (a process called polysomnography). Treatment includes special nasal masks with pumped air that increases the pressure in the throat, opening up obstructed airways (continuous positive airway pressure, or CPAP), preventing obstruction using dental appliances, and even surgery. Obese patients should lose weight.[9] CSA can be corrected by treating the underlying medical problems and stopping drug use.

After treatment, patients often experience a huge increase in their energy and overall well-being, making any other medical problems much easier to treat.[10] This is especially true for chronic pain and addiction patients, who have many of the other problems that are made worse by sleep disruption. This makes it very important to order a sleep study if there is any question of sleep disruption or symptoms, such as snoring and fatigue. At our clinic we have a very low threshold to order a sleep study, and treat out patients vigorously. This has improved the quality of life for many of our patients.

1 Dodick, D. W., Eross, E. J., Parish, J. M., Silber. M. Clinical, anatomical, and physiologic relationship between sleep and headache. *Headache*. Mar 2003;43(3), pp. 282–292.

2 Moldofsky, H. Sleep and pain. *Sleep Med Rev.* Oct 2001;5(5):385–396.

3 Sand, T., Hagen, K., Schrader, H. Sleep apnoea and chronic headache. *Cephalalgia*. Mar 2003; 23(2):90–95.

4 Skobel, E., Norra, C., Sinha, A., Breuer, C., Hanrath, P., Stellbrink, C. Impact of sleep-related breathing disorders on health-related quality of life in patients with chronic heart failure. *Eur J Heart Fail*. Jun 2005; 7(4):505–511.

5 Wang, D., Teichtahl, H., Drummer, O., et al. Central sleep apnea in stable methadone maintenance treatment patients. *Chest*. Sep 2005; 128(3):1348–1356.

6 Wang, D., Teichtahl, H. Opioids, sleep architecture and sleep-disordered breathing. *Sleep Med Rev*. Feb 2007; 11(1):35–46.

7 Teichtahl, H., Wang, D., Cunnington, D., et al. Ventilatory responses to hypoxia and hypercapnia in stable methadone maintenance treatment patients. *Chest*. Sep 2005; 128(3):1339–1347.

8 Teichtahl, H., Wang, D., Cunnington, D., et al. Cardiorespiratory function in stable methadone maintenance treatment (MMT) patients. *Addict Biol*. Sep–Dec 2004; 9(3–4):247–253.

9 Polo, O., Berthon-Jones, M., Douglas, N. J., Sullivan, C. E. Management of obstructive sleep apnoea/hypopnoea syndrome. *Lancet*. Sep 3 1994; 344(8923):656–660.

10 Chua, W., Chediak, A. D. Obstructive sleep apnea. Treatment improves quality of life—and may prevent death. *Postgrad Med*. Feb 1 1994; 95(2):123–126, 131, 135–128.

Chapter Twenty
Psychiatric Disorders and Substance Abuse

The headaches were the worst part. People talk about a hammer pounding their skulls during migraines. That's not how it happened for me. It's like nails on a chalkboard, except those four-inch razor-tipped nails are clawing at your brain, digging into the ridges like a plow in the earth. Then imagine yourself really hung over and a car alarm goes off next to your head while a baby screams an inch from your face.

Headaches that severe mean you can't do anything else. I would wake up from an agonizing dream where my head throbbed only to realize my head was actually throbbing. I would literally see spots. All I could do was take a handful of Advil and lie in a dark room with a washcloth over my eyes.

My psychiatrist was baffled. He was treating me for depression and kept giving me these different selective serotonin reuptake inhibitors (SSRIs), which were supposed to help. Nothing worked.

It was about that time that a friend gave me some Vicodin. I won't lie to you—it was great. You know how a doctor will sometimes ask you what your pain is on a level of one to 10? One means it doesn't really hurt and 10 is the most violent agony you can think of. Well, my migraines were typically at 12. They were off the scale. Vicodin brought the torture down to about a seven. You cannot understand how major that is unless you've experienced chronic and blistering pain. You literally would have shot yourself in the face to alleviate the suffering.

So I got addicted to Vicodin. Who wouldn't? They were helping. But it was also around that time my psychiatrist realized my brain chemistry was bipolar and that was probably why I wasn't responding to some of my antidepressants. That's when he hooked me up with Dr. Gracer, who used Subutex to get me off Vicodin. As it turns out, the buprenorphine in Subutex has helped lessen my depression and mood swings. I'm also on a mood stabilizer and preventative medical treatment for my headaches. I'm finally almost completely free from pain, depression, and anxiety.

Here's the main thing: the fact that I have bipolar brain chemistry is a huge deal. Doctor Gracer says the condition is called co-morbidity, meaning that many people with substance abuse problems also have a mood disorder. I've lived with violent mood swings and severe headaches for as long as I can remember. Now I can function. Now I can live.

* * *

This story is based on a patient of mine and is typical of thousands of individuals who suffer from undiagnosed bipolar disorder. What these individuals and their doctors don't realize is that this condition and similar mood disorders alter the brain's normal chemistry. Commonly these patients succumb to a substance abuse problem at some point in their lives. Whether they start due to pain or seek relief from violent mood swings, they "co-exist" with a substance abuse problem and the altered brain chemistry that probably caused their problem.

This co-existence is called co-morbidity or dual diagnosis, and it must be treated. In the same way that smoking can exacerbate the effects of drugs, a brain with altered chemistry is obviously the last place patients want to send powerful foreign substances. Doctors and patients need to recognize all the history and specifics of a patient for the best possible treatment. That means that only by viewing our patients as whole people, rather than focusing only on a specific disease or disorder, such as substance abuse, can we treat these people successfully.

Attention Deficit Hyperactivity Disorder (ADHD)

Attention Deficit Hyperactivity Disorder (ADHD) is a common problem in addicted patients. Since stimulants are an important treatment for this disease, some methamphetamine-addicted patients take the drug to self-medicate. There are new medications, including atomoxetine (Straterra) and modafinil (Provigal), that can help. It's also important to remember that this problem often co-exists with a serious mood disorder.

For an adult to have ADHD, the disorder must have started as a child. In many adults, the main symptoms are problems concentrating, rather than the hyperactivity seen in children. It is important to differentiate drug behavior possibly related to cocaine or methamphetamine use from true hyperactivity or attention problems resulting from ADHD. It may take a month or more after drug use stops to be able to tell whether the patient has a psychiatric problem or if her or his behavior is due to drug use.

Mood Disorders

Depression and anxiety are mood disorders that are very common in our society. They can severely affect functioning and quality of life. All too often patients with a substance abuse problem also have a mood disorder. This co-morbidity is also called dual diagnosis. While each of these problems has serious consequences, together they can exert overwhelming effects that impact the treatment of both. Many psychological interventions are designed to treat one or the other, but not both.

Additionally, many substance abuse practitioners have inadequate training and experience in the detection, evaluation, and treatment of mood disorders. The type often seen in patients with substance abuse issues, bipolar mood disorder, differs from the much more common types of anxiety and depression most physicians and psychologists are used to diagnosing and treating. Bipolar mood disorder may even get worse with the usual antidepressant and anxiety treatment.

Diagnosis of Mood Disorders

Many patients suffering depression come to their physicians with vague complaints. A thorough physical exam and testing fails to show a specific cause. Until recently, there were no safe and easy-to-take medications for depression. Patients suffered and some even committed suicide due to a lack of treatment.

However, with the advent of selective serotonin reuptake inhibitors (SSRIs) such as Prozac, Zoloft, Paxil, and Lexapro, and with a major effort to educate physicians about this disease, there has been a jump in the number of patients who are getting proper treatment. Even with these developments, depression remains an underdiagnosed and undertreated disorder. There are two basic types of depression, and each is treated in a different way.

Major Depression (Unipolar)

Unipolar depression is by far the most common form. It manifests in patients with at least some of the following symptoms:

- Prolonged sadness or pessimism.

- Inability to have fun or enjoy life.

- Problems sleeping or sleeping too much. Most depressed people have no problem falling asleep, but they get up in the middle of the night or early in the morning.

- Feelings of guilt or feeling worthless.

- Increased or decreased appetite.

- Problems with concentration.

- Loss of energy.

- Thoughts of death or suicide.

- Problems functioning in normal life role or job.

- Non-specific physical symptoms, such as headaches, fatigue, body aches, and stomach pains.

Anxiety is a common problem also seen in depressed patients. The symptoms of and treatments for the two overlap a great deal. Anxious patients can have several different types of problems but most are treated with the same SSRIs as for depression (Prozac, Paxil, Zoloft, and Lexapro), as well as anti-anxiety drugs like buspirone (Buspar) and benzodiazepines (Valium and Ativan). Each anxiety-based disorder has a specific set of symptoms and treatment strategies:

- **Generalized anxiety disorder:** These people feel anxious much of the time without a specific reason or trigger. They are chronic worriers. They often cannot fall asleep and have recurring thoughts.

- **Panic disorder:** These patients have attacks of dread. They have rapid heart rate, sweating, chest tightness and pain, and often feel as if they are going to die. These may be triggered by specific situations (see phobia description below) or come out of the blue.

- **Obsessive Compulsive Disorder (OCD):** These patients have thoughts that they cannot stop and must often perform rituals such as hand washing to decrease their anxiety.

- **Post Traumatic Stress Disorder (PTSD):** These patients have experienced a traumatic physical or emotional event that has changed their emotional makeup and brain function. This includes going to war, sexual abuse, or a traffic accident. Data shows that rapid identification and treatment of these people can make a big difference.

- **Social phobia:** These patients experience fear in normal social situations. They cannot express themselves, feel nervous and shaky, and usually avoid social contact as much as possible. This is a huge disability for their job performance and family life.

- **Specific phobias:** Fear of specific situations can paralyze a person. A few of the more common types are agoraphobia (fear of the outdoors), acrophobia (fear of heights), arachnophobia (fear of spiders), and claustrophobia (fear of tight spaces).

Depression and anxiety symptoms commonly bring patients to their physicians. In the past the problem has been that the doctor doesn't recognize the problem as depression or an anxiety disorder. Proper treatment is seldom offered.

Untreated episodes of unipolar depression are recurrent and can last two years or more at a time. The first episode is usually in adulthood and may or may not be triggered by a stressful event. Some of these patients use alcohol to alleviate their anxiety, while others may use opiates, marijuana, cocaine, or amphetamine to self-medicate.

Bipolar Disorder

Bipolar disorder, also known as manic-depressive disorder, causes the same depressive symptoms listed above. However, there are also symptoms of mania. In other aspects, bipolar patients act very differently from unipolar patients. Most importantly, their brain chemistry is different. Many treatments used for unipolar depression can activate an episode of mania. The symptoms of mania are:

- Racing thoughts
- Elation or euphoria
- Increased or racing speech

- Increased risk-taking or recklessness

- Poor judgment

- Eating binges

- Irritability and aggression; sudden or irrational anger

- Increased mental or physical activity

- Periods of sleeplessness

- Increased sexual activity

At times these symptoms can be severe and the patient diagnosed as psychotic. At other times, these symptoms can be subtle. Most patients don't complain about these problems; indeed, they may not think there's a problem. Substance abuse often takes place during this type of episode, leading to the type of situation experienced by my patient at the beginning of this chapter.

Unless a physician is on the lookout, these symptoms can be missed. Patients usually complain about the depressive symptoms, often leading to misdiagnosis. The following comparison differentiates between bipolar disorder and unipolar depression. Note, however, that these are not absolute.

Factors in Favor of Bipolar Disorder	Factors in Favor of Unipolar Depression
Manic symptoms	No manic symptoms
Onset in teens or early twenties	Onset in adulthood
Rapid cycling during episodes	Usually sad or depressed
When depressed, patients are very lethargic	Unless severe, lethargy is not as bad
Increased sleep when depressed	Insomnia, usually due to early morning wakening
Overeating when manic	Change in appetite up or down with secondary weight gain or loss
Psychotic symptoms	No psychotic symptoms
Severe anxiety	History of increased chronic anxiety and worry
Markedly increased risk of suicide	Increased suicide risk

20-1: Bipolar and unipolar depression chart

Over one-third of bipolar patients seek treatment within the first year of the start of their symptoms. However, over 70 percent are misdiagnosed (usually as suffering from unipolar depression) and typically see four different physicians and often wait ten years before receiving a correct diagnosis.[1]

Expanded Diagnoses

Over the past few years, the diagnosis of bipolar disorder has been expanded to include people who develop manic symptoms while on antidepressants such as Prozac or Zoloft. Many people who had some of the manic symptoms for an insufficient time or in a way that wasn't strong enough to be considered bipolar actually have bipolar brain chemistry.

Recognizing the presence of bipolar brain chemistry (even if a patient hasn't been diagnosed with the full-blown disorder) is essential to ensure proper treatment. With the old, strict diagnostic criteria, it was thought that only 1 percent to 2 percent of mood disorder patients were bipolar. With the expanded diagnostic categories (indicating bipolar brain chemistry), recent estimates suggest as many as 20 percent of depressed and anxious persons have bipolar chemistry.[2]

This is very important for treatment of substance abuse because of co-morbidity and the fact that undiagnosed bipolar patients have more than a 20 percent chance of attempting suicide. Recently, two potential patients committed suicide before they made it to our clinic. Sadly, this is not uncommon. Correct diagnoses of unipolar and bipolar depression along with better treatment can help prevent these tragedies.

Drug Treatment of Bipolar Disorder

The proper medical treatment of bipolar disorder is to use one of two classes of drugs: mood stabilizers and anticonvulsants. Mood stabilizers were originally used to treat schizophrenia, alleviating hallucinations and other psychotic symptoms. They are also very effective for bipolar disorder and are usually the first drugs used for a manic episode.

Anticonvulsant drugs are commonly used to treat seizures, but their calming effect on the brain works well for mania. Lithium is also very effective, but may not work as well for patients with substance abuse. Other medications are available, as well, but the point is that they are very different than those for unipolar depression and common anxiety. Often very low doses of mood stabilizers are effective for patients who are agitated and have trouble concentrating, but who are not truly manic.

The common mood stabilizers are:

- **Olanzapine (Zyprexa):** This is the most common medication. It is safe and effective but can cause rapid and marked weight gain.

- **Resperidone (Risperdal):** This medication is more sedating but has much less effect on weight. It may have other side effects and needs careful monitoring by a physician.

- **Ziprasidone (Geodon):** This medication is newer and has few side effects, but can be sedating.

- **Ariprprazole (Abilify):** This new medication tends to be more activating but is very effective for some patients.

The commonly used anticonvulsants are:

- **Valproic acid (Depakote):** This mainline medication is also used to treat migraine headaches. It is sedating and can cause hair loss. Blood levels and liver tests must be administered following its use.

- **Lamotrignine (Lamictal):** This medication is commonly used to treat bipolar patients who are depressed. It also helps prevent manic episodes.

- **Oxacarbazine (Trileptal):** This is commonly used when other medications are not effective. It is also sedating.

The side effects involved in bipolar depression treatment can be significant. They include weight gain, nausea, sexual dysfunction, and lethargy. Therefore, many patients stop treatment and relapse, both into drug use and into bipolar behavior. It is very important that side effects be acknowledged and vigorously addressed. It is also important that physical drug cravings be treated as they exacerbate this problem.

Co-morbidity

Over 50 percent of patients with bipolar disorder also have a substance abuse problem. There is evidence that a genetic connection exists between these factors. A positive family history for bipolar disorder makes the chance of substance abuse rise dramatically, and vise versa. Unipolar depression has a 27 percent co-morbidity rate.

Psychiatric disorder	Individuals with alcohol dependence			
	Men		Women	
	%	Odds Ratio	%	Odds Ratio
Anxiety	35.8	2.2	60.7	3.1
Mood	28.1	3.2	53.5	4.4
Drug depend.	29.5	9.8	34.7	15.8
Antisoc pers.	16.9	8.3	7.8	17.0

20-2: *National Co-morbidity Survey (Kessler, Crum, Warner, Nelson, Schulenberg, & Anthony, 1997)*

Sometimes substance abuse starts first and sometimes it comes second. At times, manic symptoms are seen during alcohol withdrawal. Many bipolar patients use alcohol to mitigate the symptoms of mania. Many depressed patients use drugs to treat their symptoms. This complicated picture makes it difficult to determine the specific relationship, but it also makes a correct diagnosis vital. Suicide is even more common for patients with co-morbidity.

Treatment

Patients often go from physician to physician undiagnosed, usually with the addiction and bipolar disorder getting worse. At other times the substance abuse is treated with detox, therapy, and then a twelve-step program referral without treatment of the mood disorder. This is bound to fail with the next episode of mania or depression.

Likewise, psychiatric treatment without cravings management and social support will not address addiction. We've seen many patients who've been working with competent psychiatrists and psychologists, sometimes for years, yet the therapist hasn't even recognized the patient's substance abuse problem.

At Gracer Medical we've found that proper treatment of the substance abuse in co-morbid patients with an emphasis on craving management can break the cycle, but that observation for manic symptoms is important. These symptoms sometimes take the form of irritability or severe anxiety.

Treatment must consider both problems at the same time with a constant eye on subtle changes in symptoms and behavior that may hint at the underlying mood disorder. I won't lie to you—scrutinizing the subtleties of a patient's depression is a delicate art. But it's a vital and necessary one in the treatment of patients who have been suffering and confused for so long. In the case of bipolar patients, taking the time to look for these subtle changes could mean the difference between life and death.

---

1 Benazzi, F. "Underdiagnosis of bipolar II disorders in the community." *Journal of Clinical Psychiatry* 2003.

2 Angst, et al. "Bipolarity from ancient to modern times: conception, birth and rebirth 2001, Journal of affective disorders" *Clinical Approaches in Bipolar Disorder.* 2002.

Chapter Twenty-One
Nutrition

B y now it should come as no surprise that whatever you put in your body affects your overall health. People suffering from addiction need to be aware that certain foods or diets can radically alter their body chemistry. Likewise, they need to know about the positive effects specific vitamins and nutrients can have on overall health while also helping control or even slow cravings.

This chapter outlines the nutritional factors that affect pain management and substance abuse and provide some specific tests and dietary suggestions. Keep in mind this is a basic introduction. Further information can be found on the Gracer Medical website. You can also sign up for our newsletter to find answers to commonly asked questions.

Study the following sections carefully and note the ideas and suggestions most applicable to you. Take this information to your doctor or nutritionist, as well as to any specialists helping you treat your addiction.

The Gracer Program features the work of clinical nutritionist Leni Felton, who has included her Surviving Withdrawal diet in

Chapter Twenty-Four and on the website. It is an excellent resource when struggling against cravings and during the early days of withdrawal.

Nutritional Factors in Pain Management and Substance Abuse

Almost all people with addiction or pain problems have serious vitamin and other nutritional deficiencies, as well as the toxicity that comes from the addiction itself. It is interesting to note that the problems caused by addictive behavior are an exaggeration of those seen in the general population that eats the regular American diet.

Of course, certain addictive behaviors such as alcoholism create serious physical problems that require specific attention. This is also true of chronic pain patients. Unless these nutritional deficiencies are corrected, people cannot be expected to return to feeling fully vital and healthy. In addition, many of the dietary habits that are often part and parcel of an addiction problem set the body up for serious metabolic imbalances that promote addictive behavior and cravings.

As Barry Sears, PhD, the well-known author of the *Zone* books, says, "You're only as good as your last meal." Let me demonstrate how your meals are either harming or helping your fight against addiction.

Silent Inflammation

Cardiovascular disease is the most common cause of death. As we age, most of us suffer from degenerative arthritis. Alzheimer's disease is affecting more and more elderly people. While these problems all involve different body systems, they all have a very important factor in common: they are caused by "silent inflammation," a concept extensively developed by Barry Sears, PhD, in The Anti-Aging Zone and The Anti-Inflammation Zone.

The fatty deposits that clog the coronary arteries of people who have heart attacks are the result of inflammation. The plaques seen in the brains of Alzheimer's patients and the increased wear in the joints of those suffering from degenerative arthritis also result from the same process.

Indeed, our body is always in a fine balance between factors that wear us down and those that build and maintain. When this balance is tipped toward destruction, the natural systems that keep us healthy are overwhelmed. The result is a gradual decrease in the vitality and resilience of various tissues. Nothing happens overnight, but when a fatty plaque in a coronary artery ruptures and then clots, the results can be disastrous. Eventually, the cartilage in one's knee joints may wear out and cause disabling pain. Knowledge of how these systems work has led to effective nutritional strategies to slow down and even prevent these processes.

It makes sense that the same system is at work in the brain. Some of the same compounds that regulate the function and integrity of blood vessels and joints do similar jobs in the central nervous system. This means that you can improve your general health while decreasing your dependence on drugs and fighting depression.

Eicosanoids and Second Messengers

Eicosanoids are compounds created from components found in cell walls. Each cell produces these vital, locally acting hormones. In a very basic way, eicosanoids can either be good or bad. The good eicosanoids promote blood flow and decrease inflammation, while the bad eicosanoids constrict blood vessels, promote clotting, and increase inflammation. The balance between these compounds determines how our cells function and how we feel.

What you eat gets into your cell walls. What you eat also regulates other important factors such as insulin levels, which set the tone for body function. The general idea is to keep your insulin level low and ingest a lot of omega-3 oils, mostly in the form of fish oil, which push the cell to produce good eicosanoids.

Eicosanoids also generate other, simpler compounds called second messengers. These second messengers cause the hormone effects that we see in cells. If there are not enough second messengers, the cell function turns faulty. The types of eicosanoids present in a given cell dramatically affect how well the body can regulate its essential functions.

The GABA receptor needs a second messenger called cyclic AMP to release its relaxing neurotransmitters. The good eicosanoids

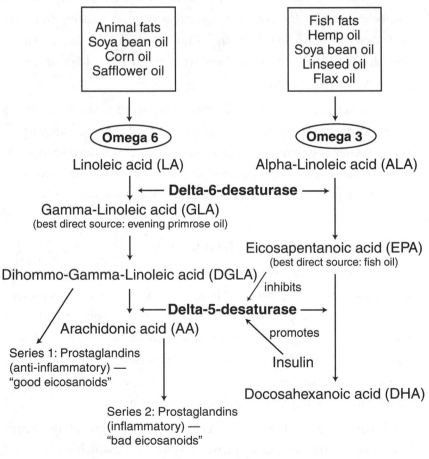

21-1: The eicosanoid story

increase the amount of cyclic AMP, making the nerve cells more efficient. During drug withdrawal, the GABA nerve cells are under-stimulated. Higher levels of cyclic AMP make the cell more likely to fire, which decreases some of the symptoms of withdrawal, like depression and anxiety.

Since a proper balance of eicosanoids is so critical, you really and truly are "only as good as your last meal."

Essential Compounds

Our bodies can make almost everything we need from basic foods. However, we must ingest specific compounds, often in very small quantities, in order to live. These are described as essential. Vitamins by definition are essential. There are also essential fats and amino acids, the building blocks for proteins. Additionally, we need to ingest adequate minerals. All of these are components of the enzymes that are vital to our existence. Deficiencies in any of these nutrients affect enzyme function and unbalance the metabolism.

When we are stressed we need even more of these essential nutri-ents. People who suffer with addiction issues and chronic pain are certainly under stress. Unfortunately they are usually also malnour-ished, making things even worse. They often suffer from a cascade of metabolic problems, such as:

- Down-regulated GABA receptors (fewer actual receptors in the nerve cell wall)

- Abnormal type of GABA receptor sites (less sensitive to endorphins and more sensitive to drugs than the normal receptors)

- Greatly decreased natural compounds that usually stimulate these receptors (such as endorphins)

- Abnormal balance of good and bad eicosanoids due to chron-ic stress, hormonal imbalances, and poor diet

- Decreased enzyme function due to amino acid, vitamin, and mineral deficiencies

- Decreased intracellular second messengers (cyclic AMP)

- Decreased ability to synthesize neurotransmitters such as dopamine, serotonin, and epinephrine (paracrine hormones)

- Decreased ability to release these neurotransmitters

- Decreased stimulation of and transmission to nerve pathways in the pleasure center of the brain

These problems cause imbalances and symptoms including withdrawal and cravings, as well as contributing to depression and anxiety and diminishing the general sense of well-being we all desire. Attacking any of these deficiencies can help with cravings and mood problems. We can achieve this in almost all cases through proper diet, exercise combined with appropriate supplementation, and the proper use of medication.

Essential Fatty Acids

We must ingest three types of essential fats to remain healthy. These are the omega-3, omega-6, and omega-9 fatty acids (FA). Omega-3 FA is found in canola, walnut, flaxseed, and fish oil. Omega-6 FA is found in the more common corn, soybean, sunflower, and safflower oils. The only major source of omega-9 FA is olive oil.

Fatty acids are made in series of chemical reactions that depend on a host of nutrients and hormones. The important thing to remember is the effect these FAs have on eicosanoid production and overall cell function.

In early times man ate a varied diet of grains and game. The ratio of omega-6 to omega-3 was about two or three to one (2-3:1). With the advent of agriculture, the types of plants eaten changed from flaxseed-related to corn and other cultivated crops. The Industrial

Revolution brought prepared foods with even less omega-3 FA. The ratio in the typical American diet is now as much as 20:1 due to the prevalence of refined vegetable oils.

In the early twentieth century, fat hydrogenation created a whole new problem. Natural oils are liquid and become rancid easily. This makes them hard to ship and store. The food industry was also looking for alternatives to butter and lard, which were loaded with saturated FAs and cholesterol. Since cholesterol is only found in animals, vegetable oils are all cholesterol-free. By adding hydrogen to the double bonds of the natural vegetable oils, a process called saturation or hydrogenation, liquid oils such as corn or safflower oil become more solid (think of Crisco) and resistant to oxidation. This makes them ideal for baking and to make margarine.

In the hydrogenation process, the carbon atoms line up opposite the hydrogen atoms. This is called trans orientation. Normally the hydrogen atoms are on the same side, called cis orientation. Humans have no enzymes for the manmade trans compounds. The trans FAs, or trans fats, as they are commonly known, maintain their straight form, making them more solid. The cis FAs fold back on themselves so they become more liquid and supple.

This difference affects cell function and structure in important ways. The manmade FAs compete with normally occurring FAs by blocking vital enzymes, especially those that convert essential FAs into a form that can be used in metabolism. They also find their way into cell walls and even breast milk. The same thing that makes them so good for baked goods—their solid form—causes cell walls to stiffen. This means it is harder for normal metabolic processes to proceed.

Many studies have shown that these artificial FAs increase the risk of heart disease and may increase the risk of breast cancer, and yet they are widely used despite the risks. Hydrogenated trans FAs are found in most commercially baked goods and in margarine. It is important to make informed decisions about the food you eat, so remember: if the label says, "partially hydrogenated oils," it means trans FAs. Fortunately, many local and even state governments have started to outlaw the use of trans FAs in restaurants.

A certain amount of an omega-6 fat called gamma linoleic acid (GLA) is also important for production of good eicosanoids. This is found in evening primrose oil, which I suggest our patients take along with fish oil. GLA is also found in borage oil, although this source contains a contaminant that blunts its effects, and in red currant seeds. The efficacy of GLA from red currant seeds, however, is unclear.

How Eicosanoids are Made

A basic understanding of the production of eicosanoids is necessary to understand how we influence which types the body makes. Basically, omega-3 FAs in canola and flax oil are metabolized into a FA called eicosapentanoic acid (EPA), the FA found in fish oil. Omega-6 FAs are converted to gamma linoleic acid (GLA), which is then metabolized into either "good" eicosanoids or into arachadonic Acid (AA), which is the source of the "bad" eicosanoids. EPA competes with and therefore inhibits the enzyme that forms AA from GLA. Therefore, the more EPA that is present, the less AA that is made and the more of the "good" eicosanoids" are produced. Therefore the ratio between these two FAs (AA/EPA) is a critical measure of what is happening in the body. Since the EPA found in fish oil is a critical factor, the best way to insure that adequate EPA is ingested is to take highly refined fish oil daily.

Evaluation and Treatments

You can also take other measures to produce good eicosanoids and avoid silent inflammation. We humans have a powerful system that controls minute by minute how our cells operate and how we feel. This system has markers we can use to see where we stand.

The famous Lyon Heart Diet study compared two groups of patients who had just suffered from a heart attack. One group got the American Heart Association diet, which is low in fat but high in vegetable oils and carbohydrates. The other group ate a diet rich in vegetables and fruits but low in omega-6 FAs. There was no difference in cholesterol or other blood tests.

The second group had a 30 percent drop in the arachadonic acid to eicosapentanoic acid (AA/EPA) ratio. A 1 percent drop in the ratio results in a 2 percent decrease in cardiac mortality. Other studies have shown that decreasing this ratio is effective in treating multiple sclerosis and there is evidence that this will also help attention deficit disorder (ADD) and depression. A recent study of teenagers showed that EPA supplementation was effective in decreasing bipolar episodes.

Lowering the AA/EPA ratio is also an effective way of decreasing cravings and depression.

I recommend that pain patients and recovering addicted patients take at least 5 grams per day of EPA and DHA in a very pure form. It is important to only take pharmaceutical-grade fish oil because the ocean is full of contaminants, including PCBs, dioxin, and heavy metals such as lead and mercury. The larger fish processed for their oil have eaten smaller fish, which themselves have eaten smaller organisms. Each step along this food chain concentrates toxins. The result is significant toxic contamination of the fish oil.

According to Dr. Sears, farmed fish are worse because they are fed a crude extract of unpurified fish oil, which is itself contaminated. The problem of mercury is so bad that the FDA requires warnings in supermarket fish departments that women of childbearing age avoid eating salmon and other deepwater fish. These are the same fish from which oil is extracted. The fish oil at the health food store may be refined, but unless is pharmaceutical grade you could be taking a huge dose of toxins.

As a reference, you can check out any fish oil that you use by checking with the International Fish Oil Standards (IFOS) program at the University of Guelph in Canada. A link is available on the Gracer Medical website. You can also find pharmaceutical-grade fish oil on our site. Vegetarians can substitute flax seed oil for the fish oil. There are also DHA products that are from vegetarian sources.

The Insulin Connection

Type II diabetes is a disease in which the cells are insensitive to insulin. To compensate, the amount of naturally occurring insulin in the early stages of this disease is higher than normal. Up to one-third of the population may have a tendency toward type II diabetes. They will therefore have insulin resistance and abnormally high insulin levels, but their glucose levels will not be high enough to be classified as diabetic. This is now recognized as a high-risk situation called the "metabolic syndrome." The treatment is the same as for early diabetes: a low-carbohydrate diet, exercise, and appropriate supplementation.

Insulin is needed to allow glucose to enter fat and muscle cells. Insulin also increases the amount of AA that is made from GLA. Therefore, we have to reduce insulin levels in order to get the most effect from taking fish oil.

Whenever the glucose levels in our blood rise, the pancreas secretes insulin. Since sugars or starchy foods that are quickly converted to sugars causes a quick rise, insulin is released in larger quantities. Limiting the quantities of sugary and starchy foods avoids insulin levels that are too high. In addition, eating protein with each meal causes glucagon secretion, which lowers insulin levels and helps fight silent inflammation. When we select our meals, we are deciding what types of eicosanoids we are going to produce. Remember that these chemicals are constantly produced in all of our cells and have potent effects. The basic strategy is to:

- Limit the amount of sugars and simple starches, eating adequate protein.
- Take pharmaceutical-grade fish oil (EPA).
- Take a small amount of evening primrose oil (GLA).
- Take proper vitamins, minerals, and amino acids to give the body the building blocks it needs for optimum function.

By strategically changing our diet, we help our bodies to create more good eicosanoids. We suffer less pain, have more energy, decrease our cravings, and recover more quickly.

Hypoglycemia

When we eat a large quantity of sugar or simple carbohydrates like bread or pasta, often too much insulin is released and an excess amount of glucose can be absorbed by the fat and muscle cells. This causes low blood sugar, called hypoglycemia. This insulin response is exaggerated in pre-diabetics and those with metabolic syndrome. Since the brain can only use glucose as fuel, when blood glucose gets low the body responds by secreting stress hormones such as epinephrine (adrenaline) and cortisol. These compounds liberate sugar from the liver and correct the situation.

Low blood sugar makes you feel shaky, tired, dizzy, irritable, sweaty, anxious, and hungry. The first thing you do is reach for a sugary snack and the whole process repeats. Since the effects of epinephrine are similar to those of low blood sugar itself, the relief you get is blunted. Addicted persons will often drink alcohol or take a pill to offset these symptoms, adding another trigger for addictive behavior. Some alcoholics drink mostly in response to hypoglycemic episodes, making this diagnosis extremely important.

Hypoglycemia is an over- and misused phrase that is applied to a myriad of symptoms and possible diagnoses. Serious medical conditions, such as tumors of the insulin-secreting cells of the pancreas (called insulinomas), can cause hypoglycemia. Many patients have several of the non-specific symptoms but only some suffer from true hypoglycemia.

It is important to find out whether your symptoms are really caused by low blood sugar. This can be done with a glucose tolerance test (GTT), in which blood glucose is measured over a five-hour period after taking a large amount of sugar. This test is now easy to do with the portable glucose monitors diabetics use to check their blood sugars. We sometimes also check insulin levels at the same time.

You may have this problem if you:

- Have severe or rapid mood swings or become irritable easily
- Binge on sweets
- Have bloating after meals
- Get sleepy after meals
- Get hungry shortly after eating
- Are frequently thirsty
- Have rapid heartbeat and get sweaty one to two hours after a meal
- Crave sweets
- Experience lack energy, feel fatigued
- Feel better after an alcoholic drink

This is only a partial list and the symptoms are nonspecific. This is why it is so important to perform a GTT to determine whether you have this problem. The treatment for hypoglycemia is identical to the anti-inflammation diet: avoid sugary foods and simple starches that are quickly converted into sugars. This prevents the need for high insulin secretion, therefore cutting off any reactive hypoglycemia.

The Common Sense Approach

You don't have to be a clinically certified nutritionist to understand that the body is affected by everything it ingests. Your general strategy to avoid the complications described in this chapter is:

- Cut down on carbs and eat enough protein.

- Start exercising.

- Take a high-quality fish oil supplement.

- Eat healthy fats to decrease inflammation.

- Take proper supplements.

These simple steps will have a significant positive effect on the symptoms of withdrawal and on many of the common complaints that arise from living in our modern, often toxic society. See our website for specific recommendations: www.gracer medicalgroup.com.

Chapter Twenty-Two
Hormones and Neurotransmitters

Our bodies are comprised of several basic systems that affect general health. Each of these systems must be evaluated and treated to ensure optimal results in any substance abuse treatment program. These include hormones such as cortisol, insulin, and thyroid; the replacement of sex hormones; and the evaluation of neurotransmitter levels.

Hormones

Various hormones regulate our body systems. You might think of them as a type of wireless communication system. Each type interacts with receptors on the walls of specific cells.

One type of hormone, called endocrine hormones, comes from specific glands. Cortisol comes from the adrenal glands, insulin from the pancreas, estrogens from the ovaries, testosterone from the testes, and thyroid hormone from the thyroid gland. These hormones spread to all the cells in the body through the blood and intercellular fluids. These hormones are regulated by other hormones made in the pituitary gland in the brain. Pituitary hormones are themselves regulated by hormones made in the hypothalamus.

Another group, the paracrine hormones, is made by each individual cell. When released, they cause specific actions in specific nearby cells. These include hormones secreted by the hypothalamus that cause the release of pituitary hormones. In turn, pituitary hormones stimulate the endocrine glands to secrete their hormones. Paracrine hormones include serotonin, dopamine, norepinephrine, GABA, glutamate, and the other neurotransmitters.

Other hormones, called autocrine hormones, are also created by each individual cells. These compounds, however, only affect the local area around the cell. They are made in tiny quantities and disappear so quickly that they are hard to isolate and measure. Eicosanoids are one of the most important groups of autocrine hormones.

Each of the trillions of cells in our bodies constantly makes eicosanoids from dietary fat. Remember that some cause inflammation, while others prevent it. Some attract immune cells and others turn off the immune process. Some promote blood clotting and others inhibit it. The balance of these hormones makes the difference between optimal health and poor quality of life. By influencing the production of good eicosanoids over the bad ones, we decrease our chances of heart disease, degenerative arthritis, depression, and Alzheimer's disease.

This also influences how we feel, the level of pain we suffer, and whether we have cravings. For example, if you have the flu and someone steps on your foot, it will probably hurt more than usual. If you've just won the lottery, though, you might not even notice. Why?

Local factors, modulated by messages sent from the brain, cause the balance of eicosanoids to change in the areas of our brain that register pain and emotions. If the cells make more good compounds due to a proper diet, exercise, and nutrition, the pain will be less.

This is an ongoing process. Eicosanoids act powerfully and quickly on nearby cells, so their effects can change rapidly. In order to be effective, a regimen that adjusts this system must be continuous and stable.

Neurotransmitters and Amino Acid Supplementation

Another important component of our program is to measure neurotransmitters by checking their level in the urine. The major neurotransmitters we measure and treat are:

- **Serotonin.** Low activity is associated with depression and anxiety. Serotonin is a major relaxation neurotransmitter and may become depleted with chronic stress. About 70 percent of our patients have low serotonin.

- **Norepinephrine.** Low activity is associated with depression, lethargy, and poor mental focus. Increased activity is seen with chronic stress and leads to irritability, shakiness, and anxiety.

- **Epinephrine.** This is made from norepinephrine and is needed to regulate glucose levels. With chronic stress, nor-epinephrine may be used up and therefore none is available for conversion into epinephrine. With chronic hypoglycemia, the epinephrine may be used up.

- **Dopamine.** Low activity is associated with depression and cravings. Its activity varies depending upon a variety of cir-cumstances and the part of the brain in which it is acting.

- **GABA.** When serotonin is low, GABA takes on more of the relaxation activity. This causes more to be released, depleting its levels in the brain.

- **Glutamate.** The excitation neurotransmitter released in response to stress, tissue injury, and chronic pain. Increased glutamate activity is responsible for some of the symptoms of drug addiction and withdrawal.

Neurotransmitters are released from bubbles called vesicles at the ends of the neurons. The chemical messengers attach to receptor sites on nearby neurons and even on the neuron they came from. Meanwhile, the neurotransmitters are reabsorbed into the vesicles. This constant release and reuptake results in a steady emotional state. If there isn't enough neurotransmitter in the synapse, depression, anxiety, or cravings can occur. If an insufficient amount is being produced in the cell to begin with, a lower than normal amount may be available in the vesicles.

Prozac and the other common antidepressants block the reuptake, increasing the concentration in the synapse. When serotonin is blocked, the medication is called a selective serotonin reuptake inhibitor (SSRI). Other drugs do the same for norepinephrine and dopamine. This results in symptom relief. It also leads to significant side effects such as sexual dysfunction, insomnia, nausea, and even anxiety as the increased amount of neurotransmitter interacts with other receptors.

A different strategy is to supplement the building blocks that make up these neurotransmitters to increase their amount. The result is more neurotransmitters in the vesicle and, therefore, more available in the synapse. Under the correct conditions and with the correct vitamins, minerals, and amino acids, this approach is a natural way to correct the underlying problem without significant side effects. This technique is often used together with drugs and is extremely effective.

A third factor is the effect of eicosanoids on second messenger production. By decreasing insulin production with a low and properly balanced carbohydrate diet, along with nutritional supplementation including pharmaceutical-grade fish oil, the quantity of cyclic AMP increases. This amplifies the effects of neurotransmitters, resulting in better efficiency and easing the effects of serotonin or GABA depletion.

By analyzing urine results, we can determine the proper prescription to replenish and rebalance this system.

Adrenal Stress and Fatigue

Cortisol is vital for normal cell function. This hormone is secreted by the adrenal gland, found just above the kidneys. A cortisol sensor in the hypothalamus closely measures the concentration of cortisol in the blood. When the level is low, the hypothalamus secretes CRH, or cortisol releasing hormone. This compound travels to the pituitary gland to cause the release of adrenocorticotropic hormone (ACTH). This stimulates the release of cortisol into the blood.

Cortisol levels change throughout the day on a schedule called the circadian rhythm. Levels are highest in the morning to get us ready for the day, and decrease while we sleep. Since cortisol blocks the body from restoring and repairing itself, the body does most of its rebuilding while we sleep. It is therefore appropriate for cortisol levels to be low at night.

With stress, the adrenal gland increases the release of cortisol. Physical factors such as exercise, infection, increased insulin levels, or emotional upheaval are all causes. In today's busy life we are constantly under stress from traffic, work, family, and the news. If you have a chronic illness or chronic pain, the problem is even bigger.

Substance abuse and constant withdrawal tax the adrenal gland. Severe adrenal deficiency causes fatigue, low blood pressure, salt craving, weakness, and can even lead to death, especially under stressful conditions such as infection. The most common cause of adrenal insufficiency comes from the prolonged use of steroids, such as prednisone (an artificial form of cortisol), which are usually prescribed for serious medical problems like severe asthma and inflammatory conditions such as rheumatoid arthritis.

High levels of these drugs shut down ACTH and, therefore, the adrenal gland. With time, the gland atrophies. When the need arises for a burst of cortisol, it cannot produce. Patients with adrenal problems often need to take small amounts of cortisol for the rest of their lives and need higher doses during times of stress. There is also a condition called Addison's disease in which the adrenal becomes scarred and ceases to function for unknown causes. In rare cases, the gland is destroyed by an infection like tuberculosis.

Chronic stress can fatigue the adrenal glands through constant stimulation. Higher levels of cortisol result in suppression of the immune system and higher glucose levels. This leads to higher insulin levels and changes in brain receptors that can lead to chronic depression and anxiety. Abdominal obesity and even an increase in the risk of heart disease can occur.

When a truly stressful situation arises, the adrenals are just not up to the task. This is not usually at a level that leads to the severe symptoms of true adrenal insufficiency, but can lead to chronic fatigue, brain fog, anxiety, depression, dizziness, increased thirst, salt craving, and a host of other non-specific symptoms. It may also lead to frequent infections and "crashing" during difficult times.

Elevated cortisol levels are part of a series of self-perpetuating consequences. Stress increases cortisol levels. This raises glucose levels through effects on the liver and by the release of norepinephrine. Insulin levels are elevated, which results in more norepinephrine release and increased fat in the abdominal area.

Abdominal fat is hormonally active. It produces thyroid-binding globulin and an enzyme that converts testosterone into estrogen. Estrogen causes the liver to make even more thyroid-binding globulin and sex hormone-binding globulin (SHBG). These transport thyroid hormone and estrogen and testosterone in the blood. The hormones bound to these globulins are not available for cell use. There is therefore less thyroid hormone activity. Since testosterone is bound by the SHBG more tightly than estrogen is, there is also less testosterone activity relative to estrogen, which is a problem for men.

The enzyme then converts much of the remaining testosterone into estrogen. This increased estrogen activity causes a condition called estrogen dominance, leading to more abdominal fat, increased

risk of certain cancers, decreased libido, increased risk of heart disease and other silent inflammation diseases, high blood pressure, and
even more stimulation of cortisol and norepinephrine.

All of the steroid-like hormones are made from cholesterol,
which is converted into the "master hormone" pregnanolone. This
is further metabolized into either DHEA or progesterone, which is
then converted to the other sex hormones or cortisol. When stress
increases, more cortisol is needed. DHEA levels decrease because
there is not enough pregnanolone to make both, so cortisol, which
is vital for life, takes priority. The resulting drop in sex hormones
causes pre-menopausal symptoms or estrogen dominance in women
and symptoms of low testosterone in men.

We test for adrenal function by looking at the level of cortisol
four times during a day to see whether there is a normal circadian
rhythm. When a person is under stress, this pattern is disrupted. In
severe cases, the morning level is low. We often see decreased levels
later in the day, when they should be rising.

The easiest way to measure this hormone, as well as the sex hormones, is to collect a sample of saliva. The concentration of hormone
in the saliva closely correlates with the active form of the hormone
in the blood. This makes these tests easy and convenient for the
patient to do at home. We also sometimes do a test in which we give
a synthetic form of ACTH by injection to see if the cortisol level
increases. We also measure the DHEA/cortisol ratio. This is usually
low in patients with high stress and adrenal fatigue.

Treatment is oriented toward the causes. It includes diet, supplementation, and, if warranted, low doses of cortisol.

Sex Hormones and Hormone Replacement

Before starting this discussion, I want to clearly define some
important concepts. Natural means any substance that comes
from an organic source—that is, ones that are not man-made. Just

because a hormone is natural that does not mean it is human. Until recently, the most common drug used for estrogen replacement was hormones purified from pregnant horse urine (the source of brand name Premarin).

Although effective, Premarin increased the risk of breast cancer. It was also impossible to measure hormone levels while a person was on this drug. Gracer Medical uses bio-identical hormones for replacement. They may be made in a lab, yet they are comprised of exactly the same molecule as is found in the human body. These have the least side effects, act predictably, and can be measured with routine lab tests.

Estrogen, progesterone, and testosterone have important functions in both men and women. Estrogen and progesterone are secreted by the ovaries and testosterone is secreted by the testes. The adrenal glands of both genders secrete small amounts of all three. Therefore, men normally have a low level of female hormones and women normally have some testosterone.

In women, these compounds drive sexuality and regulate the menstrual cycle. Testosterone has important functions in both sexes related to libido and bone density. As we age, our hormone levels normally decrease. With this decrease can come significant symptoms and metabolic problems.

Men with metabolic syndrome almost always have low testosterone levels, as do many chronic pain patients. Symptoms include lack of energy, fatigue, decreased libido, problems attaining and maintaining an erection (erectile dysfunction), hair loss, feeling cold, depression, decreased ambition, obesity, and muscle weakness. Women can also have a decreased testosterone level. This can give similar but usually less dramatic symptoms, the most common being decreased libido. It can also contribute to osteoporosis.

Gracer Medical usually aims to replace testosterone to the level of a normal thiry- to forty-year-old. Effective gels and patches exist, but the best way to treat many men, especially if they are obese, is with an injection every two weeks. It is important to check estrogen levels before prescribing testosterone for men because in some males, testosterone is converted into estrogen. Since pituitary hormones regulate testosterone secretion from the testes, this system should also be evaluated.

The easiest way to check sex hormone levels is in the saliva. It is very important to screen men for possible prostate cancer before prescribing testosterone because this hormone stimulates the growth of prostate cancers. There is no evidence, however, that testosterone supplementation causes prostate cancer. In fact, for many men the PSA level actually goes down after they start using testosterone. In women the doses are much smaller, of course, but the effects on libido, energy, and even bone density can be dramatic.

DHEA (dehydroepiandrosterone) is the hormone from which all other sex hormones are made. In chronic fatigue patients, and probably in chronically depressed and addicted patients, the DHEA level is often very low. In chronic stress there is more need for cortisol, which decreases DHEA production.

Recent studies have indicated that this hormone is effective in improving energy and perhaps the immune system. Because it is the "mother" sex hormone, it is important to check DHEA and other sex hormone levels before and after supplementation. In some women, DHEA is converted into testosterone and can cause unwanted side effects such as hair growth and acne. In men it is wise to check for prostate cancer before using DHEA.

During a normal menstrual cycle, the lining of the uterus is stimulated by estrogen secreted from the ovaries. Around day 14, an egg is ejected from an ovary and progesterone is secreted. Progesterone causes the uterine lining to become thicker. If the egg is fertilized progesterone levels rise through the pregnancy. If the egg is not fertilized progesterone secretion stops and the uterine lining sloughs off, resulting in menses.

This process is regulated by pituitary hormones. As a woman nears menopause, the first hormonal change is usually a failure to ovulate, causing low progesterone levels. Later the ovaries stop making estrogen. Measurement of these hormones during different times of the cycle determines if hormone replacement is needed. If so, we use bio-identical hormones so that the levels can later be measured and dosages regulated accordingly. We also measure testosterone in women and provide small doses if needed.

These hormones are available in several forms. They are readily absorbed through the skin and are often prescribed in cream or gel form. They can also be taken as a capsule or as a lozenge that is placed under the tongue. For testosterone, injections give good blood levels for about two weeks. It can also be implanted under the skin as pellets that work for about two months. The type of follow-up test required depends on the type of dosage. As this whole area is complex, and as there are significant possible side effects and medical complications, you should consult with a physician familiar with these treatments.

Thyroid Dysfunction

The thyroid gland in the neck regulates the body's furnace. Thyroid hormone is needed for cellular metabolism and is particularly critical for energy production and oxygen utilization. Without adequate thyroid function we slow down and feel cold and tired. Hypothyroidism is a common cause of depression. Other symptoms are constipation, dry skin and hair, heavy menstrual periods, and brain fog. Because of slow metabolism, cholesterol levels are high and there is high risk of heart disease.

There are two types of thyroid hormones: thyroxine (T_4), which has four iodine atoms, and triiodothyronine (T_3), the active form of

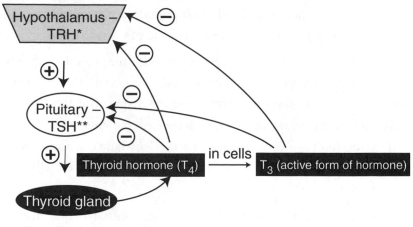

*Thyroid releasing hormone
**Thyroid stimulating hormone

22-1: Hypothalamus and thyroid action

the hormone, which has three iodine atoms. T_4 is secreted by the thyroid and is converted to T_3 in the cells. When there is not enough T_4, the level of thyroid stimulating hormone (TSH) hormone increases and stimulates the thyroid to make more T_4. Testing TSH then, is a specific and sensitive way to determine thyroid function. If the T_4 is low, the TSH is high and visa versa.

Many people have a problem converting T_4 into T_3 in their cells. Since the hypothalamus measures T_4, these and TSH levels may be normal but the person functionally has hypothyroidism. There is also evidence that low serotonin levels common in fatigued and/or stressed people decrease the pituitary's ability to release TSH, further compromising thyroid function and making diagnosis more difficult.

When this occurs, giving the patient T_4 is not effective, or the dose needed is much higher than what lab tests indicate. It is vital for the physician to know that this is a possibility. Often, treatment must be based on observation rather than lab findings. T_3 is what the patient needs, not the usually prescribed T_4. T_3 is found in natural products such as Armour thyroid or desiccated thyroid, which is ground, dried beef or pork thyroid glands. T_3 can also be given in a pure medication called Cytomel. Compounding pharmacies formulate it into longer-acting capsules by specific physician order.

It is truly amazing how many patients with the typical symptoms of hypothyroidism get well after taking T_3. This is so effective that I often use T_3 as an important treatment for depression. Psychiatrists have known for years that many depressed patients with normal TSH levels improve with T_3 but not with T_4. Many do not respond to the usual antidepressant medications and only get well with this treatment.

There is evidence that T_3 acts as a neurotransmitter and may be needed for proper brain function. Another problem in depressed patients is the fact that TSH release is at least in part dependent on serotonin. The decreased serotonin often found in depressed patients blunts the usual increase in TSH, further confusing the clinical picture.

The way to test for thyroid function is to measure the free (unbound) T_3 and T_4 as well as the TSH. I look for the T_3 to be in the high to normal range. Since TSH cannot be trusted to tell the whole story, the levels must be interpreted while looking at the whole clinical situation.

Other lab tests can indicate abnormal thyroid function. The most common cause of hypothyroidism is an autoimmune condition called Hashimoto's or lymphocytic thyroiditis. This disease affects women much more commonly than men and is usually asymptomatic. It may leave the thyroid unable to create thyroid hormone. The first indication is the onset of hypothyroid symptoms. Thyroid antibody tests can show if this condition is present.

Another screening method is to measure body temperature. Broda O. Barnes, MD, described this in his book, *Thyroid: The Unsuspected Illness*. It is also used by E. Denis Wilson, MD, who developed a whole system for evaluating and dealing with thyroid problems. They believe that when thyroid function is low, so is the body temperature. When the proper thyroid supplementation is prescribed, body temperature returns to normal.

In my experience, almost all patients with hypothyroidism have low body temperature. Many others with low temperature have normal thyroid function. This makes body temperature an excellent screening test for thyroid problems. If temperature is normal, you probably do not have low thyroid function; if temperature is low, you may have a thyroid problem or the low temperature could be caused by something else. I have also found that temperature can stay abnormally low even when thyroid function is restored and the patient feels well.

Wilson believes that the enzyme that converts T_4 to T_3 is itself abnormal in cases of low thyroid function, and that it can be restored with T_3 treatment. If this is true, the patient may not need long-term supplementation. He uses T_3 in cycles of increasing and then decreasing dosages. I have had some success with this regimen, but most patients must take thyroid replacement on an ongoing basis.

Finally, there are further problems with traditional thyroid lab tests. TSH is sensitive to T_4 and T_3. The TSH may therefore indicate that the patient is taking too much thyroid medication at the dose needed to alleviate symptoms. Because of this, many patients suffer with doses that are too low because the physician treats the lab test instead of the patient.

Our program determines the correct dose using symptoms and other physical findings, as well as lab tests. It is important to check bone density when starting thyroid treatment, as there is evidence that thyroid medication levels that are too high may lead to osteoporosis. Patients must be warned and their bone density tested, although I do not feel it is a real problem with correct dosages. Another caveat is to be sure that the patient does not have significant adrenal fatigue, as increasing thyroid function requires adequate cortisol production. In this case, the adrenal dysfunction must first be corrected.

Chapter Twenty-Three
Supplements

S upplements can make a big difference in your overall nutritional status even if you are healthy. Most addicted persons have major deficiencies in their diets and also have unique needs caused by the changes in brain chemistry that accompany this problem. I have therefore broken down the information in this chapter into general health suggestions, strategies for withdrawal and detoxification, and support for specific problems. You can always check our website for the latest suggestions and the best way to get high-quality, reliable supplements.

Basic Support

I recommend that most of my patients take a basic set of supplements that support their overall body function. Since the readers of this book have special needs, I will just say that we can all benefit from a comprehensive multivitamin/mineral supplement. Pharmaceutical-grade fish oil is also very important. After these, each of us has specific needs that depend on our health risks and habits. Please see the recommendations below.

Detoxification

Remember that you should only detox from heavy drug use under the direction of a physician. At the very least you should have a close friend or relative stay with you. After you are stable, continuing with this program will decrease cravings and make withdrawal much easier.

This concept was developed by Joan Mathews Larson, PhD, in her groundbreaking book *Seven Weeks to Sobriety*. After Leni Felton and I decided on the best ingredients for this regimen, we consulted Dr. Larson's book. It was no surprise that our independent ideas closely shadowed her excellent suggestions. I also consulted with Dr. Larson in my research to write the nutritional sections of this book. I highly suggest that you read her book for more specific guidelines, especially for the treatment of alcoholism.

These ingredients will support your body's normal functions and help restore the nutrients and natural compounds, such as neurotransmitters, that are depleted by substance abuse. For this book, I am going to recommend a basic regimen that will work for almost everyone. At our clinic, I often test for specific abnormalities and modify the prescription as needed.

Basic Detox Formula

Supplement	How Taken
Multiple vitamin/mineral in the form of four to six capsules or tablets daily (not the usual "One a Day").	Take two tablets with each meal (three times each day).
Pharmaceutical-grade fish oil: Two to 5 grams of EPA plus DHA daily.	Ten to 15 cc of liquid with a meal once each day.
GLA (gamma linolenic acid) in the form of evening primrose oil (EPO) 45 to 100 mg. (With some types of problems much higher doses may be used.)	Take once in the morning with breakfast.

Vitamin C: 1000 mg as ascorbates.	Take two, ½ hour before each meal.
Vitamin D (in the form of D₃): either as 400 IU drops or tablets/capsules 400 IU to 1000 IU	Take 1600 to 2000 IU twice daily (more is needed if you are deficient)
Calcium/magnesium supplement: 500/250 mg.	Take one with each meal.
Glutamine: 500 mg.	Take two, ½ hour before each meal.
Pancreatic enzymes and, for some, betaine hydrochloride to supplement deficient stomach acid.	Take two, ½ hour before each meal.
Amino acids: 500 to 1000 mg.	Take one in the AM, ½ hour breakfast, and ½ hour before dinner.
Tyrosine: 500 mg.*	Take two, ½ hour before each meal.
5 hydroxy-tryptophan (5HTP): 500 mg.	Take two, ½ to one hour before bedtime.
DL-phenylalanine (DLPA): 500 mg.*	Take one or two ½ hour before meals

*People who have high blood pressure, hyperthyroidism, schizophrenia, PKU, or melanoma, who take an MAO inhibitor, or who are pregnant should not take these amino acids unless it is under the direct supervision of their physician.

23-1: Basic detox formula chart

At our clinic we use combination products that make getting these supplements a bit easier. We also use some specific products with additional ingredients for some of our patients. There are huge discrepancies in the quality of nutritional supplements available in health food stores and markets. It is very difficult to tell which products to buy. We therefore have specific suggestions. See our website for specific recommendations: www.gracermedicalgroup.com.

Vitamins C and B and Mineral IV Infusions

We use high-dose vitamin C IV infusions at our clinic for detoxification and to support other types of medical treatments. At these doses vitamin C can remove heavy metals and has also been used for drug detoxification, especially for alcohol. We give a mixture of vitamin C at doses of 25 grams or more along with magnesium, calcium, and other vitamins and minerals. We can also infuse amino acids and other important nutrients. This can make a huge difference in how quickly one can start to feel better during withdrawal. Most of these patients have depleted their stores of these minerals and vitamins. If you cannot get IV treatment, the vitamin C flush alone can really help.

Vitamin C Flush

It is safe to take large amounts of vitamin C. Dr Linus Pauling, the famous double Nobel laureate, advocated huge doses of vitamin C as a way of delaying aging, increasing immune status, and fighting illness. Vitamin C has also been used as a detoxification agent and even helps remove heavy metals like mercury from the body.

The most serious side effect of oral vitamin C is diarrhea. This usually occurs with doses over 10 grams per day. The concept of a vitamin C flush is that the body will absorb as much as it can use and that the diarrhea starts after this amount is exceeded. The diarrhea also flushes out toxins and acts a cleanser for the GI tract.

Start with a gallon of non-sweetened juice, distilled water, or Aloe Vera (aloe to drink). Put 1,000 milligrams of powdered vitamin C in the form of Ester C or any other good buffered C in 4 to 6 ounces of liquid and drink it. You can also take a capsule or tablet of vitamin C and drink the liquid with it. Repeat the procedure every half-hour, counting how many times you have taken the dose. Continue until you develop diarrhea.

Once you know how many doses it takes for diarrhea to develop, subtract two doses (if you took ten doses before diarrhea developed, then subtract two to arrive at eight). Now you assume that you can probably take 8,000 milligrams of vitamin C without causing diarrhea.

Wait four hours, then prepare an 8,000-milligram dose of vitamin C, and take it with as much liquid as you can comfortably drink. Repeat this procedure every four hours for the next 44 hours (counting your beginning doses, this means you will be flooding your body with vitamin C for two days). If you develop diarrhea during the treatment, cut back little by little to find the dose you can sustain without diarrhea developing. If treating a chronic condition you should, of course, consult a health professional; you could elect to repeat this process every month or so.

Description of Ingredients

There are specific reasons for taking each of the compounds that I suggest. They each have a role to play in helping you restore and then maintain your health.

Multivitamin and mineral: Most of us do not get the basic recommended amount of vitamins and minerals in our daily diets. In fact, our bodies can use much higher doses than what you get from an excellent, well-balanced diet. If you add the stresses of addiction and withdrawal, you can suffer significant deficits in many vital nutrients.

The usual one-a-day vitamin has many important components, but the actual amounts are low. The FDA's recommended minimum daily requirements (MDAs) are designed to avoid deficiency diseases, such as rickets and scurvy, rather than to give the optimal amount. This is especially true for those who have the stress and relative malnutrition caused by substance abuse.

The vitamin that I suggest is split into six doses. There is simply no way to fit all of this into one small tablet. The B vitamins are crucial for the treatment of addiction, as well as for detox and withdrawal. There is evidence that, along with the relative decrease in the ingestion of foods high in omega-3 fatty acids, there has also been a decline in the intake of B vitamins. Both these factors cause deficiencies.

Drug takers are even more likely to be deficient. This may increase anxiety, compulsive behavior, irritability, and the likelihood of addiction. The B vitamins and the impact of deficiencies in this group are listed below.

- **Thiamin,** vitamin B1, is commonly depleted in alcoholics. Acute deficiency causes a very severe condition called the Werneke-Korsakoff Syndrome, which can lead to permanent brain damage if thiamin is not given promptly. In the emergency room, we often give this vitamin as an injection to intoxicated patients as a precaution.

- **Niacin,** vitamin B3, has been used to treat a variety of conditions, including high cholesterol, degenerative arthritis, and psychiatric illness. Edwin Hofer, MD, has done extensive studies on patients with severe psychiatric illnesses. He found that high doses treat schizophrenia and severe anxiety. It can reduce cravings and compulsive behavior.

- **Pyridoxine,** vitamin B6, is vital for the production of neurotransmitters. It is a key vitamin in the methylation pathway described earlier in this book. Pyridoxine is converted by the liver into the active form called pyridoxal 5 phosphate. This form of the vitamin is becoming more available, as some people have problems with this conversion. Some studies show that very high doses of pyridoxine can actually cause nerve damage.

- **Folic acid** is used in methylation and deficiency can lead to confusion, nerve damage, and anemia. There are individuals in whom the enzyme that converts folic acid to the active form is underactive. For this reason we give high doses. Note that even this high dose is just a few milligrams.

- **Vitamin B12** is unique among the B vitamin in that it is absorbed into the body by a complex route that needs proper stomach acid and function. High doses are required to ensure proper absorption. It is often given by injection to aid absorption. B12 deficiency can cause anemia and nerve damage.

- **Vitamin B5,** inositol, choline, and PABA are other important vitamins included in the multivitamin.

Fish oil (source of omega-3 fatty acids): As described in the nutrition chapter, the EPA (eicosapentanoic acid) found in fish oil reduces the amount of inflammatory prostaglandins and reduces "silent inflammation." This reduces the risk of many chronic conditions, such as heart disease. It also acts in the central nervous system to increase the efficiency of the systems that regulate the balance between activation and relaxation (glutamate and GABA).

DHA (dodecahexanoic acid): DHA is a basic building block for brain cell walls. This fish oil must be pharmaceutical grade, as the deepwater fish from which the oil is derived concentrate heavy metals such as lead and mercury, as well as other contaminants like PCBs, in their tissues. It is important to check sources carefully before you buy. Since it is expensive to purify fish oil, in this case you get what you pay for.

GLA (gamma linolenic acid): This is source of the specific omega-6 fatty acid that the body converts into the anti-inflammatory Group 1 prostaglandins. Dr. Joan Larson has found GLA to be very effective in decreasing cravings and alleviating mood disorders.

It is important to make sure the GLA you take is made from evening primrose oil (EPO), as the other common source, borage oil, is not effective. It is surmised that a trace component in borage oil blocks GLA's beneficial effect. The dosage that I suggest for most patients is less than that suggested by some other physicians, including Dr. Larson, because GLA can increase the inflammation in certain patients. In other patients much higher doses may be needed, but this must be assessed individually. This is fully described in the Nutrition chapter.

Vitamin C: This vitamin has been shown to decrease the withdrawal symptoms from alcohol and other drugs. It is safe to take large amounts of vitamin C without ill effects. I suggest that you take it in the form of mineral ascorbates instead of the usual ascorbic acid, as the latter can cause stomach irritation. Ascorbate is not acidic. It is also beneficial, as other important minerals like magnesium, potassium, calcium, and zinc are attached. Another excellent product is Ester C, which is also buffered.

Vitamin D: This vitamin is crucial for the formation and maintenance of our bones. It allows the absorption of calcium from the intestines and its incorporation into the skeleton. More recently it has been found to be very important in the prevention of various types of cancer, including pancreatic, breast, and colon cancer. It also plays an important role in immune system and musculoskeletal function. Some studies show that it reduces the chance of multiple sclerosis. It most likely plays a role in brain function. Vitamin D is produced in the skin with exposure to the UV rays in sunlight. Fifteen minutes is probably enough, but in northern latitudes in the winter months this is often impossible. In addition, sunscreen products of SPF 8 cut out 95 percent of the UV rays, as does regular window glass. Since there is very little vitamin D in our food, even though it is added to milk and other products, it is not surprising that vitamin D deficiency is extremely common.

Vitamin D is measured in the form of 25 hydroxy vitamin D. Any level under 40 nmol/l is too low and under 25 is extremely low. Since I have been routinely measuring vitamin D levels I have rarely found a patient with a level over 40. The lowest level that I have seen in one of my patients is 6.2! A recent study showed that 80 percent of elderly over 65 years have vitamin D insufficiency, 44 percent of nursing home residents have severe vitamin D deficiency (< 12 nmol/l) 75 percent of hip fracture cases have vitamin D insufficiency, 25 percent have vitamin D deficiency and 5 percent have severe vitamin D deficiency. For this reason I now recommend that all patients with serious medical problems or who are over 65 years old have their vitamin D level checked and supplement vigorously. The usual RDA of 400 IU daily is not even close to being enough, and many experts are suggesting very high doses. Vitamin D comes in two forms, D_2 and D_3. Although it is harder to find, D_3 is the one to get. The usual dose is at least 1000 IU daily for healthy persons, but if there is a low vitamin D level I recommend at least 1600 IU three times per day and will often give much higher doses under my direct supervision for some time. Of course, an addicted person will almost always be deficient, so it is a good idea to supplement vitamin D at the higher level as part of any program.

Calcium/magnesium supplement: Many of us have a chronic magnesium deficiency. In addition, alcohol markedly increases excretion in the urine of both these minerals. Magnesium is used in our cells for many of the most important metabolic processes. The cell pumps out calcium and takes in magnesium as part of its usual function. The magnesium inside the cell is depleted. Regular supplementation over time is required to replenish the level.

Magnesium causes relaxation of muscles and the nervous system. It is used in patients with heart attacks and decreases the risk of irregular heartbeats. It also helps the tight chest found in asthma and even helps with migraine headaches.

Low blood levels of calcium can trigger severe muscle spasm and seizures. In acute drug withdrawal these minerals are often given in an IV (along with the vitamins C and B and minerals). Taking these will really help you get through detox.

Glutamine: This is the most common amino acid in the blood and extracellular fluids. While it is made by our bodies, there is often a relative deficiency, especially during times of physical and/or emotional stress. Glutamine is the main fuel for the upper GI tract and is an important component of glutathione, the main antioxidant found in the liver. This is very important for liver support, especially for alcoholics.

Glutamine has another very important property: it can satisfy the brain's need for glucose. During a diet, 500 milligrams of glutamine placed on the tongue to dissolve quickly reaches the brain and stops sugar cravings. Other data indicates that glutamine can reduce cravings. Feeding glutamine to rats has been shown to decrease their alcohol consumption by 33 percent, while giving them other amino acids has no effect.

Joan Larson, PhD, uses glutamine as part of her craving management program at her Health Recovery Center. According to Dr. Larson, dissolving a 500-milligram capsule of glutamine on the tongue quickly quenches alcohol cravings.

Pancreatic enzymes and betaine hydrochloride: Most people with addiction problems have abnormal pancreatic function. Again, this is most pronounced in alcohol abuse. The addition of pancreatic enzymes ensures that the body can absorb more of what is eaten.

Many patients also do not produce enough stomach acid. For them I prescribe betaine hydrochloride, a source of hydrochloric acid. This can stimulate the stomach to empty more quickly, decreasing bloating and increasing the efficiency of digestion. (If you have had bleeding ulcers or other serious GI problems, please check with your physician before taking betaine hydrochloride.)

Amino acids: Amino acids are the building blocks for proteins. They are usually depleted in addicted persons. Many amino acids have special roles to play in the metabolism and the brain and should be taken separately. A simple supplement is very effective in replenishing your stores of many of them.

5 hydroxy tryptophan (5HTP): This amino acid is the building block for serotonin and melatonin. These chemicals are important in preventing depression and anxiety, and for promoting normal sleep.

We originally used tryptophan, the amino acid from which 5HTP is made. Unfortunately, a production contaminant in Japan caused many people to develop a very painful and chronic condition called eosinophilic myalgia syndrome. The FDA banned tryptophan, and the ban remains in place even though tryptophan was proven not to be the cause. You can get tryptophan by prescription, but 5HTP is readily available and works as well.

Tyrosine: This is the amino acid building block for the activating neurotransmitters dopamine, norepinephrine, and epinephrine. It acts as an antidepressant and increases energy. It is also an important constituent of thyroid hormone.*

DL-Phenylalanine: This amino acid is a building block for norepinephrine and epinephrine. It also is effective in some for pain reduction. Another important function is its blocking action on the enzyme that breaks down endorphins. This means that endorphin levels go up and withdrawal symptoms go down.*

* People with high blood pressure, hyperthyroidism, PKU, schizophrenia, or melanoma, who take an MAO inhibitor, or who are pregnant should not take these amino acids unless it is under the direct supervision of their physician.

Probiotics

The normal bacteria found in the colon have many important purposes. In fact, without these bacteria we would die. They digest some plant foods and create some of the B vitamins. They also prevent abnormal bacteria from infecting the bowel.

In many of us this "normal flora" is suppressed due to poor nutrition or from taking antibiotics. This can allow abnormal bacteria to grow that cause severe diarrhea, or even allow an overgrowth of yeast. By taking capsules that contain cultures of these normal bacteria (acidophilus, bifidobacter, lactobacillus, and certain strains of e. coli) we can re-establish the normal balance. Combined with pancreatic enzymes and other specific nutrients, such as fructo oligo saccharides (FOS), these bacteria support normal bowel function. This is evaluated using the Comprehensive Digestive Stool Analysis (CDSA) test.

Liver Support

Many drug users either have liver disease from alcohol abuse or are infected with hepatitis C. For these individuals we use specific supplements for liver support.

- **Silymarin** from milk thistle is a specific herbal remedy for liver problems. It lowers liver enzymes and probably prevents liver damage.

- **Turmeric and artichoke** are effective anti-inflammatory herbs.

- **N-acetyl cysteine** is a vital component of glutathione, the main antioxidant used by the liver for processing toxins.

- **Glutamine** is another of the components of glutathione. Please see more in the detox section.

See our website for specific recommendations: www.gracer medcalgroup.com.

Chapter Twenty-Four
The Surviving Withdrawal Diet

*Created by Leni Felton in conjunction
with the Gracer Medical Group*

A strong body will face the challenges of withdrawal and avoid relapse better than one weakened by poor nutrition. Whether you're kitchen-savvy or need to rely on outside sources for your food, this chapter will help guide you toward better choices that support overall health.

The Surviving Withdrawal Diet/Detox Program

Upon stopping the use of an addictive substance you will pass through an initial detox phase, during which you will suffer a variety of withdrawal symptoms depending on your specific medical situation. Leni Felton, our clinical nutritionist, has developed what we call the Surviving Withdrawal Diet. Foods and nutrients can be powerful tools for easing some of the physical and mental symptoms associated with withdrawal. They can help you begin to unburden your body of the ill effects of addiction. They can also help to address some of the underlying health issues that may have prompted you to look for relief by utilizing drugs or alcohol. Dietary and lifestyle changes provide excellent proactive gear for your withdrawal toolkit.

By following the Surviving Withdrawal Diet, you will discover increased energy and decreased cravings. The underpinning of the Surviving Withdrawal Diet will be to accomplish the following:

1. Maintain consistent and balanced blood sugar and low insulin levels.

Avoiding sugars and simple starches is the best way to keep your insulin levels low. Simple starches, such as potatoes, white rice, most breads, and pastas are converted to sugar in the stomach. These sugars are then quickly absorbed into the blood, where insulin is needed to clear them into the fat and muscle cells. High levels of insulin shift the body toward inflammation and can make some of the relaxation neurons less responsive.

2. Reduce exposure to foods that commonly produce food intolerances.

3. Provide nutrient-dense food so that you will feel more deeply nourished and have the vitamins, minerals, phytochemicals, and other nutrients you need to feed your body's rebuilding pathways.

4. Open the doors of elimination in your body: liver, kidney, colon support.

5. Develop routine and normalcy in your daily food and lifestyle program.

For the purposes of this diet, it will help to think of withdrawal as two phases:

Phase I usually lasts only a few days, but can last up to 10 days. This is when you get to see, in Technicolor, the impact an addictive substance has had on your body. As you might imagine, food is often the last thing on people's mind during this phase.

Phase II, while not as dramatic, lasts for several weeks to three months. During this time your body continues to eliminate the toxic byproducts of the addictive substance. We suggest that you utilize the Phase II dietary recommendations as a framework to rebuild and cleanse your system as much as possible. During that time you will be forming new, healthier eating habits.

We have two plans to help you pass through these periods as easily as possible:

- **Kitchen Savvy Survival** is geared toward people who are savvy in the kitchen or who have a kitchen-savvy support person.

- **Survival to Go** suggestions are for individuals who are challenged in the kitchen, or whose support people aren't the best cooks. This plan suggests healthy choices from both the grocery store and restaurants once you have passed through Phase I.

Keep in mind that a lot of this information may be new to either the support person or the withdrawal patient. That's okay—what's vital here is that the recovering patient moves toward healthier nutritional choices. The idea is to change your eating habits as you begin your recovery.

Phase I–Surviving Withdrawal

During Phase I you will feel severe withdrawal symptoms. Due to these extreme problems, food may become unappealing. Fluids are the easiest way to survive this difficult time.

During this Phase it is important to:

- **Keep your bowels moving.** Some people will experience diarrhea, while others may have constipation. If you are not taking in much besides fluids, bowel movements may be irregular.

- **Keep your body hydrated.** Drink liquids like water, vegetable broth, vegetable juices, herbal teas (hot or cold), homemade lemonade, or fruit juices diluted in water (¼ cup juice to ¾ cup water).

- **Keep your blood sugar as steady as possible.** Don't spike your blood sugar with sweets or sweetened sodas, which can contain as much as nine teaspoons of sugar per can. If you want a carbonated drink, try the calorie-free flavored carbonated waters now popular on the market.

A handy rule of thumb is to drink half your body weight in ounces of fluid daily. If you weigh 160 pounds, you will want to drink 80 ounces of water. A quart is 32 ounces, so a 160-pound person will want to drink 2.5 quarts of fluids. This is about 2.5 liters daily in the metric system. If you are drinking less water than this per day, slowly increase your fluid intake instead of boosting it all at once. Since you will be taking in primarily fluids during this time, a portion of that amount will be water and a portion the vegetable juices, broth, and herbal teas that comprise the Phase I plan.

Vegetable Juices

Vegetables juices are the premier way to support your body through Phase I. They are rich in vitamins, minerals, antioxidants, and phytochemicals (plant–based nutrients). Carrot juice is soothing and rich in natural sugars. A person can sail through Phase I drinking water and vegetables juices. Possible juices and combinations include carrot juice; carrot, celery, and beet juice; carrot, celery, and apple juice; and carrot, celery, and dandelion green juice. Add fresh ginger for a warming quality if you feel cold.

Vegetable Broths

Vegetable broths are naturally rich in vitamins and minerals. You can add any other vegetables that you want to the following recipe.

Survival Broth

Yield: 8 cups of broth

1–2 tbsp. olive oil

3 stalks celery

3 large carrots (or 2 carrots and 1 parsnip)

1 burdock root (optional, if you can't find this then do without). This can be found at Whole Foods and many other such markets. Burdock root has liver healing properties.

1 large onion, or 2 leeks, or 1 bunch of scallions (including greens)

Garlic–5 cloves (or more, to taste)

Ginger–1 tsp. freshly grated

Parsley–6 stems with leaves

2 Bay leaves

2 quarts of water

Directions: Clean vegetables and cut in large pieces (after preparing the broth, the vegetables will be discarded or used for another purpose). Heat the oil; add garlic, onions, celery, carrots, bay leaf, and parsley. Heat for 5 minutes stirring frequently. Add water, bring to just boiling, then reduce flame and let soup simmer for 30 minutes. Strain the broth from the veggies and refrigerate. This will yield about 8 cups of broth.

Prior to serving, add a pinch of sea salt (rich in minerals).

During Phase I you'll probably want to make a fresh pot of broth every other day. As Phase I progresses and your withdrawal symptoms become less severe, you can add vegetables to the broth. Finely chop the vegetables and simmer them in your soup stock.

Your body will likely feel uninterested in oils or fats.

> **Survival To Go:** A number of companies make vegetable stocks in a jar or can, or as bouillon. Choose something low in salt and fat to better tolerate it during this time of detoxification.

Herbal Teas

Herbal teas can soothe the nervous system as well as the digestive system. Commonly available herbal teas include spearmint, peppermint, and chamomile. To aid sleep or reduce anxiety you can try passionflower or skullcap tea. Brands include Celestial Seasonings, Traditional Medicinals' Yogi Tea, Mighty Leaf, Stash, and others.

Getting through Phase I

Drink the teas, broths, and other suggested fluids throughout the day. Try to consume half your body weight in ounces of the broth, teas, juices, and water. You can supplement with easy-to-digest foods, such as oatmeal, toast, or brown rice.

Moving To Phase II

Phase I is over when you suddenly "wake up" and you're ready for food. You have made it through the severe withdrawal phase and are now ready to move into a phase of healing and restoration.

You can start on solid, healthy foods. Think of food as a way to nourish and cleanse your body. I suggest following this diet for at least two months. This gives you time to change some old habits. You may find a newly acquired sense of what foods feel right for you.

Your diet goal is whole foods: a diet rich in vegetables and lean proteins, and low in fat. This will give you proteins to boost the immune system, help the liver detoxify, and provide the building blocks for rejuvenation. The carbohydrate sources you choose during this phase of the diet will be vegetables, fruits, nuts, and seeds. Fats will be healthy oils, such as olive, coconut, and butter.

Your lunchtime and dinner motto will be "at least 2.5 cups." Eat at least 2.5 cups of vegetables with each meal. This can be 2.5 cups of salad, 2.5 cups of one kind of vegetable steamed, or 2.5 cups of mixed sautéed vegetables. Just get in 2.5 cups!

If you have grown to like vegetable juices during Phase I, continue to have at least one glass of fresh juice per day. Some people find that the foods or juices they ate during Phase I have become scapegoats. The taste reminds them of their difficult experience. If you find this to be the case, know that this association will change over time. One day you'll once again look forward to a glass of fresh vegetable juice.

You may wish to add protein powder or have some nuts when drinking vegetable juices like carrot or beet juice, which are high in sugars. The addition of this protein will blunt the release of insulin and help avoid hypoglycemia in susceptible people.

Beverages

Drink one glass of each daily:

Lemon "Aid"

Squeeze one lemon into a quart of water, add a touch of black strap molasses or maple syrup to taste (mildly sweet—remember, you are still attempting to balance your blood sugar).

Dandelion Tea

Steep in one quart of hot water. Several brands now make a dandelion tea (Traditional Medicinals, Mighty Leaf, Alvita).

Green Food (such as "Superfood" or our suggested intestinal support powder, found in health food stores or on our website. These products contain chlorella and spirulina.)

One heaping teaspoon in a glass of water.

Fresh Vegetable Juice

Typical combinations include:

- Carrot, beet, and celery
- Carrot, beet, and cucumber
- Carrot, celery, parsley
- Celery, apple, walnut
- Try your own combinations

Meals

Think fresh, nutritious, delicious, and satisfying. Plan to eat three meals and two snacks a day. This will keep your blood sugar stable. You will be amazed at how much energy you have. The strategy is to avoid high-sugar foods and those that contain starches that are rapidly converted to sugars. These include potatoes, white rice, most breads, and pastas. It is also important to have an adequate amount of protein with each meal, as this helps to keep insulin levels low. We do not advocate large amounts of saturated fats and we definitely want you to stay away from trans fats. The protein should mostly come from poultry, fish, and lean meats.

The Surviving Withdrawal Diet for the Kitchen Savvy plan is the framework for your meals. It is meant to give you suggestions of vegetables that combine well. You can season these to your satisfaction. Below is an example of a typical day of the Phase II diet. More suggestions and advice are available on the Gracer Medical Group Website.

Phase II Diet

Kitchen Savvy:

Breakfast

Eggs (2) any style, spinach and mushroom sauté (use olive or canola oil)

Snack

Almonds–take 24 of them, or 12 if with vegetable juice

Lunch

Garden Salad (2.5 cups) with olives, cooked chicken breast, 1 tbsp. of olive oil, and lemon juice

Snack

Hummus (garbanzo bean dip) with celery sticks

Dinner

Broiled or baked salmon, broccoli (2.5 cups), green salad

Survival to Go: For those who don't cook and need to go to restaurants for their meals, choose restaurants that you know to emphasize quality over quantity, slow food over fast food. For lunch and dinner, think of Asian restaurants and their abundant vegetables or restaurants that serve healthy dishes, essentially steamed or sautéed vegetables and fresh fish or other meat protein. Think of the whole picture and don't get lost in small details.

On either diet plan, if you find that you are having difficulty sleeping through the night, try drinking a small protein shake before bed. Choose a protein powder that has a higher ratio of protein to carbohydrate. Mix ½ serving of protein powder with 8 ounces of rice or almond milk. Shake well or mix in a blender and drink.

These plans are just suggestions. The idea is to emphasize highly nutritious fluids to get through detox and then shift to low carbohydrate, higher protein foods, which keep insulin levels low and which also help the rebuilding process that is so important during the early recovery period. Please see the appendix of this book as well as www. gracermedicalgroup.com for other resources to help with this aspect of your recovery.

Chapter Twenty-Five
Acupuncture and Alternatives

Gracer Medical sometimes uses other methods to help patients battle addiction. Although this chapter focuses on acupuncture, two important factors are demonstrated here:

- **Every patient is unique.** Sometimes patients feel uncomfortable taking certain medications or undergoing surgery. To treat patients effectively, doctors must understand and be able to recommend alternatives.

- **Many alternative medicine methods work.** It's easy for Western practitioners to think that their ways are superior to the rest of the world's. The focus on technology and science leads us to believe that Western medicine is correct and other methods are backwards. True science examines any methodology that can help, if it's deemed safe and done with patient's informed consent. When empirical evidence suggests that there is merit to these alternative practices, rejecting them is backwards.

Acupuncture

My colleague Alon Marcus, DOM, licensed acupuncturist, author, and 1997 recipient of the Educator of the Year Award by the American Association of Oriental Medicine, lends his thoughts to the subject of alternative medicine and addiction treatment.

To successfully treat an addicted patient it is imperative to understand the entire physical, emotional, and spiritual reality of that patient.

A 1993 study published in *The New England Journal of Medicine* found that the American public spent almost as much out of pocket money on alternative medicine ($10.3 billion in 1990) as they did on hospitalizations ($12.8 billion). The study estimated that people made more visits to unconventional therapy providers (425 million) than to primary care physicians (388 million). Clearly patients understand the limitations of conventional care and seek alternatives.

One system is Chinese Medicine. This form of medicine has a written tradition containing tens of thousands of medical texts and vast clinical experience. Artifacts have dated acupuncture possibly as far back as 1,000 BC, and acupuncture/Chinese medicine was well described as a medical system by about 200 BC.

One modality that has become popular in the West for the treatment of pain as well as chemical dependency is acupuncture. Acupuncture has been shown to affect many of the systems that control pain, emotions, and addictive behavior. Acupuncture pain relief has been described as the stimulation of small and medium nerves that send impulses to the spinal cord. Then, the spinal cord, midbrain, and pituitary centers are thought to release neurochemical substances that create the pain relief or analgesic effect.

Acupuncture can be used as a natural and non-addictive method to address pain and help patients with drug detoxification.

Alon presents a compelling argument that acupuncture is both efficacious and relaxing. Compare this to surgery, which no one finds terribly calming. The irony that people can't imagine small needles poking their skin but will tolerate hours of a scalpel carving their flesh is fascinating. But here again, we see how tradition and culture play such a major role in how we seek out care.

I'm not trying to sell you one specific type of treatment. Rather, you should know that just as twelve-step programs alone have not proven successful for every addicted patient, Western medicine also has its limitations. While I am comfortable practicing and recommending Western treatments, my comfort is derived from understanding the context of the care I provide. If I prescribe buprenorphine, it's because that's the best treatment for that patient. I won't dole it out haphazardly to just anyone suffering from addiction. This is why our comprehensive assessment tools are so important.

Doctors and patients alike should take a balanced outlook toward their care. We need to learn to embrace practices that have healed in other cultures. Fear of new techniques is no reason to stop exploring and investigating—especially when lives and good health are at stake.

While each patient is unique and must be treated individually, an accepted form of ear acupuncture is almost always indicated, as it causes relaxation and decreases cravings. It is easy to teach to patients and can be used several times per day if needed.

Acupuncture for Addiction and Detoxification

The National Acupuncture Detoxification Association (NADA) auricular (ear) acupuncture protocol is used around the world to help people deal with and recover from substance abuse. The protocol has been shown in a variety of clinical settings to be beneficial in detoxification as well as to help with the emotional, physical, and psychological attributes of addiction.

Because this protocol involves no diagnosis and is usually not modified, many localities allow non-acupuncturists to administer these treatments. Please check the local laws in your community before using this modality on your own. Generally, the protocol is administered on its own without other ear or body acupuncture points. The length of the treatment depends on the setting in which it is administered and the status of the patient.

Clinicians apply fine-gauge, sterilized, one-time use stainless steel needles to five points on each ear. The needles are inserted just under the skin and remain in place for between 25 minutes up to an hour. Groups of patients may sit together during this time. Benefits include improved program retention, a more optimistic and cooperative attitude, and a reduction in cravings, anxiety, sleep disturbance, and need for pharmaceuticals.

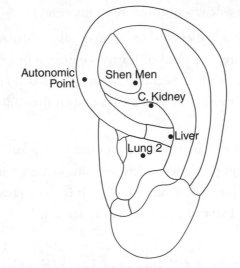

25-1: Ear diagram with NADA acupuncture points

Chinese Herbal Remedies

Chinese medicine is the most documented form of herbal medicine in the world. Chinese herbs have been used to treat both alcohol and drug abuse for many centuries. Ten Chinese medicines for the treatment of opiate addiction have been approved by the Chinese State Food and Drug Administration (SFDA), and at least six are in clinical trials. Traditional formulas can be used in the detoxification process as well as to reduce cravings. Herbal formulas are also effective in treating anxiety, insomnia, depression, and irritability associated with drug use and withdrawal.

The following are common Chinese herbal formulas you can use. Note the very different types of symptoms that are used to decide on the proper remedy.

- Insomnia associated with night sweats, thirst, and heart palpitation: take Emperor of Heaven's Special Pill to Tonify the Heart (Tian Wang Bu Xin Dun).

If irritability, dizziness, and sore throat are more pronounced use Sour Jujube Decoction (Suan Zao Ren Tang).

- For Irritability and/or anger associated with fullness or discomfort in the chest, use Bupleurum plus Dragon Bone and Oyster Shell Decoction (Chi Hu Jia Long Gu Mu Li Tang).

For more severe agitation and bad tamper, use Iron Filings Decoction (Sheng Tie Lou Yin).

- Depression often associated with digestive symptoms: use Rambling Powder (Xiao Yao San).

If anger and agitation is also a problem, use Augmented Rambling Powder (Jia Wei Xiao Yao San).

Chapter Twenty-Six
The Culture and
the Cure

How can one person change the world? By starting with themselves. Whom do you know who is suffering from dependence on or addiction to prescription medication? What about cocaine? Or meth, alcohol, or even marijuana? Is it your mother or husband? Your child? Your best friend?

Is it you?

I mentioned early on that the first step in conquering addiction is not admitting that you have a problem, but realizing that you have a problem. Now that you've read this book you understand what the problem is: a disease that affects the neurotransmitters and receptors in the brain. Addiction isn't a moral failing; it's a medical reality. That fact needs to be shouted from the rooftops so the stigma can be replaced by truth. Millions of people—many of them middle-class or white-collar workers—need the facts to be made public so they can come out of hiding and begin treatment.

That's why I wrote this book. I want the Gracer Program to start a revolution in our country and all over the world. And I need your help.

I need you to start talking with your doctor about the issues raised in this book so you can find specific help for yourself or your loved ones. I need you to brave the ignorance of friends and family and tell them that addiction is a complex, chronic disease. I need you to risk leaving your physician if he or she can't treat your pain properly or considers you a drug seeker.

I need you to stop keeping your problem to yourself.

And, finally, remember that there's hope. The Gracer Program is designed to treat you in a holistic, comprehensive fashion, to examine and treat every aspect of your specific situation so you can return to your life as whole and healed as the day you were born.

Join the revolution. Make *A New Prescription for Addiction* the last thing you ever get hooked on.

What to Do Right Now

- *Just ask* yourself or your loved one the tough questions surrounding addiction.

- *Take the tests* included in this book. Be brutally honest so you can begin getting treatment now.

- *Ask yourself* where you are on the Readiness Quadrant (RQ).

- *Remember* that there are many doctors, therapists, specialists, and other caring individuals who understand that addiction is a disease. You can receive *private, in-office* care.

- *Remember* that new medications and medical technology have blown the lid off traditional addiction care. Success rates have never been higher.

- *Visit* my website at www.gracermedicalgroup.com.

- *Subscribe* to our newsletter.

- *Link* to other websites from our site and discover a community of people discussing addiction issues as a disease, not dementia.

- ***Take comfort*** in knowing that you are on the road to recovery.

- ***Utilize*** the resources in this book and on our website.

- And most of all: Embrace your New Prescription for Addiction.

Appendix A

Resource List

You can always find the latest recommendations and information on our website: www.gracermedicalgroup.com.

Suggested Books

The Anti-Inflammation Zone by Barry Sears, PhD (Harper Collins, 2005)

The Anti-Aging Zone by Barry Sears, PhD

Seven Weeks to Sobriety by Joan Mathews Larson, PhD (Ballantine Wellspring, 1997)

End Your Addiction Now by Charles Gant, MD, PhD (Warner Books, 2002)

It Will Never Happen to Me and *Changing Course: Healing from the Loss, Abandonment and Fear* by Claudia A. Black, PhD

Marijuana: What's a Parent to Believe? by Timmen Cermak, MD

Self-Help Support Groups

AA–Alcoholics Anonymous, a worldwide organization serving millions of alcoholics, dates back to the mid-1930s. The individual's recovery journey centers around acceptance of their illness, increasing sense of spirituality, personal inventories of strengths and weaknesses, and connection to a supportive fellowship. A personal mentor called a "sponsor" helps members learn practical strategies to avoid drinking.

www.AA.org
AA World Service, Inc.
P.O. Box 459
New York, NY 10163
(212) 870-3400

NA–Opiates Anonymous (also known as Narcotics Anonymous) is patterned after AA but focuses on the broader illness of addiction. Addiction to chemicals such as opiates, marijuana, cocaine, crack, crystal meth, and multiple drugs are addressed. Support for total abstinence is an organizing principle. NA is also worldwide and holds conventions in the US and abroad.

www.NA.org
NA World Services, Inc
Van Nuys, CA 91409
(818) 773-9999

Secular Organizations for Sobriety–SOS is also known as "Save Our Selves" and was developed in the 1970s as an alternative to AA. The SOS approach is not reliant on a higher power, but seeks to emphasize one's own ability to become sober.

www.secularsobriety.org
Secular Organization for Sobriety
4773 Hollywood Blvd.
Hollywood, CA 90027
(323) 666-4295

SMART Recovery–A support group that focuses on building coping skills, such as problem-solving, craving management, and lifestyle balance. Unlike AA, SMART groups have a facilitator who guides participants without becoming overly demonstrative. Members learn successful coping strategies from each other in a non-confrontational atmosphere.

www.smartrecovery.org
7537 Mentor Ave.
Suite 306
Mentor, OH 44060 USA
866-951-5357
(440) 951-5357

Life Ring is secular and maintains a "here and now" approach. The central theme is "How did my last week go in terms of coping with my addiction, and how will I get through the next week without drinking or using drugs?"

www.unhooked.com
LifeRing Service Center
1440 Broadway, Suite 312
Oakland CA 94612
800-811-4142
(510-763-0779
Fax: 510-763-1513
service@lifering.org

Women for Sobriety understands that substance abuse and recovery differ for men and women. The approach works on positive reinforcement as well as emotional and spiritual growth. Their thirteen-statement program empowers the women they guide toward abstinence.

www.womenforsobriety.org
WFS, Inc
Women For Sobriety, Inc.
P.O. Box 618,
Quakertown, PA 18951-0618
Phone: (215) 536-8026
Fax: (215) 538-9026

National Organizations

National Institute on Alcohol Abuse and Alcoholism
www.nih.NIAAA.org
5635 Fishers Lane, MSC 9304
Bethesda, MD 20892-9304

National Institute on Drug Abuse
www.drugabuse.gov
6001 Executive Boulevard
Room 5213
Bethesda, MD 90892-9561

Substance Abuse and Mental Health Association
www.samhsa.gov
1 Choke Cherry Rd.
Rockville, MD 20857

Other Resources

- NARCANON (www.addictionca.com)
- National Alliance of Advocates for Buprenorphine Treatment (naabt.org). This is the premier website for information on buprenorphine (Subutex/Suboxone). There are extensive discussion groups and a wonderful free newsletter. There is also an advanced patient/physician matching program to help you find a doctor who is certified to use buprenorphine in your area and also notifies her/him that you are looking and to contact you.

- www.drugstory.org

- *Addiction Treatment Homework Planner* by James R. Finley & Brenda S. Lenz. Provides exercises and homework, the type of materials handed out at an addiction center. Assignments include: early warning signs of mania, correcting distorted perceptions, and anxiety profiles.

Recovery Resources

- National Association of Alcoholism and Drug Abuse Counselors, www.naadac.org
- Alcoholics Anonymous World Services, Inc., www.alcoholics-anonymous.org
- Cocaine Anonymous World Services, Inc., www.ca.org
- Opiates Anonymous World Services, Inc., www.na.org
- Join Together Online, www.jointogether.org
- Al-Anon-Alateen World Service, Inc., www.al-anon.alateen.org

Research Organizations

- American Society of Addiction Medicine (ASAM), www.asam.org
- Center for Alcohol and Substance Abuse at Columbia University, www.casacolumbia.org
- National Council on Alcoholism and Drug Dependence, Inc., www.ncadd.org
- Agency for Healthcare Research and Quality, www.ahrq.gov
- Center for Substance Abuse Research, www.cesar.umd.edu
- Alcohol Medical Scholars Program, www.alcoholmedicalschol-ars.org
- The American Association for the Advancement of Science, www.aaas.org
- Brain Disorders Network, www.brainnet.org
- Center for Alcohol and Addiction Studies, www.caas.brown.edu
- Center for Interventions, Treatment, and Addictions Research, www.med.wright.edu/citar

- Drug Abuse Treatment Outcome Study, www.datos.org
- RAND's Drug Policy Research Center, www.rand.org/multi

Government Organizations

- National Alcohol & Drug Addiction Recovery Month, www. recoverymonth.gov
- National Institute on Drug Abuse (NIDA), www.nida.nih. gov
- Office of National Drug Control Policy, www.whitehouse-drugpolicy.gov
- Department of Health and Human Services, www.os.dhhs. gov
- National Institute on Alcohol Abuse and Alcoholism, www. niaaa.nif.gov
- Substance Abuse and Mental Health Service Administration, www.samhsa.gov
- Healthfinder.gov
- Medline Plus (National Library of Medicine and National Institutes of Health), www.nlm.nih.gov/medlineplus
- US Department of Labor–Workplace Substance Abuse, www. dol.gov/workingpartners
- Centers for Disease Control and Prevention, www.cdc.gov

Treatment Center Information

- **American Council on Alcoholism**–Features treatment referral assistance. www.aca-usa.org
- **Cri-Help**–Drug and alcohol treatment services located in Los Angeles and North Hollywood, California. www.cri-help.org

- **Drug Rehab Services**–Drug Rehab Services is a drug rehabilitation, addiction treatment center help line and referral service. The help line is free to the public to help with the process of getting someone into treatment that will work. www.drugrehabservices.com

- **Focus Healthcare**–Focus Healthcare is a national provider for the treatment of Chemical Dependency and Psychiatric Disorders. www.focushealthcare.com

- **Legacy Sober Living**–Legacy Sober Living is located in Los Angeles, California, and provides an organized clean and sober living community. www.legacysoberliving.com

- **Sober.com**–Directory of drug treatment centers, alcohol rehabilitation centers, halfway houses, sober houses, eating disorder clinics, and recovery related products. www.sober.com

- **Sober Living House**–Sober living homes are affordable, alcohol- and drug-free environments that provide a positive place for peer group recovery support. www.soberville.com

Help, Support, and Referral Resources

- **Alcoholism News**–Latest news, research, and developments, http://alcoholism.bongomedia.com

- **Addiction Intervention Resources**–Addiction Intervention Resources (AIR) is a national addiction consulting company that specializes in helping families and organizations in crisis. www.addictionintervention.com

- **AddictionLA**–Provides professional outpatient psychotherapy treatment in a safe and private atmosphere. www.addictionla.com

- **Addiction No More-Drug Rehab**–Drug rehabilitation referral services. Drug rehabilitation centers, also know as drug rehabs, provide crucial care for the drug user. www.addiction nomore.com

- **Addiction Resource Guide**–Directory of addiction treatment facilities and resources. www.addictionresourceguide. com

- **Empowered Recovery**–Candidly helping the family and friends of alcoholics recognize, understand, and resolve an alcoholic relationship. www.empoweredrecovery.com

- **Intervention Center**–Family Intervention for Addiction. Intervention resources for alcoholism, drug addiction, gambling, computer addiction, other self-destructive behavior. www.intervention.com

- **Join Together**–A project of Boston University School of Public Health, provides publications and news regarding addiction. www.jointogether.org

- **National Institute on Chemical Dependency**–Articles and directories for: Addictions, Prevention, Recovery, Medical, Health and Wellness, Mental Health, Professionals, Education, Family, Spirituality, and Other Social Issues. www.nicd.us

- **The Penn Foundation**–Founded in 1955, the Penn Foundation is a private not-for-profit corporation dedicated to providing comprehensive mental health and drug and alcohol services for southeastern Pennsylvania. www.penn foundation.org

- **Sober 24**–Alcohol and addiction recovery resources. www. sober24.com

- **Sober Recovery Resources**–Offers extensive information and resources for a variety of recovery issues. www.soberrecovery. com

- **The Institute for Authentic Process Healing**–A community of peers, peer-practitioners, psychotherapists, counselors, psychologists, and physicians who are committed to the practice of Authentic Process Healing (APH). www.theinstitute.org/addiction.shtml

Addiction Recovery–General Resources

- **Daily Dose**–A compilation of substance misuse articles from the World Wide Web; includes such categories as: Government, Education, Medicine, Press, Science, Organizations & Agencies, Law and Research, and so on. www.dailydose.net

- **National Association of Alcoholism & Drug Abuse Counselors (NAADAC)**–Committed to enhancing patient care. www.naadac.org

- **National Association of Alcohol, Drugs, & Disability (NAADD)**–The mission of NAADD is to create public awareness of issues related to alcoholism, drug addiction, and substance abuse faced by persons with other co-existing disabilities. www.naadd.org

- **Opiates Anonymous Info.**–NA meetings online, message board, and much more. www.narecovery.org

- **Addiction Technology Transfer Center Program (NATTC)**–National network of centers improving skill levels of treatment practitioners. www.nattc.org

- **National Council on Alcoholism and Drug Dependence (NCADD)**–Provides public education services and operates referral service. www.ncadd.org

- **Center for Substance Abuse Treatment**–Offers publications, manual, and guides that assist in treatment of substance abuse. Excellent coverage of special topics on addictions. www.treatment.org

- **Way2Hope**–Advice, information, research, and links about a variety of issues, including alcoholism, debt, and drug addiction. www.way2hope.org

Appendix B

Psychological Questionnaires and Worksheets

The following list includes the questionnaires and score sheets that are used in this book, as well as the most common questionnaires used by mental health professionals to determine not only the diagnosis, but also the progress of treatment for the most common mood disorders. Either the questionnaires themselves, or links to them on the Internet, are available at our website, www.gracermedicalgroup.com.

Gracer Substance Use Questionnaire

Change Plan Worksheet

Readiness Quadrant Evaluation test rulers and scoring sheet

Hamilton Depression Scale

Beck Anxiety Scale

Mood Disorder Questionnaire

Everyone has some of the symptoms and characteristics of most of the problems assessed with these tools, so do not worry if you "see yourself" in some of the questions. Just be as honest as possible in your responses and then use the results to see where you are. By knowing what kind of problems you have, you can seek proper help. You can also retake these tests after you begin treatment to see how you are progressing.

Appendix C

Laboratory Tests

Lab testing is an important part of our evaluation. Some of the lab tests we use are routinely performed by most physicians and are vital to evaluate basic health as well as screen for dangerous conditions. We also use some special laboratory tests that help us assess other conditions that impact the treatment of drug addiction, withdrawal, and craving reduction. The theory behind these tests is found in the nutrition chapter. Please see our website, www.gracer-medicalgroup.com, for the most up-to-date recommendations for the best labs and direct links. As with most medical tests it is important to have a health professional evaluate and guide you through this process.

1. **Routine tests.** This should be part of the basic evaluation and can be done at any medical laboratory

- CBC
- Chem. panel with liver function tests and lipids (cholesterol and triglycerides)
- Urinalysis
- Vitamin B12 level
- Vitamin D (total 25 hydroxy vit D)
- Thyroid evaluation
- Free T4
- Free T3

- TSH

- Anti-thyroid antibodies

Salivary Hormone and Antibody Testing

A. What to use this test for:

- Adrenal Stress Testing.

- DHEA–This is used to assess system stress and is used to compare with cortisol levels as well as to see if specific supplementation is needed.

- Sex hormones are tested as a single test in men and in women who are in menopause. For menstruating women we use a series of samples over the whole cycle.

- Antibodies for specific food allergies. We usually test for allergy to soy, egg, casein (milk), and gliadin (gluten), as well as for the total quantity of these antibodies called sIGA. We do this to be sure that you have a properly functioning immune system that can respond to allergic stimulation.

B. Labs to use:

- Aeron Laboratory, www.aeron.com

- Diagnos techs, www.diagnostechs.com

- Genova Lab (formerly known as Great Smokies Diagnostic Lab) www.gdx.net

Comprehensive Digestive Stool Analysis

A. What to use this test for:

- Use this test to check for abnormal bowel bacteria as well as for as for a number of other GI functions, such as the adequacy of digestive enzymes. This test gives a comprehensive overview of GI function and allows the health professional to prescribe the best regimen to restore normal bowel function.

Routine labs do not usually perform these types of tests and most physicians are not familiar with them.

B. Labs to use:

• Genova Lab

• Diagnos Techs

• Doctor's Data, www.doctorsdata.com

Measurement of AA/EPA
(arachadonic acid/eicosapentanoic acid)

A. What to use this test for:

• This test looks at the make up of the fatty acids in cell walls, which reflects the types of eicosanoids that your body makes ("good" vs. "bad"). This is a measurement of silent inflammation, the underlying cause of heart disease, degenerative arthritis, and most other chronic illnesses. A lower ratio can make withdrawal and recovery easier.

B. Labs to use:

• Meridian Valley Lab, www.meridianvalleylab.com (425) 271-8689

• SIPTesting (Silent Inflammation Panel), www.siptesting.com

Index

diabetes, 296
diabetics, 298
Diagnostic and Statistical Manual-IV
  (DSM-IV), 55
Diazepam, 147
digestive stool analysis, comprehensive,
  360
Dilaudid, 120, 123, 135, 138
disulfiram (Antabuse), 229, 232, 235–36
DL-phenylalanine (DLPA), 317, 325
DNA, 116
docosahexanoic acid (DHA), 290, 321
dopamine, 107, 109, 110, 247–48, 292, 303
  in the mid-brain, 249
  nerve cell, 142–44
  receptor, 141–43
  system, 202
Drug Enforcement Administration
  (DEA), 60
drug
  addiction, 106
  addiction and physical dependence, 268
  detoxification, 166
  holiday, 271
  overdose, 139
Duragesic, 120, 123, 131

E
eicosanoids, 289, 291, 302, 304
eicosapentanoic acid (EPA), 232, 290,
  295, 321
  measurement of, 361
empathetic models, 82, 190, 199
empathy, 189, 192, 195–97
  therapist, 198
endocrine,
  hormones, 301
endorphins, 122–27, 211
epinephrine, 292, 297, 303
Epstein-Barr, 269
eszopicione, 150
essential fatty acids (EFAs), 229, 231, 292
  cis, 293
  trans, 293
estrogen, 301, 306, 308–09
  dominance, 306
  replacement, 307
ethanol, 228
evening primrose oil, 294, 297, 316, 321

F
5-hydroxy-tryptophan (5HTP), 317, 324
factors leading to treatment,
  emotional importance, 175
  health concerns, 174

legal issues, 174
positive results of quitting, 175
relationship problems, 175
vocational and employment
  consequences, 175
fat hydrogenation, 293
FDA, 138, 215–16, 233, 251, 325
Felton, Leni, 287, 316, 327
fentanyl, 46, 120, 123
fentanyl as patch, 102, 131, 265
Fentora, 120
fetal alcohol syndrome, 163
fibromyalgia, 270, 272
Five-step program, 66
fish oil, 294–95, 297, 304, 315–16, 321
flaws in the mainstream treatment
  model, 77
frontal cortex, 240
fructo oligo saccharides (FOS), 326

G
gamma amino butyric acid (GABA),
  107–08, 110, 112–15, 205, 213, 215, 239,
  246, 291, 303–04, 321
  See also spectrum of GABA activity
  receptors, 147, 230, 236, 290
  system, 202
gamma hydroxybutyrate (GHB)/Xyrem,
  204, 214–215
gamma-linolenic acid (GLA), 231, 290,
  294, 316, 321
gambling, 54
Gant, Charles, MD, PhD, 347
genetic factors, 114, 115
genetic predisposition to addiction, 104
Ghalie, Richard, MD, 138
Gladwell, Malcolm, 33, 54, 62–3, 93, 250
glucose, 296
  tolerance test (GTT), 298
glutamine, 323–24, 326
  supplement, 317
glutamate, 107–08, 110, 112, 303, 321
Gracer/Peterson Readiness Quadrant (RQ)
  evaluation, 165, 171
  confidence, 172
  importance, 172
Gracer Substance Use Questionnaire, 357
Gracer Treatment Protocol, 165

H
habituation, 163–64
Hashimoto's thyroiditis, 312
heroin, 47, 119–20, 122, 138, 140, 211
Hidden, The, 58, 61, 74
Hillbilly Heroin, 119, 137
  See also Oxycodone